1988

# "AUTHORS TO THEMSELVES"

# "AUTHORS TO THEMSELVES"

## MILTON AND THE REVELATION OF HISTORY

### MARSHALL GROSSMAN

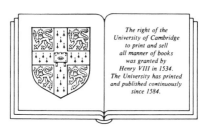

The right of the
University of Cambridge
to print and sell
all manner of books
was granted by
Henry VIII in 1534.
The University has printed
and published continuously
since 1584.

CAMBRIDGE UNIVERSITY PRESS

CAMBRIDGE

NEW YORK   NEW ROCHELLE   MELBOURNE   SYDNEY

*For AKG and JLG*

Published by the Press Syndicate of the University of Cambridge
The Pitt Building, Trumpington Street, Cambridge CB2 1RP
32 East 57th Street, New York, NY 10022, USA
10 Stamford Road, Oakleigh, Melbourne 3166, Australia

© Cambridge University Press 1987

First published 1987

Printed in the United States of America

*Library of Congress Cataloging-in-Publication Data*
Grossman, Marshall.
Authors to themselves.
1. Milton, John, 1608–1674, Paradise lost.
2. Milton, John, 1608–1674 – Knowledge – Psychology.
3. Milton, John, 1608–1674 – Knowledge – History.
4. Self in literature.   5. History in literature.
6. Psychoanalysis and literature.   I. Title.
PR3562.G77   1987      821'.4      87-9357

*British Library Cataloguing in Publication Data*
Grossman, Marshall
"Authors to themselves": Milton and the
revelation of history.
1. Milton, John, 1608–1674. Paradise lost
I. Title
821'.4      PR3562

ISBN 0-521-34037-3

# CONTENTS

# PREFACE

My topic is a certain textual inscription of the self in the second half of the seventeenth century. The experience of history as progress, proclaimed by Bacon and demonstrated by technological advances that were changing the economics of agriculture, marks the birth, in the seventeenth century, of the modern conception of the self as at once coherent and unified, yet developing, as capable of making and being made by history. In the third book of *Paradise Lost,* Milton has the Father describe Adam and Eve as "authors to themselves in all / Both what they judge and what they choose." This use of writing as a model for the structure of the self-information reflects a conception of history as a progress of second causes inscribed within a providential design. My book studies how the narrative form of *Paradise Lost* projects this new concept of the historical self through a dialectic that locates the narrated events at the intersection of prospective and retrospective points of view.

The notion that the modern conception of the individual was born in the Renaissance has long been a scholarly commonplace. Recent studies have described the textual traces of this birth in sixteenth-century English literature and have begun to outline in some detail the stages of its gestation. Stephen Greenblatt has described the appearance in sixteenth-century texts of the self as an object to be fashioned by an interior subject and submitted to a world of external forces, and Anne Ferry has charted the development of a vocabulary of "inwardness" with which this new self, composed of an authentic interior and an always inadequate outward expression, began to be explored in sixteenth-century sonnets. Greenblatt's notion of a self that can be fashioned, manipulated, and revised according to the tensions of a particular historical situation is in many ways the starting point of my study. I have sought to describe how this tension between the self as subject and as object is manifest in a narrative representation of inwardness that appears nearly a century after the sonnets in which Ferry traces the earliest poetics of the divided self.

The intervening century was a tumultuous one, and it is a certain assumption that English culture after the Glorious Revolution represents the transformation into a modern commercial state of the feudal world in which the Tudor monarchy began. The self-fashioned selves studied by Greenblatt reflect the tensions of a society whose explanations of power in relation to individual men lag behind the forces of historical change that such explanations must accommodate. The present study examines a textual constitution of the self in England in the second half of the seventeenth century, after the Commonwealth and the Protectorate have irreversibly broken the link with the feudal past.

The self-authored subject of *Paradise Lost* accumulates experiences through a series of judgments and choices that extend over the period of its life. As a fully historical conception of the self, it faces the problem of changing in response to temporally unfolding events while maintaining an essential continuity with its own past. Self-authorship, therefore, may be understood as the temporal recuperation of the tension between self-fashioning and self-cancellation – the alternating experience of oneself as mastering and mastered – described by Greenblatt. This modern subject substitutes for the continuity provided by a stable and repetitive network of power relations, the individual and internal integrity of the Cartesian cogito. The subject of self-authorship substitutes its internal coherence, its ability to understand itself as developing in continuity with a personal past, for the social continuity that is effaced by the technological dream of progress and its vision of "improvement by tract of time." Representing itself to itself as additive, as accumulating experiences through which it grows and changes, the self-authored subject imagines the recuperation over time of the instantaneous self-identification that had previously been afforded by a stable network of social, political, and familial roles. It offers, at the dawn of bourgeois

*Preface*

social and political hegemony, the prototype of the self-made man, carefully modifying and retying the knot that binds this entrepreneurial self-purveyor to God and to history.

The method of this study reflects my belief that literary history errs when it constitutes the history of literature as an autonomous, self-generating system responsive only to intertextual processes like imitation or the exhaustion of generic possibilities or, conversely, when it treats literature as epiphenomenal to some extratextual "reality." The problem for the literary historian is to specify the relationship of text to history and to understand as far as possible how change in one affects change in the other, without reducing textual to literary events or reducing historical to textural processes. To navigate between this Scylla and Charybdis, I propose a dialectical analysis that uses the experiential and textual aspects of time to mediate material and literary history. Time, as Thomas Aquinas noted, is implicit in the verb. Literary texts, therefore, necessarily articulate a time of reading and a sense of duration interior to their discourse. Verbs have subjects as well as tense, and every narrative necessarily represents a series of choices in the linking of subjects to verbs. In his brilliant and comprehensive study of the redescriptive powers of rhetoric, *The Rule of Metaphor*, Paul Ricoeur has shown that the operation of rhetorical tropes depends upon predication. Following his argument, while resisting the ontological value he accords to metaphoric redescription, I have understood Milton's narrative as a sequence of tropes relating grammatical subjects and verbs in definite temporal sequences. The representation of time and the grammar of predication mediate between historical actions and the narrative episodes that recount them. Therefore, I have followed the episodes of *Paradise Lost* in sequence and charted the poem's representation of the self in relation to time as a method of exploring the boundary between world and literary events and of studying the dialectical interaction between experience and narrative. It is part of my argument that for Milton the temporal unfolding of human events is part of a signifying system in which the meaning of any human action is always provisionally anticipated in the act but ultimately deferred until the eschaton. The sequential reading of the poem respects and thematizes this representation of semantic deferral as narrative form.

## Preface

It has not been my intention to provide a revisionary reading of Milton's epic or to reinterpret its major cruces or fix its historical meaning, although on occasion such interpretive efforts have been an inevitable outcome of my procedure. Rather, I have sought as much as possible to displace the question What does this mean? in favor of the question How does this mean?; further, I have situated the latter question in the sequence of the narration, paying special attention to how a specific textural feature may mean differently at different points in the poem. In practice the answer to this question has taken the form of a description of the rhetorical tropes that organize the narrative configuration of the epic and form the basis of the text's representation of judging and choosing subjects moving through time. Seeking a vocabulary with which to fashion this description of Milton's rhetoric and its historical and social context, I have referred to a broad spectrum of philosophical and narratological studies. Underlying this range of reference is my conviction that each of these apparently disparate discourses reinscribes, within its own context, logical and temporal relations implicit in a dialectic internal to the tropes themselves. I have thus used several frames of reference, not heterogenously, but relying on their homogeneity for the freedom to exploit each to its appropriate effect.

A special instance of this procedure is my juxtaposition of psychoanalytic and rhetorical analyses. In some ways my text may be taken as an inverting mirror image of William Kerrigan's *The Sacred Complex*, a work with which any study of the representation of the self in *Paradise Lost* ought come to terms. Kerrigan provides a sophisticated and sensitive study of the "psychogenesis of *Paradise Lost*" in the personal history of John Milton, and of the poet's particular use of Christian myth as a vehicle for the resolution of the tensions to which that history gives rise. Since the subject of psychoanalysis itself is the very configuration of the self or ego whose formation is exemplified in Milton's narrative, my study may be thought of as presenting the psychogenesis of John Milton in the text of *Paradise Lost*. Where Kerrigan seeks the origin of *Paradise Lost* in the life history of its author, I seek to trace in the text an early articulation of the form "life history" presupposed by psychoanalytic explanation. Psychoanalytic discourse presupposes the experience of a self in search of the continuity between its past and present, such as the one I have sought to locate in the developing response of men and women in the seventeenth century to the changing conditions of their lives. As I have suggested, this configuration of the self was already in the making by the second half of the sixteenth century. Psychoanalysis can thus be situated within a historical formation of the self of which Milton's narrative is exemplary. The unique form of Milton's narrative–and its realignment of theology, hermeneutics, and experience–makes *Paradise Lost* the epic of the origin of Freudian man, discovering at once the form and subject of psychoanalytic inquiry. It is a trope of psychoanalytic discourse to place the origin of the text in the ego and its history, but this temporal priority is an effect of the discourse, not an ontological necessity. Because our interests interrelate in this way, my text parallels Kerrigan's at some points, approaching the same issues and reading the same passages, but always with a strategic reversal of direction. In the notes, I have traced these points of contiguity with the psychoanalytic reading and allowed Milton's texts to comment on, in effect, to historicize, Freud's and Lacan's.

In the preparation of this study, I have incurred more debts than I can properly chronicle. C. A. Patrides and Anthony Low introduced me to the serious study of Milton's work, and conversations with Hayden White and Joel Fineman led me to study the vicissitudes of the subject in Renaissance poetry. Mary Ann Radzinowicz, Anthony Low, Bernard Gilligan, and Lee Erickson provided meticulous readings of the entire manuscript, saving me from many embarrassments. Ernest B. Gilman read this material in various stages of production, engaged in a discourse on the issues raised in it, functioned as a critically acute bibliographic resource, and, finally, offered a careful and generous reading of the whole. Patricia Clough, Lee Erickson, Bernard Gilligan, Lia Lerner, Robert O'Brien, and Herman Rapaport listened attentively to endless formulations and reformulations of my thoughts and commented perspicaciously. Andree Hayum advised me on parallel developments in the visual arts. I have a special debt to Richard Harrier for his long-standing encouragement of my efforts, for his generosity, and for the example of humane humanism he provides.

I should also like to express my appreciation to the staffs of the New York Public Library and of the Elmer Holmes Bobst Memorial

*Preface*

Library of New York University and, in particular, to Ann M. Finnan and Clement J. Anzul of the Lowenstein Library of Fordham University at Lincoln Center and to Robert Underbrink of the Lumpkin Library of Blackburn College.

Finally, I am indebted to my wife and son for tolerating my sporadic absence and my constant preoccupation over a long period of time.

Parts of Chapters 5, 6, and 8 of this study have appeared, in different forms, in *Milton Quarterly*, *Milton Studies*, and *Modern Philology*, respectively. I thank the editors for permission to reprint this material.

Claude Mellan's engraving (frontispiece), *Title Page for the Bible*, after Poussin, is reproduced with the permission of the Fogg Art Museum, Harvard University.

# 1

## INTRODUCTION

I

> They themselves decreed
> Thir own revolt, not I: if I foreknew,
> Foreknowledge had no influence on their fault,
> Which had no less prov'd certain unforeknown.
> So without least impulse or shadow of Fate,
> Or aught by me immutably foreseen,
> They trespass, Authors to themselves in all
> Both what they judge and what they choose; for so
> I form'd them free, and free they must remain,
> Till they enthrall themselves.[1]

The fate of Adam and Eve in *Paradise Lost* is at once divinely foreknown and historically contingent. As "authors to themselves," they write their own life histories with the actions they freely chose to take, and without interference from the Father's foreknowledge of the as yet unwritten chapters. Why should Milton choose the metaphor of authorship to represent the freedom within providence enjoyed by the first parents? It shall be my contention that we may take this metaphoric association of authoring and acting within time very seriously, drawing out its implications until they form a modus operandi for the reading of *Paradise Lost*.

The word "author" is used variously to refer to authority, creator, and writer in the late seventeenth century. The different meanings accruing to it are all related through its Latin antecedents: *auctor* (writer, progenitor), derived from *auctus* (magnified), the past participal of *augere* (to increase).[2] When Milton has God, the Father, say that Adam and Eve are "authors to themselves," he clearly means that they have authority over their own destinies. But the form that this authority takes is the ability to determine the narrative of their lives by judging and choosing. They have the authority of authors, that is, of writers, and they will augment or magnify the life histories they write as they accumulate experiences. As progenitors of the human race, they will similarly magnify human history by augmenting, magnifying, authoring a "race of worshippers" (VII.630). By becoming progenitors they will augment God's authority and their own. Created "in the Image of God / Express" (VII.527–8), they will "be fruitful, multiply, and fill the Earth, / Subdue it, and throughout Dominion hold" (VII.531–2). As my argument develops it will become clear that Milton's text activates the varied aspects of authorship, integrating and articulating authority and augmentation through the analogy of writing a narrative and living a life. The shared authorship and authority of God and man requires of Adam and Eve an intricate reading of human action and divine revelation, issuing in a collaboration of history and providence. I shall further argue that the projection of this collaboration as a relationship of accumulation to experience and authority is conditioned by the material social relations characteristic of the late seventeenth century.[3]

It is in the nature of metaphor in general to join two signifiers in mutual reference and of the metaphor of self-authorship in particular to project tenor and vehicle as two sides of the same phenomenon as seen from two temporally opposed points of view: that of the author who stands within the story he or she writes and who constructs each episode out of the judgments and choices he or she makes, and that of the reader who follows a familiar story, assigning significance to each episode by relating it to his or her conception of the plot as a whole.[4] The analogy of action to text implied by Milton's metaphor suggests that there is an underlying structure common to the foundation of the self through action in the world and of character through plot in fiction. Beyond the suggestion that morally responsible human beings author themselves, as poets (for example) author texts, is the peculiar relationship of

Adam and Eve's life history to the always already-written text of divine providence. I shall argue that the rhetorical structure of *Paradise Lost* performs a dialectical reversal of the tenor and vehicle of the metaphor of authorship so that providence becomes the author, and the free creature the reader of his or her own life story. This rhetorical reversal at once defines and represents Christian liberty in Milton's narrative.

Within this dialectic, the Christian fathers himself by actions conformable to a providential text that God not only foresees but also reveals – in the form of a set of narrative patterns. These patterns, the characteristic structures of biblical narrative, are revealed to Adam by Michael in the final two books of the poem. The recognition of these scriptural patterns in everyday life provides a context for moral action, for the judgments and choices through which Milton's Christians are to author themselves. The way in which the narrative structure of *Paradise Lost* establishes this superimposition of an eternal pattern and a dramatically developing situation is the principal theme of my study. The revision of Adam's own brief (auto)biography, when it is reread in light of the patterns provided by Michael's synopsis of biblical history, provides a model for the application of scriptural narrative to moral choice and for the narrative strategy of Milton's poem. The mediation of experience by a narrative revelation is represented in Milton's text by a temporal structure that projects St. Paul's distinction of the letter and the Spirit in a peculiar and unexpected way.

Michael tells Adam that in the time of the apostles, the moral application of the Gospels was made through the living witness of their authors, but

> at length
> Thir Ministry perform'd, and race well run,
> Thir doctrine and thir story written left,
> They die; but in thir room, as they forewarn,
> Wolves shall succeed for teachers, grievous Wolves,
> Who all the sacred mysteries of Heav'n
> To thir own vile advantages shall turn
> Of lucre and ambition, and the truth
> With superstitions and traditions taint,

Left only in those written Records pure,
Though not but by the Spirit understood. (XII. 504-14)

The written word is at once the only pure record of Christ's ministry, yet subject to corruptions. The superstitions and traditions that taint the Gospel must be presumed to enter the pure writings when they are preached. After all, it is the corrupt clergy who are the grievous wolves that succeed to teach the holy word. Corruption enters the tradition when the texts are "read," as they are returned from the silence of the letter to the living word of the preacher. Bereft of the authentic preaching of those who witnessed the events they preach, the written word becomes an archive of a truth that can enter living discourse only in corrupt form. Egress from this predicament is through the displacement of the "reading" from an exterior to an interior voice.[5] The written text is to be collated with "what the Spirit within / Shall on the heart engrave" (XII. 523-4). Self-authorship, in so far as it depends upon the use of revealed truth, requires a dialectical process of double readings. One authors oneself by acting out a story already written in the regenerate heart.[6] The Christian is released from the self-enthrallment of the fall by conforming his or her personal mythos to an internalized logos. The community of Christians is founded on a sort of silent reading: The Spirit voices the letter in the heart.

Reason and affection are the faculties through which the Spirit is heard and the community joined. The Father's foreknowledge does not impair the authorship (or authority) of Adam and Eve; they enthrall themselves by their disobedience. When Eve calls Adam "My Author and Disposer" (IV. 635), she recognizes him as her origin and acknowledges his authority over her, but, we learn in the separation and temptation scenes in book IX the extent to which her judgments and choices express and determine her moral ethos. God, as "Author of this Universe" (VIII. 360), is situated as Adam's authority as Adam is Eve's. The sharing of authority in this way is a precondition of but not an infringement on the freedom to write one's story out of one's acts. Adam and Eve participate with each other and with God in "authoring" the history of this world until the fall, when "exorbitant desire" takes control. In the

4

postlapsarian world, authority over the self is restored when the individual fathers the Father in himself, by writing out in actions the story the Spirit both writes and reads in the human heart.

The use of writing as a model for the structure of the self-information and the ambivalence of individual action and communal destiny implicit in the notion of joint action through obedience to a common, yet interior, voice reflect a conception of history as the progress of second causes that is becoming dominant in the seventeenth century.[7] Milton's chiasmic reversal of the metaphor of authorship – through which an individual authors himself by acting out a story foreseen and revealed by God – marks *Paradise Lost* as the narrative expression of a sense of the historical self coming into being in Milton's time.

As we shall see, the characteristically Protestant poetics so carefully reconstructed in recent criticism of seventeenth-century religious poetry may be understood as the adaptation of traditional hermeneutics to the needs of this newly developing conception of the individual as an actor on the historical stage.[8] Before proceeding to a reading of *Paradise Lost*, I want to elaborate further these two claims: 1) that the metaphor of authorship discloses a rhetoric common to the reading of a narrative and the formation of the self-inaction as Milton understood it; and 2) that the assertion of this common structure reflects a specifically Protestant and seventeenth-century experience of time and history. I shall consider the more general case first – that of a common structure underlying the metaphoric identification of writing and historical action.

II

The most important of these [elements of tragedy] is the arrangement of incidents, for tragedy is an imitation, not of men but of action and life, of happiness and misfortune. These are to be found in action, and the goal of life is a certain kind of activity, not a quality. Men are what they are because of their characters, but it is in action that they find happiness or the reverse.[9]

For Aristotle, plot is a feature of life as well as art. Tragedy imitates actions because "character is a by-product of the action."[10] The view from within the fiction would be different. The individual who acts experiences action as a by-product of character, sees what he or she does as a function of who he or she is. If we return now to the passage from *Paradise Lost* III with which I began, we can say that Adam and Eve are free to act according to their judgments and choices but that once they act, an ethos or a moral character is disclosed. The Father foresees their acts and so knows the nature of that character before they do. However, there is a serious ambiguity concealed in the difference between his point of view and theirs. Do actions simply disclose character or do they form it? Is the individual destined to live out the consequences of his innate characteristics, or does character develop in response to experience? It is here that the authorship of creator and creature overlap. If we are to take seriously the Father's claim that Adam and Eve are "authors to themselves," we should see the judgments and choices they make in response to what they experience as contingent circumstances as not simply calling for the exercise of an innate capacity for judgment but as exercising and developing that capacity. Presumably, it is through such exercise of the judgment that Adam and Eve might have "improv'd by tract of time" (V.498) had they remained obedient.[11] Thus a person moving through a sequence of temporal actions both forms and discovers his or her character through and within the medium of his or her experience. To form and recognize character in this way, one must conceive of oneself as a subject moving through time, both self-consistent and capable of change.[12] It is this relation of the self to time that I shall call historical consciousness. An individual conceiving of himself in this way, evaluates his actions not only in relation to an immediate situation but also in relation to his image of himself as a particular sort of person, author of a particular sort of life story, and actor in the broader world history of which his personal story forms a part.

In *Paradise Lost,* the inability to function *historically* is manifest in Satan, who boasts of "a mind not to be chang'd by Place or Time" (I.253). In contrast Adam recognizes the irreversibility of historical action when he laments the finality of Eve's disobedience, "past who can recall, or done undo? / Not God Omnipotent, nor Fate"

(IX.926–7). While Adam and Eve begin to regain authorship by cultivating the lands of the "subjected Plain," that is by re-forming themselves in the medium of history, Satan, unable to enter history except as an agent of providence, retreats into the false autonomy of the objectless or nondialectical "subject," the unchanging mind that is "its own place, and *in itself* / Can make a Heav'n of Hell, a Hell of Heav'n" (I.254–5; my emphasis).

Thus, in Book XI, Michael advises Adam to make judgments not in terms of what seems immediately gratifying but for the benefit of the self he is both creating and discovering:

> Judge not what is best
> By pleasure, though to Nature seeming meet,
> Created, as thou art, to nobler end
> Holy and pure, conformity divine. (603–6)

Adam's "nobler end" has both a logical and a temporal sense. It is the realization of the divine archetype that is his formal cause and the "conformity divine" ultimately enjoyed by the renovated soul, the completion of history as the fulfillment of providence. If Adam is to author himself by judging and choosing, he must temper his judging with knowledge of his "nobler end" as both formal and final cause, intention and terminus. Such knowledge – available in the Scriptures in correlation with the law engraved in the heart – must guide the judgments he makes as his temporal history unfolds. (Self)knowledge of the "nobler end" of "conformity divine," that at which all action should aim, specifically supersedes and displaces judgments made according to Nature, which, because it is instinctive and not subject to development, excludes freedom and responsibility. Adam by taking the writing of the Spirit in the heart as his ideal is able to sublimate his natural appetites and aspire to conformity with the image of God. In fact it is this image of the self to be constructed that raises Adam above the beasts and endows him with the moral responsibility necessary to self-authorship.[13]

In practice, the informed judgments of Adam and Eve require two steps. They must first imagine that the events they experience seriatim form a discernible and meaningful pattern, and then make such choices as will conform that pattern to their understanding of the revealed patterns of providence. They must author a life history conformable to that which God desires. To judge and choose well, it is necessary to match the story one is writing to a revelation of providence's story of all things.[14]

The identification of text and action implicit in *Paradise Lost* is made explicit in some recent investigations of the ways in which history may be known. Philosophers working in the tradition of phenomenological hermeneutics and others pursuing "the analytical philosophy of history" have converged on "the logic of narration" as a means of characterizing historical knowledge.[15] For example, Paul Ricoeur, a major exponent of contemporary hermeneutics, argues "that in one way the notion of the text is a good *paradigm* for human action, in another the action is a good referent for a whole category of texts."[16] This is so partly because human action leaves a mark on subsequent historical developments that are beyond the reach of the actor's intention:

> Human action is in many ways a quasi-text. It is exteriorized in a manner comparable to the fixation characteristic of writing. In becoming detached from its agent, the action acquires an autonomy similar to the semantic autonomy of a text; it leaves a trace, a mark. It is inscribed in the course of things and becomes an archive and document. Even more like a text, of which the meaning has been freed from the initial conditions of its production, human action has a stature that is not limited to its importance for the situation in which it initially occurs, but allows it to be reinscribed in new social contexts. Finally, action, like a text, is an open work, addressed to an indefinite series of possible "readers." The judges are not contemporaries, but subsequent history.[17]

Ricoeur argues that the "dialectic of understanding [*Verstehen*] and explanation [*Erklaren*]" governing the interpretation of texts may be similarly used as a model for the interpretation of human actions, and he distinguishes *understanding,* which seeks insight into the "historical human subject," from analytic or "scientific" knowledge, which is "objective" and ahistorical.[18] In Ricoeur's dialectic, historical episodes are *explained* in terms of causation but *understood* in terms of intention: "The human phenomenon is situated . . . between a causality that requires explanation and not understanding, and a motivation requiring a purely rational understanding."[19]

Thus a narrative plot may be *explained* as a causal series of connected episodes, but it will be *understood* as the disclosure of character, of the motives and intentions of a fictive subject. Milton's presentation of Adam and Eve as author-readers of their own life histories implicitly anticipates Ricoeur's argument for a homology of the structure of the narrative text and historical actions. We may take for an example the interpretation of the daughters of Cain episode in Book XI. Adam's recollection of his "nobler end" and "conformity divine" leads him from natural explanation – the daughters of Cain are good because they give delight – to historical understanding – although delight in beauty is not evil in itself, delight in the daughters of Cain is misplaced because these "fair Atheists" (625) are "bred only and completed to the taste / Of lustful appetence" (618–19) and will spoil the Sons of God "for which / The world erelong a world of tears must weep" (626–7). The historical episode is understood only when placed in the prospect of the completed narrative of history itself. Only the long or retrospective view discloses the motives and intentions, the interior "truths," that determine the quality of the sequence of actions.

In a fictive narrative *or* a narrativization of experience, cause and motive may be expressed as a dialectical synthesis of prospective and retrospective points of view. Milton's text uses metaphor to project these two points of view in a hierarchical structure so that the "eternal" or retrospective experience of time rhetorically masters the immediate or, as I shall call it, dramatic experience of time. In the dialectic of plot and action of the historical text Adam and Eve write, present action is motivated in part by anticipated result. In fact, we can say more generally that the meaning of any action resides in its consequence. The meaning of an action is its historical effect.[20] Because the consequences of an act remain in question as long as history continues to be written, meaning depends upon a proleptic view of history as complete. For Milton, the eschaton of Christian revelation supplies this view.[21]

The Christian view of history, reaching back to creation and forward to the apocalypse, provides the model according to which the apparent contingencies encountered in the temporal unfolding of individual human experience may be rendered meaningful. Each episode in Milton's poem or in the life of the Christian believer becomes significant in two registers. It is understood *contingently*, in a dramatically developing situation, as a link in an unbroken chain of causes and effects connecting episode to episode, and *significantly* as an episode in "the Race of time, / Till time stand fixt: beyond is all abyss, / Eternity, whose end no eye can reach" (XII. 554–6).

Christians living in dramatic time know their own mortality and therefore understand the historicity of their actions as forming episodes on the way to the final terminus of death.[22] Similarly, collective life has an end point when "The World shall burn, and from her ashes spring / New Heav'n and Earth" (III. 334–5). Mediating individual destiny and collective destiny – life history and world history – are the incarnation, passion, resurrection, and second coming of Christ. As Adam realizes, when integrating his life into the world history supplied by Michael in the final books, "to the faithful Death [is] the Gate of Life" (XII. 571) and apocalypse the beginning of new heaven and earth.[23] The individual Christian is then situated at the point where prolepsis and analepsis cross; he or she performs acts from within time that are to be evaluated sub specie aeternitatis. This rhetorical crossing or chiasmus is made historical by Christ's cross, on which the temporal and eternal realms are materially joined for all time by a sacrificial act performed *within time*. Because revelation previews the history of the future, the Christians authoring themselves through their mundane actions are in the position of readers who at once read and reread a story. Louis Mink, writing on the cognitive use of narrative, clarifies what is at stake in the distinction between these two activities:

> What I mean to suggest is that the difference between following a story and *having followed* a story is more than the incidental difference between present experience and past experience. . . . [T]o know an event by retrospection is categorically, not incidentally, different from knowing it by prediction or anticipation. It cannot even, in any strict sense,

be called the "same" event, for in the former case the descriptions under which it is known are governed by a story to which it belongs, and there is no story of the future.[24]

Christians, for whom the history of the future is available, *know* the events of their own lives in a peculiar and complex way, for they experience them seriatim, necessarily using prediction and anticipation to fashion the judgments and choices upon which their actions are based, but Christians also place these same experiences in the cosmic context of revealed, providential history and so are enabled, as it were, to evaluate them retrospectively. They produce the story of their lives – as far as possible – by conforming their lives to a story they have already followed many times.[25]

The knowledge of the end, the experience of rereading, allows us to draw the episodes of any text into a structure within which each individual episode is modified by its perceived relation to every other episode. Mink calls this specifically narrative cognition the "configurational mode of knowing":

> It is in this *configurational* mode that we see together the complex of imagery in a poem, or the combination of motives, pressures, promises and principles which explain a Senator's vote, or the pattern of words, gestures and actions which constitute our understanding of the personality of a friend. . . . The *totum simul* which Boethius regarded as God's knowledge of the world would of course be the highest degree of configurational comprehension.[26]

Mink's reference to the *totum simul* returns us to the omniscient gaze of the Father in Book III. As the Father argued, knowledge of the configuration of things beyond time does not compromise the authority of human action within time. But revealed knowledge of that omniscient view provides the context within which those who have enthralled themselves to history, to dramatic time, may be redeemed to the "nobler end" of "conformity divine." But how is revelation to be known in this dynamic fashion? How does one join the letter of the sacred text to the developing patterns of a semantically open life history? To answer these questions we may recur to the "theory of the text" as it was promulgated in the seventeenth century.

## III

> Medieval four-level exegesis had of course provided for the personal application of the scripture text as the third or tropological level of meaning – *quid agas,* moral allegory, in the familiar formula. . . . But this formula was discredited by the Reformation insistence upon the "one sense of Scripture" and also by Reformation theology: the Protestant sense of the desperate condition of fallen men dictated a shift in emphasis from *quid agas* to God's activity in us. And this in turn led to some effort to assimilate the pattern of individual lives to the pervasive typological patterns discovered in Old and New Testament history.[27]

This statement by Barbara Lewalski, along with its supporting documentation, has had a large influence on recent readings of seventeenth-century religious poetry, and I do not intend in any way to oppose it. Rather I want to pose a question in the margin of *Protestant Poetics:* What becomes of the question *quid agas* after the tropological tradition is rejected?

Tropological or *moral* allegory served an eminently practical and immediately necessary purpose. It enabled Christians, usually with the aid of a priestly interpreter, to draw from Scripture advice about how to behave in daily life, about the judgments and choices out of which the pattern of their moral beings would take shape. When the two dialectically linked contexts of judgment and choice I have just outlined are juxtaposed and distinguished by the Father in *Paradise Lost* III, humankind's obligation to *act* morally is specifically proclaimed. Milton's text raises the issue of just how *quid agas,* the daily acts for which humankind is held morally responsible, and "God's activity in us" are to be reconciled in a properly Protestant – that is, a literal and historical – interpretation of God's will.[28] It is my contention that the Protestant emphasis on "God's activity in us" remains largely theoretical (or one might just as well say theological). Apart from the fringes of extreme predestinarianism (and obviously not in Milton's explicitly Arminian epic), the theoretical question of God's activity in the individual is posterior to the practical question of moral choice.[29] Whether one understands oneself to be moved by God's grace or one's own (more or less regenerate) will, physical action in the world must issue from a certain transaction of mind and muscle – and is normally experienced as having done so. Thus I think we may more accurately understand the Protestant interest in typological *patterns* not as evidence of a rejection of the question of moral action and the tropological tradition that answered to this concern, but as a displacement of the traditional function of tropology onto a revisioned and revisionary typological hermeneutics. Through this displacement, the Protestant is able at once to meet the pressing need for moral guidance and to save the appearance of a theological insistence on the literal interpretation of Scripture. In the specific context of *Paradise Lost,* the Father's remarks on the self-authorship of Adam and Eve in Book III and the dialectic of experience and revelation they imply suggest that the distinction between *quid agas* and "God's activity in us" becomes, in practice, undecidable. Once we have put in question the purely doctrinal explanation of the observed preference for and widening application of typology among seventeenth-century Protestant poets, we may consider what this hermeneutic reformation may tell us about the changing experience of time and its impact on literary genre in the period.

We may begin to reevaluate the association of typological hermeneutics and Protestant poetry by grounding both in the broad currents of social change and technological innovation that underlie the competition in the seventeenth century between two contradictory conceptions of history. The first of these conceptions, which places little value on mundane human action, is conveniently epitomized in John Donne's *First Anniversary*:

> . . . mankind decayes so soone,
> We're scarse our Fathers shadowes cast at noone.
> Onely death addes t'our length: nor are we growne
> In stature to be men, till we are none. (11.143–6)

The second is just as conveniently represented by Francis Bacon's claim that the study of second causes will restore, even in this life, the dominion over nature from which man fell by Adam's sin.[30] The first of these views looks back to a long tradition of Christian thought that sees Adam's fall and Christ's passion as punctuation marks in a homogenous human history, winding down to the appointed moment of messianic apocalypse. The second view looks forward to the notion of history not as a prolongation of man's exile from the light of heaven but as a progress toward regeneration – a sort of postlapsarian improvement "by tract of time." Paradoxically the same group that disputed the efficacy of works in its theology, oversaw and reacted to the beginnings of a technological control of "second causes" that replaced the ancient cycle of the agricultural calendar with a notion of the steady accumulation of wealth through fen drainage, enclosure, wintered-over livestock, and international trade.[31]

The displacement of the seasonal cycle of growth and harvest by the expectation of continued accumulation – of arable land, of livestock, of wealth in its varied commercial forms – occurs over an extended period of time. It is well underway in the second half of the sixteenth century and decisive by the 1650's. The ideological change that follows upon such a reorganization of social production also occurs over an extended period of time. I would suggest that one aspect of the reorganization of English culture that takes place in the sixteenth and seventeenth centuries is a gradual transformation of the experience of time. The seasonal cycle in which productive activity is annually repeated until it culminates, after an indeterminate number of such repetitions, in a decline toward the death of the individual and the concurrent decay of the world, slowly yields to an experience of time as a continual progress, marked by the accumulation of wealth through ever greater mastery of natural law. While Bacon's view of progress is an optimistic one, the "progressive" view of time to which I refer may be held in varying moods. What is at issue is not the expectation that things will necessarily get better over time, but that they grow into their proper or complete forms. The nature of a thing, an event, or a person is thus displaced from its origin to its end. The meaning of history is no longer the expression of an essence, humor, or defect in varied contexts, but rather the continuous motion of development toward the discovery of a final and definitive state of affairs.

Representations of the self within this temporality become less *iterative* expressions of an original predisposition or humor (Odysseus's cunning or Volpone's slyness would be examples) and more *additive* conceptions of a temporal development, articulating change within continuity. *Paradise Lost* is not a *bildungsroman,* but it introduces a relationship of narrative to character that sketches the *bildungsroman* on the horizon. The notion of self-authorship presented in Milton's narrative reflects and consolidates this change. In it, the human individual is understood to author himself or herself over the course of a lifetime by accumulating judgments and choices and the experiences that follow from them, just as the human race authors itself over the course of history, accumulating a "Race of Worshippers" (VII.630) through the biblically enjoined activities of propagation and work.

It is against this background that Reformation hermeneutics play a role in the shaping of poetry and thought. To understand the notion of history implicit in the seventeenth-century religious poets' adaptation of typology, it is necessary to see the typological tradition in relation to the most popular of the pre-Reformation allegorical modes, tropology or *moralitas*. As I have suggested, both tropology and typology function, in different social contexts, as methods for evaluating individual human actions. The theological shift from an emphasis on human action to an emphasis on God's actions in man does not obviate the need for scriptural assistance in the making of moral choices, but it does open the way for a creative revision of mundane action in the direction of the newly important notion of historical progress.

This revision may be observed in the passage of *Paradise Lost* that includes an explicit application of typological hermeneutics. When Michael's narration of the future reaches the Mosaic law, Adam remarks:

> This yet I apprehend not, why to those
> Among whom God will deign to dwell on Earth

So many and so various Laws are giv'n;
So many Laws argue so many sins
Among them, how can God with such reside? (XII.280–4)

Michael's reply illustrates the way in which Milton's typology understands God's activity in man as an internal correlate of man's
activity in time. By the grace of God, man is reempowered to work
on the material world so as to bring it and himself into conformity
with a revelation of the Divine will:

> Doubt not but that sin
> Will reign among them, as of thee begot;
> And therefore was Law given them to evince
> Thir natural pravity, by stirring up
> Sin against Law to fight; that when they see
> Law can discover sin, but not remove,
> Save by those shadowy expiations weak,
> The blood of Bulls and Goats, they may conclude
> Some blood more precious must be paid for Man,
> Just for unjust, that in such righteousness
> To them by Faith imputed, they may find
> Justification towards God, and peace
> Of Conscience, which the Law by Ceremonies
> Cannot appease, nor Man the moral part
> Perform, and not performing cannot live.
> So Law appears imperfet, and but giv'n
> With purpose to resign them in full time
> Up to a better Cov'nant, disciplin'd
> From shadowy Types to Truth, from Flesh to Spirit,
> From imposition of strict Laws, to free
> Acceptance of large Grace, from servile fear
> To filial, works of Law to works of Faith.
> And therefore shall not *Moses,* though of God
> Highly belov'd, being but the Minister
> Of Law, his people into *Canaan* lead:
> But *Josua* whom the Gentiles *Jesus* call,
> His Name and Office bearing, who shall quell
> The adversary Serpent, and bring back

*Introduction*

Through the world's wilderness long wander'd man
Safe to eternal Paradise of rest. (XII.285–314)

The revelation of laws looks forward to that of Love. By evincing
the "natural pravity" of the Jews, laws teach them that fallen men
cannot perform "the moral part" and "not performing cannot live."
Laws thus prepare men – through the long historical tenure of the
covenant – for Grace. Historical experience is the medium in which
fallen man is "disciplined" "from shadowy Types to Truth, from
Flesh to Spirit." The distinction between the two covenants is that
between external adherence to a written text and regeneration of
the heart. When the Spirit writes on the heart, man can be released
from the self-enthrallment incurred by Adam's fall and once again
perform his moral part.

Michael's words accord well with Lewalski's association of typology and the Protestant emphasis on "God's activity in us." Still,
we may note that while under the law man cannot "the moral part
/ Perform, and not performing cannot live"; the effect of "God's
activity in us" is to restore our ability to act morally and thus to
re-pose the question *quid agas*. To perform the moral part, Adam
must follow a *narrative* progression from Moses through Joshua to
Jesus. To follow this narrative, Adam imaginatively occupies the
positions from whch these fictive subjects judge and choose, and,
as his reading progresses, he moves closer to the "conformity divine" that is the goal of his own temporal actions. Since the story
is "foretold," each historical sequence is already placed in the context
of the future fulfillment toward which it tends. Adam is thus afforded the opportunity to act proleptically to regain the moral part.
He transforms Michael's prophecy into a set of moral principles
that he derives from its narrative patterns:

Henceforth I learn, that to obey is best,
And love with fear the only God, to walk
As in his presence, ever to observe
His providence, and on him sole depend,
Merciful over all his works, with good
Still overcoming evil, and by small
Accomplishing great things, by things deem'd weak

Subverting worldly strong, and worldly wise
By simply meek; that Suffering for Truth's sake
Is fortitude to highest victory,
And to the faithful Death the Gate of Life. (XII.561–71)

Michael makes the requirement of moral action in the fallen world an explicit element of the lesson when he instructs Adam to "add / Deeds to thy knowledge answerable" (XII.581–2).[32]

This return to moral action in the world from a detour to the end of time marks a formal alliance between typology and narrative. The favored Protestant hermeneutic and the situation of *Paradise Lost* as the end of an epic and the beginning of a novelistic tradition may be seen as the theological and literary reflections of the rise of historical consciousness and the progressive view of history, as the seventeenth century made its knowledge answerable to its experience. Typology emphasizes the historical development of the Christian revelation. Christ's career is anticipated by the Old Testament prophets, whose prophecies are, in turn, fully realized by his acts. Since the Old Testament types are recognized as such only after the New Testament records their fulfillment or antitype, the typological reading of Scripture always refers the interpretation of one Scriptural passage to a subsequent Scriptural passage. Milton's statement in the *Christian Doctrine* of "the right method of interpreting the scriptures" suggests the degree to which the procedures of Scripture interpretation come to emphasize the narrative nature of the biblical text:

> The requisites are linguistic ability, knowledge of the original sources, *consideration of the overall intent,* distinction between literal and figurative language, *examination of the causes and circumstances, and of what comes before and after the passage in question, and comparison of one text with another.* It must always be asked, too, how far the interpretation is in agreement with faith. (*CP*.VI.582; my emphasis)

One import of the Protestant interest in the text as a completed narrative to be read with constant reference between episodes is a movement away from the notion of a word immediately invested with significance and toward the more modern apprehension of language as a transaction of words with other words. Thus William Whitaker justifies including the typological in the literal sense by arguing that the type and antitype are the metaphoric vehicle and tenor of a single text:

> [The Jewes] had indeed many things of a typical nature, the cloud, the passage through the sea, the water from the rock, the manna; which all were symbols to the pious of heavenly things. . . . These were all sacraments to them, and so the pious understood them. When, therefore, these are expounded literally of the things themselves, spiritually of celestial graces, we do not make two diverse senses; but, by expounding a similitude, we compare the sign with the thing signified, and so bring out the true and entire sense of the words.[33]

Revelation of the truth signified in the Old Testament is deferred until the continuation of the narrative supplies a second term. Out of the conjunction of two episodes – one the metaphoric prolepsis of the other – truth emerges in the course of historical time.

The seventeenth-century Protestant emphasis on the linking of biblical episodes to form a continuous narrative contrasts with the earlier Catholic dependence on tropology or *moralitas* as a way to personalize the biblical text as a guide for moral choice in contemporary contexts. The tropological reading of Scripture distills from the scriptural text a universal moral. This moral, everywhere and always, reveals a universe that is divinely *ordinatissima*. Tropology thus seeks an insight into the eternal decrees of God as they are reflected in the ordered structure of his creation. The individual Christian applies this insight by harmoniously ordering his or her own behavior. Tropology draws from the historical episodes of the Bible timeless truths about the structure and nature of the universe, and these truths are then available for the governance of human actions.

It is precisely this atemporal universality that comes under pressure from changes in the rhythm, governance, and organization of life in the seventeenth century.[34] The problem of moral choice is more complex in a world in which history itself is felt to be man-made, a constant flux of second causes, than it is in a world of moral verities, a world understood as *essentially* unchanging. The nature of an act comes to seem less inherent in its harmonious relationship to unseen, yet omnipresent, eternal decrees and more dependent on its, frequently unforseeable, consequences. Against this background, the type displaces the *moralitas* as the means by which an individual assesses the moral quality of his or her actions. As Lewalski observes, the emphasis of seventeenth-century typology is moral – the Christian understands his or her present condition by referring it to a biblical precedent and understands the moral choice as that choice which conduces to the fulfillment of divine providence. The Christian assimilates not only the moral precepts of Scripture but also its narrative patterns to his or her own ongoing life story. Thus, when Milton refers to the parliamentary engineers of the Restoration as "chusing them a captain back for Egypt" (*CP*.VII [rev.].463), he applies the pattern of the Exodus from slavery through hardship in the wilderness to entry into the promised land to the contemporary voyage of England from Laudian monarchy through the Puritan interregnum, and he evaluates the morality of those who bring England back to monarchy by imputing to them an act that refuses the biblical pattern and leads England away from the promised, regenerate republic and back into bondage.[35]

The historically conditioned emphasis on the type in the seventeenth century does not cancel the tropological emphasis on the divine order of the universe so much as relocate it within history and especially within contemporary historical experience. Since the biblical types represent both historical actors and events *and* an eternal, divine order, typological hermeneutics confirm the Thomistic notion that God writes with things as well as words. Properly understood, contemporary historical experience discloses the ongoing progress of revelation. In a sense, typology replaces the gnosis of God's ways achieved through *moralitas* with the experience of those ways disclosed in time. Typology encourages the reading of Scripture as a narrative of historical events and resists the reduction of biblical history to a series of moral exempla. Revelation itself comes to be appreciated as a process whose completion will occur in a more or less remote future. As the New Testament reveals the true meaning of the historical events narrated in the Old Testament, the indwelling holy Spirit may, in time, reveal the meanings of contemporary historical events: Events that are now experienced as contingent may later be recognized as providential.

A clear presentation of Milton's belief that revelation continues to unfold through mundane history may be found relatively early in his work, in a famous passage of *Areopagitica*:

> Truth indeed came once into the world with her divine Master, and was a perfect shape most glorious to look on: but when he ascended, and his Apostles after him were laid asleep, then strait arose a wicked race of deceivers, who as that story goes of the *AEgyptian Typhon* with his conspirators, how they dealt with the good *Osiris,* took the virgin Truth, hewd her lovely form into a thousand peeces, and scatter'd them to the four winds. From that time ever since, the sad friends of Truth, such as durst appear, imitating the carefull search that *Isis* made for the mangl'd body of *Osiris,* went up and down gathering up limb by limb still as they could find them. We have not yet found them all, Lords and Commons, nor ever shall doe, till her Masters second comming. (*CP*.II.549)

Christians are to collect truth where they can find it and, through the medium of their experience and the faculty of reason, make such judgments and choices as will conform their moral character to the divine body of Truth whose return they await. That return, when it comes, will write the conclusion to historical time and human action.[36]

## IV

What I wish to explore in the chapters that follow is the implication of historical consciousness, as I have defined it and as it is doctrinally represented by the characteristic hermeneutic procedures of Milton and his contemporaries, in the narrative structure of *Paradise Lost*. Milton's epic is the success at the end of a line of attempted English epics stretching back to the Elizabethan period.[37] Somewhere near the heart of that success is Milton's explicit rejection of the dynastic romance as a generic model (IX.24–47). What seems to me to be involved in the formal revision Milton undertakes is precisely the historical sense of action taking hold in the social relations of Milton's time. A very brief consideration of the differences in narrative form between Spenser's epic romance and Milton's dramatic epic underlines the emphasis on revelation in history and the temporal unfolding of historical events exemplified in the latter. In Spenser's poem events occur in a place that cannot be located with respect to human geography and the narrative is often interrupted by emblematic tableaux.[38] In Milton's poem events tend toward the clearly defined narrative goals given in the opening lines. The internal geography and timing are precise, and the historicality of the fictional locales is reinforced by references to details of mundane geography. While Spenser's poem is literally endless, Milton's is clearly proportioned by the dimensions of his argument.[39] I would suggest that the experience of historical time changed between the composition of these two poems – that Spenser's poem transforms time into space to form an allegorical landscape in which all times and places signify God's divine order, while Milton's presents a sense of time conditioned by cause and effect, the committing of acts the meanings of which are disclosed in their consequences. This is not to imply that *The Faerie Queene* lacks a historical dimension. Spenser's juxtaposition of real and imagined worlds, of the history of Britain and of Faerie Land, explicitly engages his readers in the assessment of contemporary historical events. But the relationship of the British and Elfin "histories" is Spenser's alternative to the fully temporalized configuration of episodes that structures Milton's narrative. In *The Faerie Queene* the key to British history is to be found in the parallel history of an allegorical location not in the rigorously worked out linkage of contingent causes. Despite his own Protestantism and his use of typological figures, Spenser's narrative bends the "arrow of time" in a tropological mirror, turns always back to the court of Glorianna and the origin of the knightly quests, an origin that is itself displaced to the missing terminus of the nonexistent twelfth book.[40]

This summary account of the differences between Spenserian and Miltonic narrative may be challenged by recent studies of the interpretation and imitation of Vergil's *Georgics* in the Renaissance. Arguing that the *Georgics* provide a model of dignified labor, under-taken by many hands and issuing finally in the fulfillment of a collective destiny, these studies find in *The Faerie Queene* a historical consciousness quite close to that of *Paradise Lost*.[41] William Sessions, for example, argues that the various quests of the knight-virtues in *The Faerie Queene* represent, through a plurality of examples, "the definition of a native English hero," who labors within history to attain a transcendent, national destiny. The heroism of each knight is to suggest the activation of some aspect of Arthurian "magnanimity" as called forth by a particular set of historical circumstances. Thus "the formal allegory now provides the courtiers [of Spenser's audience] with a clarifying transformation of their own consciousness of perspectives for heroism," much as Milton's depiction of judgment and choice promotes a transfer of biblical patterns to everyday situations.[42]

Such an apparent conceptual harmony between Spenserian and Miltonic narrative serves to bring into focus the sharp formal differences between *The Faerie Queene* and *Paradise Lost*. Although Spenser and Milton both combine exemplary patterns and concrete circumstances in their narratives, Spenser does not imbricate his narrative episodes in the way that Milton does. The unity of *The Faerie Queene* lies not in the logical implication of the various actions portrayed in it but in its delineation of an ideal character, expressed variously in each quest.[43] Spenser's presentation of character remains iterative. The virtue for which a knight is named is always prior to the events that test it, figuring by its presence or absence in response to different contexts, the readiness of the knight to undertake the actions that will at once confirm his character and his destiny.

Milton joins the epic's accumulation of exemplary episodes – illustrating repeatedly the single, just man's defense of the Godly, as Homer illustrates the cunning of Odysseus, and Vergil, the *pietas* of Aeneas – with the dramatic causality of tragedy to produce the focus on judgment and choice that discloses characters who understand themselves to be self-authored. Milton's narrative joins its principal characters to one another through a series of acts that contribute to the connected actions of fall and restoration announced in the poem's opening lines. *The Faerie Queene* offers a plurality of actions differed in space and unifies those actions by invoking their exemplarity. *Paradise Lost* presents an *integrated* series of actions differed in time and projects a unity of action and history, destiny and choice.[44] Its presentation of character is additive rather than iterative; Milton's characters author (augment) themselves in and through a sequence of historically contingent actions, discovering their peculiar virtues and vices in the backward glance of historical time. The modern historical subject is doubtless emergent in *The Faerie Queene*, but it has not yet found its commensurate literary form. The version of Genesis presented in *Paradise Lost* is the genesis of that peculiar individual who is at once God's creature and author to himself or herself.

In his seminal study "Figura," Erich Auerbach sees in typological hermeneutics the three-way articulation of a historical event (*historia*), the rhetorical use of that event as a type (*figura*), and the truth that will come into view at a later time, when the singular event is fulfilled by a subsequent and transcending event (*veritas*):

> Beside the opposition between *figura* and fulfillment or truth, there appears another, between *figura* and *historia; historia* or *littera* is the literal sense or the event related; *figura* is the same literal meaning or event in reference to the fulfillment cloaked in it, and this fulfillment itself is *veritas,* so that *figura* becomes a middle term between *littera-historia* and *veritas.* In this connection *figura* is roughly equivalent to *spiritus* or *intellectus spiritalis,* sometimes replaced by *figuralitas.*[45]

As an example of the theory of the text, Auerbach's argument is an exercise in philology, but if we apply Ricoeur's homology of text and actions we can see in Auerbach's argument the situation of Milton's Christian hero authoring himself in history.[46] The Miltonic subject writes his history in actions based on choices made in the light of *intellectus spiritalis,* knowledge of the future understood through the mediation of the interior voice of the Spirit. Temporal experience will give way to *veritas,* when Truth's master returns to "bring together every joint and member, and mold them into an immortal feature of loveliness and perfection" (*CP*.II.549). To succeed, the Christian acts within time to mold his or her image in "conformity divine" to that future revelation of Truth beyond time.

24

It is this pattern of historical revelation, the slow learning of the double dialectic of immediate experience and spiritual understanding, that I wish to trace through a sequential reading of the twelve books of *Paradise Lost*.

In considering *Paradise Lost,* I shall be looking closely at the interactions of three elements in its structure: the episodes, which are the building blocks from which it is assembled; the narrative itself, by which I mean the working out of the story through the integration of the episodes; and the network of allusions both to the cultural background outside the text and, as the poem develops, to previous episodes within it, especially when a given word or passage is revised by a subsequent word or passage. For example, in Book IV, Adam and Eve are conversing in Eden, when Adam remarks on the munificence of their creator and the single rule they must obey:

> hee who requires
> From us no other service than to keep
> This one, this easy charge, of all the Trees
> In Paradise that bear delicious fruit
> So various, not to taste that only Tree
> Of Knowledge, planted by the Tree of Life.
> So near grows Death to Life, whate'er Death is,
> Some dreadful thing no doubt. (419–26)

In this scene, the projection of Adam's innocence is mediated by the reader's awareness that Satan, who overhears the conversation, is supplied by it with the weapon he seeks. But the jarring difference in the apprehension of the word "death" by innocent Adam and experienced Satan is the more arresting element. The signification of "death" slips among three different points of view, Adam's, Satan's, and the reader's. "Death's" meaning "in truth" is deferred to the end of time when "Death his death's wound shall then receive, and stoop / Inglorious, of his mortal sting disarm'd" (III.252–3). Eventually Adam's "so near grows Death to Life" will be rewritten as "and to the Faithful Death the Gate of Life" (XII.571). In the chapters that follow, I wish to trace the mediations through which Adam's *historia* figures this *veritas*.

25

# 2

## EXORBITANT DESIRES

Of Man's First Disobedience, and the Fruit
Of that Forbidden Tree, whose mortal taste
Brought Death into the World, and all our woe,
With loss of *Eden,* till one greater Man
Restore us, and regain the blissful Seat,
Sing Heav'nly Muse (I. 1–6)

In the opening lines of *Paradise Lost,* a series of transformations
from metonymy to synecdoche projects a double movement of fall
and restoration. The poem's second word, "Man's," stands metonymically for "Adam's." But Adam himself stands for "mankind," as the "one greater Man" of line four stands for the "second
Adam" of Christian Typology. As Adam includes mankind in his
fall, Christ includes mankind in his resurrection. When understood
from the retrospective view of revelation, first and second Adam
are identified with each other because each *acts* for all men.

The logical force of this transition from metonymy to synecdoche
is the introduction and reduction of difference. The centrality of
this rhetorical transformation to the architecture of *Paradise Lost*
will be discussed in Chapter 8, but I want to pause at this point to
notice briefly the relationship of rhetorical tropes to narrative action
that subtends my argument. If we think of narrative as transitive
discourse, that is to say, discourse that records a change from one
state of affairs to another, we may recognize the role of tropes in
envisaging an articulate account of experience and motivating the
transitions from one state to another. The figures of metonymy

and synecdoche (along with metaphor and irony) each represent a distinct way of relating elements within poetic discourse. Metonymy substitutes one term for another, contiguous, but different. Synecdoche relates two terms in a hierarchy of part and whole. The organization of relationships among actors and objects in any discourse may be opposed to a different organization that represents a different tropic configuration, and thereby, an alternative notion of relatedness. Narrative discourse in particular may be thought of as a series of alternative descriptions, joined to each other through transitions from one trope to another. Milton's narrative offers these alternative configurations as a temporal series, in which narrative closure represents the final configuration as synecdochially including all the others. A narrative that asserts such a hierarchical privilege for its closure resolves the discontinuities internal to its characters as they move through it by envisaging successive actions as stages through which the characters pass on their way to self-realization.[1]

To read Adam and Christ as metonymies is to posit a succession of distinct individuals appearing at specified times in the linear unfolding of history. To read them as synecdoches of the whole of mankind is to elide the distinctions between them and to attribute their acts to a unified essential man who recuperates the losses of disobedience by his subsequent restoration. The rhetoric of Milton's invocation, metonymic in the prospective view and synecdochic in the retrospective view, performs the cycle of alienation and rapprochement between man and God that is its theme. In the poem's first four lines the act of an individual man is first projected as irreversible and decisive, then negated through the transcending act of a second man, yet finally preserved in the form of its effects within a history that is itself inscribed within a transcendent providence. Providence anticipates – through divine foreknowledge – the general shape of human history and intervenes – with the incarnation – to provide a synecdochic resolution that guarantees the integrity of human action, while deferring the discovery of that integrity to the end of time. Milton's text invests this succession of rhetorical redescriptions with ontological authority. As a prophetic poet, he engages a rhetoric that asserts itself as a description of what will be at history's end. The force of this assertion comes from the formal assimilation of history to narrative form and the

27

consequent assumption that the apocalypse will provide history with a synecdochic narrative closure. Since the events of the eschaton and the general patterns of providential narrative have been given to man by divine revelation, human actors may actively participate in the motion of history toward this narrative closure, thus becoming "authors to themselves." The reader of *Paradise Lost,* constructing and revising the meaning of each episode according to his or her recollection of what has been revealed and anticipation of what is to come, collaborates with its author in a representation of his or her collaboration with providence.

The principal theme of Books I and II of *Paradise Lost* is the exclusion of the fallen angels from this dialectical transformation of difference into identity. In terms of Milton's dialectical rhetoric, Satan and his followers are presented as subjects of a desire that cannot realize an identity with its object. The exorbitance of their desire, which always exceeds its object and seeks to set up its own fantasy image in the place of the other, precludes the historical mediation of the individual self and the eternal and unitary image of God that is the thesis of Milton's theme. The fallen angels are thus constituted as absolute difference. Their damnation is eternal because they are what remains at the end of time; the repressed underworld of Milton's universe, their acts motivate a narrative that is structured as a series of motions to exclude them. Unable to interpret the dialectic of difference and identity represented by the transformation from an excluding metonymy to an including synecdoche, they are cast out of the orbit of divine creation. The reader, initiated into the universe of *Paradise Lost* through the infernal corridor of Books I and II, first confronts and learns from the inhabitants of hell a set of rhetorical patterns that constitute the thesis of difference.

When the narrative action of Book I begins, the pattern of alienation and reunion apparent in the invocation is replaced by images that equate prospective and retrospective views. The fallen angels are cast into hell "to bottomless perdition, there to dwell" (I.47). The adjective "bottomless" transposes the infinite time of eternal damnation to an equally infinite space that prolongs indefinitely the action of the latinate "ruin." The prosody of the passage effectively transforms this fall through endless space into a sudden exhalation as the aspirates of "him . . . hurl'd . . . headlong . . . hideous," are released in the clustered glottal stops of " . . . com*b*us*t*ion *d*own / *T*o *b*o*tt*omless *p*er*d*ition, there *t*o *d*well / In A*d*aman*t*ine Chains and *p*enal Fire, / Who *d*urs*t d*efy th' Omni*p*o*t*en*t t*o Arms" (I.44–9). The realization of time as space symbolically arrests the temporal movement of the fallen angels as the long exhalation converts the living rhythm of breath into an infernal wind.[2]

This equation of space and time is ascribed to a subjectivity peculiar to the fallen when Satan, awaking to the double torment of present pain and the memory of lost pleasure, "throws his baleful eyes / That witness'd huge affliction and dismay" (I.56–7). What the reader sees through Satan's eyes is an external world that mirrors in physical terms Satan's internal distress. The boundary between Satan's subjectivity and its objects is breached and obscured so that what he sees is "mixt with obdurate pride and steadfast hate" (I.58). Described as a "dismal Situation" (I.60) before it is established as a place, hell is at once the location and the future of the fallen angels.

Satan's intellect, formidable in its dimensions, is crippled by his exile from God's light, for in the universe of *Paradise Lost,* it is God's light that discloses a world other than and independent of the pseudoworld projected by internal desire. The darkness into which Satan is ultimately cast is the shadow world of self-generated need, and the "dismal situation" of the damned is the logical projection of a rupture in the dialectic of desire and the material conditions in which it seeks its object. His link with a stable reality severed, Satan faces a proliferation of hypothetical projections, each hypothesis superseded by the next before a significant conclusion is reached. These projections pour through the breach in the boundary between self and world to constitute the "darkness visible" (I.62) that fills the space from which light has been withdrawn.[3]

The metonymic substitution of objects produced by fantasy for the desired identity with God obscures Satan's view of the light and marks his language with a characteristic syntax.[4] Just as movement in space and time in hell can only reproduce the same "dismal situation," Satanic discourse sacrifices the positive to the conditional statement. Thus, of all the named characters in *Paradise Lost*, Satan has the first word and that word is "if."[5]

If thou beest hee; But O how fall'n! how chang'd
From him, who in the happy Realms of Light
Cloth'd with transcendent brightness didst outshine
Myriads though bright. (I.84–7)

The change Satan perceives in Beelzebub marks the culminating effect of the devils' denial of divine creation: their inability to articulate their own past and present and thus to constitute a sense of themselves as able to remain self-identical while differing over time. This final disruption of the articulation of self and world implies a loss of the thing they most desire – self-possession – or, to return to the metaphor governing the present study – self-authorship. What they were is somehow no longer what they are. The dialectic of the developing self that unifies an individual as the sum total of his experiences is reduced to an interminable present and an irretrievable past. Their very nostalgia for this past is maintained only as a retrospection that blurs the boundaries of past and present and makes Beelzebub at once himself but not himself, a hypothetical "hee" whose relationship to an authentic but no longer present self is problematic.[6]

A clue to the complicated temporality of this rupture lies in what might at first appear to be a nostalgic idealization of the past. Why would Satan and Beelzebub revolt if they were "cloth'd with transcendent brightness" in "the happy Realms of Light"? The acute sense of loss that defines the painful nostalgia of the fallen covers over the paradoxical impulse to measure the transcendent upon which satanic logic is built. For Satan, Beelzebub's glory inheres not in transcendent brightness of itself but in the fact that he "didst outshine / Myriads though bright." Thus, even in the presence of an absolute God, Satan appears to have measured merit on a scale both relative and competitive.

I do not want to engage here the old canard about the temporal placement and motivation of the fall, but only to suggest that it is a peculiar transcendence that is only achieved at the expense of another and that it would be as impossible to describe Lucifer without a prolepsis of Satan as to describe Satan without a retrospection of Lucifer. The point to be underlined is that this problem can arise at all. The need to motivate the fall, to render a unified satanic psychology, arises only because Milton's narrative portrays a historical rather than an essential subject. Lucifer has broken free of his origin in God and been subjected to history. Satan is determined by his action of rebellion and his predisposition to measure value on a relative scale, and he can only return to his happy past in the gloomy guise of his present self. Heaven is the scene of his childhood viewed by a rigid adult self who stares at the impenetrable innocence of his own lost image.[7]

Satan and his followers understand the fall as the tragic result of an ambitious experiment. Joined once in hopes, they are now joined "in equal ruin" (I.91). Satan addresses to Beelzebub a retrospective interpretation of their recent common experience, asserting that their fall has finally proven God the stronger: "till then who knew / The force of those dire Arms?" (I.93–4). The force of "knew" is revised by Satan's fall. He, along with his legions and the two-thirds of the heavenly host that did not fall, had direct experience of God's love, goodness, justice, and light. Satan's "need" to oppose these attributes and so bring out their opposites looks forward to the "need" of Eve to acquire knowledge of good and evil by losing good. Fallen knowledge results from an act of appropriation in which the inherent qualities of things are made dependent on the subjectivity of a perceiver. God's inherent power becomes subject to Satan's proof and Eve's diet. In each case the result is to elide the absolute substantiality of God in favor of an internal economy of desires. Milton's falls are in one sense falls into history, because they record the founding of the historical subject in its subjection to temporal events. But in another sense they are ironic negations of history, because they result in a negating self-involvement that leaves the historical actor incapable of further action. Satan argues that his desire to test God's strength is also the ground of his tragic nobility: "that fixt mind / And high disdain, from sense of injur'd merit, / That with the mightiest rais'd me to contend" (I.97–9). But the contradiction inherent in Satan's pose as an existentialist in the sight of God suggests compulsive rationalization and repetition rather than the freedom acquired through the existential project. Satan's claims have meaning only after the fall and cannot motivate

31

it. He is a creature who cannot author himself because he is condemned by virtue of his "dismal situation" to repeat the act of rebellion on which his sense of self is based.[8]

In Hell, Satan's attempts to understand, structure, and test his environment seem admirable. But the more we search his speech, the more we understand the compulsion behind his rationalizing rationalism. Satan claims he revolted "from sense of injur'd merit," but his perception of injured merit cannot be divorced from his peculiarly competitive and relativistic value system. To him God is "so much the stronger prov'd" by "his Thunder" (I.92–3). Satan perceives merit not as a moral quality but as the ability to dominate. He believes he is elevated by the mere act of challenging God's dominance, and he exults in the domination of his own legions. Satan seeks to be the subject of the history he initiates and is, ironically, subjected to. Satan's desire misses its target in a way that recapitulates (or anticipates) the change in the usage of the word "subject" that takes place toward the end of the seventeenth century. Satan wishes to be a subject in the modern philosophical sense by asserting the primacy of consciousness over the material world, but instead becomes a subject in the older (feudal) sense of being ruled by an outside force.[9] This philological trope on the meanings of "subject" is especially apposite because Satan's subjection to external forces is immediately seen as his captivation by his own language. There is in Satan's speeches an insistent, underlying pattern of compulsion, a language of justification that culminates in direct and verifiable lies. For example, there was never any "dubious Battle on the Plains of Heav'n" (I.104) (at least not taking "dubious" in the sense Satan intends), nor did he ever shake God's throne. That the devil is a liar is not particularly revealing, but the context of his lie is. Since Beelzebub knows the facts of the war as directly as Satan, Satan's lie to him can only be an effort at self-deception or mutual deception.

Satan's empiricism then rises not out of the desire for knowledge but for power. He wishes to understand his environment only to manipulate it and remake it in his own unstable image. Writing in the first phase of the technological age, Milton engages in an effort to distinguish knowledge and power that is already nostalgic. The

32

attempt of the devils, under the direction of Moloch and Mammon, to make a heaven of hell recalls (perversely) Bacon's claim that Eden might be restored through mastery of second causes (a claim echoed by the young Milton in his seventh Prolusion). But because he makes his own will the arbiter of reality, Satan is himself unable to construct a social subject. His perceptions remain his own and the transformations of the material world that he brings about are never those he intends, but rather reiterations of his own psychic economy. He sets out to impose his angelic face on the landscape of hell but can only learn (in Book IV) to recognize as his own the face reflected in hell's mirror. Refusing to accept his place in the intersubjective society of heaven, Satan prefers to enact his fantasies of power. God responds by throwing him into a world where those fantasies are unrestrained by material creation. In such a world the dialectic of metonymy and synecdoche, of part and whole, outlined at the start of this chapter, cannot be achieved, and Satan is condemned to pursue eternally his own image, lost in the metonymic objects seized by his desire. Satan uses rhetoric not only as a tool to persuade others, but to shield himself from the truth. He is mastered by language and imprisoned by the persistent patterns of his own speech, patterns that reflect not choice but compulsion.

Because Satan can only conceive of reality in his own image, he projects himself onto God and makes of God a stronger Satan, whom he invests with "the Tyranny of Heav'n" (I.124). He cannot sue for grace because, lacking it himself, he assumes that the "tyrant" God must lack it as well. Satan, applying his subjective standard, implies that his submission would somehow "deify" (I.112) the power of the Father. Seeing only the projections of his own desires, Satan appropriates to himself the power to deify God by submitting to him or to make him a tyrant by resisting.

We find in Beelzebub a similar tentativeness toward external objects. Beelzebub, too, adverts to logic and experimentation (I.134–55) and puts the syllogism to curious use. According to Beelzebub: 1) God has defeated Satan's angels; 2) only an almighty power could have defeated them; therefore, 3) God is almighty. Like Satan, Beelzebub begins with the fiction of a quest for certainty and then argues that it is his experiment that in fact constitutes God's divinity.[10] As Satan believes that his submission or resistance defines God's political nature, Beelzebub implies that the rebellion has finally settled the "issue" of God's omnipotence. What had been understood as the eternal expression of God's essence is redefined by the fallen angels as a historically contingent reaction to their actions. Of more general importance is their penchant for seeking the nature of things not in created essences, but in historical consequences as they are encountered seriatim.

Like Satan, Beelzebub believes glory to be an extrinsic quality derived from one's position with respect to others. Thus, he can say "vigor soon returns, / Though all our Glory extinct" (I.140–1). The converse of the fallen habit of projecting internal states into the exterior world is the investiture of external panoply with intrinsic value. Again, the constant state of doubt caused by the "darkness" of hell represents the specifically epistemological failures of its inmates. Even though they talk of experimental verification, the devils boast paradoxically of the immutability of their minds and wills. When they do not obtain the results they hope for, instead of altering their views, they become petulant.

The narrator's poetry is not often as exciting as Satan's, but it offers a contrasting pattern against which Satan's speech may be evaluated. Satan's rhetoric generates a fictive universe in which he may constitute himself as heroic, but the narrator's rhetoric is grounded on confidence in the unfolding of a history that remains within the control of providence:

> So stretcht out huge in length the Arch-fiend lay
> Chain'd on the burning Lake, nor ever thence
> Had ris'n or heav'd his head, but that the will
> And high permission of all-ruling Heaven
> Left him at large to his own dark designs,
> That with reiterated crimes he might
> Heap on himself damnation, while he sought
> Evil to others, and enrag'd might see
> How all his malice serv'd but to bring forth
> Infinite goodness, grace and mercy shown
> On Man by him seduc't, but on himself
> Treble confusion, wrath and vengeance pour'd. (I.209–20)

Here the conditional statements, projected realities, and appeals to empirical knowledge that characterize fallen rhetoric are replaced by calm declaration of truth reached through reason and revelation. The narrator's faith satisfies the needs that Satan seeks to fill with words.

Milton never presents Satan as "a worthy Antagonist of Heaven," nor does he first glorify and then degrade him.[11] From the beginning, Satan is presented as a character without volition, whose range of action is limited to attempts to negate divine initiatives

> As being the contrary to his high will
> Whom we resist. If then his Providence
> Out of our evil seek to bring forth good,
> Our labor must be to pervert that end,
> And out of good still to find means of evil. (I.161–5)

Satan can no more be free of God than a reverse image in a mirror can be free of the object that it reflects. His role as a distorting mirror of God further discloses his particular mode of subjectivity. Satan perceives God as his alter ego and reacts aggressively to God's creative activity as if it were an attempt to appropriate his power of action.[12] But this aggression only confirms the appropriation, since it leaves him reacting to or parodying divine actions. Just as Satan's attempt to establish himself as a free subject results in his subjugation, his attempt to establish a revolutionary state in exile results in the "reactionary" monarchy of hell.

Since my purpose is to explicate the rhetorical configuration that defines Satanic subjectivity, I will put the case in rhetorical terms. In the previous chapter we saw that Milton defines the historical subjectivity of Adam and Eve under the metaphor of authorship. As "authors to themselves" Adam and Eve write their lives in actions and become characters – that is, personalities – in the same way that fictional characters do. But just as fictional characters perform actions that are written by an author who transcends the text, Adam and Eve act within a specifically metaphoric relation to providence. They understand themselves to be authors insofar as they are like God, yet different. They recognize the difference between analogy and identity, and they write in a language supplied

by God. Satan is unable to recognize the divine language of providential patterns that supplies the motives of self-authorship. God
supplies the context of all actions by creating the universe. It is
precisely this context that Satan rejects. By denying divine creation,
he, in effect, challenges the medium of discourse. His message of
self continually exceeds and subsumes the context. In rhetorical
terms he personifies irony, a challenge to the efficacy of language
so general as to be able to manage only negation. The ironic cannot
generate a narrative because it can only say this is not true. At best
it generates a shadow narrative dependent upon the story it challenges, and this is precisely what Satan does.[13]

Under the metaphors of discourse and authorship that control
the presentation of subjectivity in *Paradise Lost,* Satan is a monol-
oguist, who attempts self-affirmation by negating the very language
in which the self is constituted. It is in this precisely rhetorical way
that his evil always redounds upon him. The reader who has noted
Satan's habit of projecting his internal state onto the exterior universe
will be aware of the ironic literalness of his claim that "the mind
is its own place" (I.254). Because hell is Satan's place, the infernal
parody of God's monarchy serves only to illustrate that heaven is
heaven because God and not Satan is its king. In Book IV, when
he once more confronts creation in God's light, Satan will rewrite
his assertion that "the mind is its own place" as "which way I fly
is Hell; myself am Hell" (IV.75).

What is extraordinary is that Milton's portrait of Satan anticipates
the development of literary subjectivity over the next three centuries.
As Adam and Eve's self-authorship represents the subject of the
realistic novel, the self developed in conflict with a given set of
historical circumstances, Satan's free-running fantasies represent the
autonomy of the self achieved through the rejection of history characteristic of modernism. A brief consideration of Georg Lukács's
distinction of realism and modernism should clarify this point.[14]
Lukács distinguishes between abstract and concrete potential in literary characters. Abstract potential is bounded only by the individual
imagination:

> The possibilities in a man's mind, the particular pattern, in-
> tensity and suggestiveness they assume, will of course be

characteristic of that individual. In practice, their number will border on the infinite, even with the most unimaginative individual. It is thus a hopeless undertaking to define the contours of individuality, let alone come to grips with a man's actual fate, by means of potentiality. The *abstract* character of potentiality is clear from the fact that it cannot determine development – subjective mental states, however permanent or profound, cannot here be decisive.[15]

Over against this "abstract potential" Lukács places what he calls "concrete potential," that is, not what the subject can imagine but what, given a concrete set of material historical conditions, he can achieve: "Situations arise in which a man is confronted with a choice; and in the act of choice a man's character may reveal itself in a light that surprises even himself."[16] Lukács's language in describing this dialectic through which the concrete emerges from the confrontation of desire and possibility is remarkable for its resemblance to the language Milton uses in the third book of *Paradise Lost* and in *Areopagitica*. Adam and Eve are confronted by situations, by a created universe. Satan generates situations. Adam and Eve emerge from their choices, but Satan dwells within his abstract potential and cannot confront situations at all. Thus two very different kinds of actors are at work in the narrative of *Paradise Lost*. That Lukács, arguing for "socialist" realism and against modernism, should define and evaluate them so aptly is neither surprising nor coincidental. The coexistence of the "realistic" and the "modernist" subject in Milton's epic is a function of the temporality of his narrative, for the "modernist" subject, like Satan in *Paradise Lost,* is the ironic double of the realist subject and therefore always implicit in it. History is not elided in the consciousness of Satan or of his modernist descendants; it is repressed. Indeed this genealogy of the modern privilege accorded to the "triumph of the will" and the unbounded self at once suggests the origin of the romantic infatuation with Milton's Satan and the continuity between romantic and modernist versions of the imagination.[17]

The construction of the self, whether abstract or concrete, remains a social phenomenon, and Milton does not neglect to place Satan within the social community of hell. After Satan and Beelzebub complete their conference on the Stygian lake, Milton widens his focus to include the infernal body politic. The social structure of hell projects the fallen sensibility as the pattern of earthly tyranny. The catalogue of fallen angels that Milton presents when Satan calls his apostles from the burning lake identifies the chief devils – anachronistically – as the pagan gods of postlapsarian Earth (I. 376–521). The projection of the devils into human history again defines their character from a double temporal perspective. What they are now – in the fictive present – is understood through a retrospective knowledge of what they will become in the narrator's present.

When Satan, now monarch in his own realm, reviews his troops, the value of "transcendent brightness" is forgotten as he is overwhelmed by his numerical strength:

> He through the armed Files
> Darts his experienc't eye, and soon traverse
> The whole Battalion views, thir order due,
> Thir visages and stature as of Gods;
> Thir number last he sums. And now his heart
> Distends with pride, and hard'ning in his strength
> Glories. (I. 567–73)

These lines are followed by a series of similes comparing the infernal legions to mythological and historical armies (I. 575–99). As in the catalogue of pagan gods, the devils are again proleptically translated out of hell and into human history. Here the dialectic of temporal views is quite complex. As much as the earthly concept of warlike heroism dignifies the devils, so much is that concept deprecated by its hellish origin.[18] The past is understood by comparing it to a less remote past and each term of the simile undercuts the other, reiterating the pattern by which the future discloses the meaning of the past.

Satan's address to his troops (I.622–34) reveals the same patterns of thought observed in his private dialogue with Beelzebub. Satan begins with Beelzebub's syllogism: Only omnipotence could defeat the infernal horde; it was defeated by God; therefore God is almighty. Satan asserts that only the empirical test of war could prove

God's omnipotence, for God's power was unknown, "from the Depth / Of knowledge past or present" (I.627–8). Having proven that God is omnipotent, however, Satan refuses to accept the proof and proposes to repeat the experiment. Having confronted the resistance of a material reality, he can only reiterate his desire. Does he dissemble or does he forget what he has previously learned (I.249–63)? As his oratory becomes increasingly hyperbolic the distinction is blurred. Satan becomes his own audience. The public and private Satan are compatible.

Demonstrating in the political sphere what he has already shown in private conversation, Satan projects onto heaven the structure he will establish in hell when he appears in Book II, "High on a Throne of Royal State" (1). In his perceptions of his surroundings, in his understanding of the social organization of heaven, in his insistence on the immutability of his own personality, Satan consistently projects his desire – indeed his image – onto his surroundings. We may understand this nondialetical subjectivity as the negation of the "conversation" engaged in by the intersubjective community of God's creatures.[19] Embodying the trope of irony, Satan ironically speaks the truth. Because he is always that which is in excess of the communal system, that which must be excluded to maintain the discourse, Satan, despite his rebellious intentions, can only affirm God's system. His actions, aimed at challenging the discourse, take the place of negation within it. In this sense he is, indeed, the other of God. Unable to maintain the necessary distinctions of self and other, interior and exterior, Satan creates, in hell, a mirror of the slipping and contingent embodiments of his own desire, a desire for self that is necessarily elusive because discourse locates the self always in the speech of the other. Irony is the collapse of this relocation of the self in the other. Satan loses the image in the mirror by trying to go behind it.[20]

Milton's portrait of hell begins with an invocation of heaven. The opening lines of *Paradise Lost* enact the rhetorical dialectic of metonymic substitution and synecdochic identity that form the background of the sliding metonymies of hell, Satan's parody kingdom, which can never be more than an antiheaven. In this parody, metonymy remains metonymy, and Satan sits in for God, on a demented throne that is always specifically not the judgment seat. The polity of hell reflects this metonymic displacement on the level of social organization. It is, so to speak, the ideology of satanism.

The narrative form corresponding to the demonic rhetoric of metonymy and irony is patterned or periodic repetition – a fact that will later be figured in the divine discourse by the condemnation of the devils to the yearly reenactment of the temptation of man (X. 575–7). This narrative of repetition is, however, enclosed in the narrative of Milton's epic through the narrator's adjustments of perspective, through the displacement from the fictive present to the anticipated end of time, which we have already discussed, and through a series of mediating shifts in point of view. The whale simile of I.200–8 warns that Satan is massive and dangerous but ultimately unstable by transferring him from the mythological setting of the Stygian lake to the historical context of the mistaken seamen, "the Pilot of some small night-founder'd Skiff" (I.204).[21] Similes like this one quite literally "naturalize" Satan by looking forward to the ways in which he will be translated from his own unresisting realm to the more mediated venue of the postlapsarian world. Through them the prolepsis of the devils' manifestation as pagan gods is rendered more meaningful. The pagan gods are accorded a substantial reality but, at the same time, the fallen angels are subjected to diminution because they are forced to present themselves to men in fictive disguises and false myths. Similes such as the comparison of Satan to a whale diminish the devils further by carrying forward the chronicle of their appearances in human history.

At the close of Book I, another famous simile extends the transformation from myth to nature, from Satan to the entire polity of hell: The hordes of devils crowd the entrance to Pandemonium like bees about a hive in springtime (I.768–88), when, "the Signal giv'n," the devils

> who seem'd
> In bigness to surpass Earth's Giant Sons
> Now less than smallest Dwarfs, in narrow room
> Throng numberless. (I.777–80)[22]

The reader who has imagined the awesome palace of the devils is suddenly asked to reenvisage it as the "suburb of thir Straw-built Citadel" (I.773). The fallen angels, previously translated into human history as pagan gods, now take the forms they will have in the Christian world: bees, pygmies

> or Faery Elves,
> Whose midnight Revels by a Forest side
> Or Fountain some belated Peasant sees,
> Or dreams he sees. (I.781–4)[23]

This series of similes attenuating the fallen angels from "Earth's Giant Sons" to bees, pygmies, and faery elves has an implicit temporal thrust in relation to mundane history, carrying the devils through their careers as pagan gods and later images of homely naturalism to their folklore manifestations as elves and goblins. It is worth noting in this context that when Satan presents himself to the human world it is not in his horrific giant form but first as a toad and then a serpent. In the world of God's light the abstract form of Satan's ambition is moderated by confrontation with a reality his mind cannot subsume.

The comic decorum of Book II continues to revise the demonic appearances in the *light* of a more worldly point of view, culminating when Satan confronts his "proud imaginations" (II.10) substantially realized in the forms of Sin and Death. Rather than an attempt to degrade an initially heroic Satan, this shift indicates the narrator's increasing understanding of Satan's limitations. As a fallen man, the narrator stands in for the reader, and as a fallen man journeying toward salvation, he stands in the synecdochic line of the Old and New Adams as a certain kind of reader, one for whom worldly experience and scriptural revelation combine to form a progressive revelation that facilitates the transformation of the self toward its promised identity in Christ. The shift in the narrator's handling of the devils from preaching warnings to open scorn indicates a new assurance that begins with the bee simile at the close of the first book. The narrator is initially assured and calmed by faith, but, as he (and the reader) grows to understand the providential patterns his narrative enforces, faith is strengthened by experience.[24] The reduction of devils to pygmies thus signals a tonal change in the narration of the poem.

Satan's address to his troops at the beginning of Book II (11–41) reiterates patterns already observed in his exchange with Beelzebub in Book I. The narrator and reader possess knowledge of the demonic leadership unavailable to the devils and are thus placed in a position of superiority to them. The speech is at once exalted rhetoric and crude politics, depending on whether one is situated in Satan's audience or Milton's. The relationship of the reader to Satan is thus modified in the same direction as that between Satan and the narrator. The reader, with the benefit of human history and the revealed truth of scripture, knows more of Satan's fate than Satan does. Such a reader will not credit his parody of the *felix culpa*:

> From this descent
> Celestial Virtues rising, will appear
> More glorious and more dread than from no fall
> And trust themselves to fear no second fate. (II. 14–17)

The narrative of repetition that characterizes Satan is dramatically enacted in the devil's consult when each speaker elaborates a position already discussed privately by Satan and Beelzebub. Each infernal leader expresses, in his own fashion, Satan's thought, because each repeats, in less complete form, the thought patterns that define the fallen subject – patterns that equate virtue and domination, inside and outside, essence and attribute. Milton's narrative renders evil as a sensibility, a mode of being in relation to others and dramatizes the binding and reiterating force of evil on those who are captivated by its discourse.

The deflation of satanic pretension by the reader's knowledge of subsequent human history and biblical revelation is supplemented and completed by the representation of Satan's own increasing awareness of his "dismal situation" as he moves out of hell across the no-man's-land of "unessential Night" (II.439) and into a world in which his projections are confronted by God's creation. Milton's curious concatenation of adjectives to suggest the substantive character of chaos in the phrases "vast abrupt" (II.409) and "palpable obscure" (II.406) comments concisely on the relationship of Satan's subjectivity to the space it occupies. The *OED* gives one definition for "abrupt" as a substantive and cites Milton's phrase as its unique occurence: "An abrupt place; a precipice, chasm, or abyss." The word "abrupt" derives from the perfect past participle of the Latin *abrumpere,* to break, to dissociate, to sever. The "palpable obscure" Satan must cross is an area broken off, dissociated, severed from creation. Chaos is a space of adjectives turned into nouns, of a qualitative beinglessness. Satan does not recognize the negativity of his being until he sees his reflection in the mirror of the newly created world.

While Satan's journey reflects his psychological limitations, it is also an important event in the causal chain presented by the narrative. He does travel to and arrive in Eden, where the effects of his activity are tragically real. An intensification of the ironic–comic decorum of Book II occurs when Milton introduces for this double journey through real and symbolic space the traditional poetic mode for discourse on two levels, allegory. The tendency in allegory is to hierarchize the two levels so that one becomes the obscure signifier of the other: The allegory is grasped only when the narrative of events becomes transparent to reveal the spiritual truth *embodied* in it. Milton's allegory of Sin and Death resists this tendency. The moral truth and literal events of Milton's allegory intersect each other just as the interior condition of the damned intersects the infernal universe of hell. The peculiar transformation that Milton works on allegorical narration, here and elsewhere in *Paradise Lost,* once again reflects the founding rhetoric of the historical subject.

We may begin with William Empson's remark that "Milton regarded the words Sin and Death in the poem, as the names of two supernatural persons, and wanted us to gather that the abstract ideas were named later from the predominant activities of those persons."[25] What has been introduced into the allegorical discourse is precisely a temporal dimension. The evaluative hierarchy of obscure sign and luminous truth that characterizes atemporal allegory gives way, in Miltonic allegory, to a temporal ordering in which the narrative of events presents the founding moment of a historical revision. Sin and Death enter the world as allegorical figures and are disseminated in time as repeating patterns of action. This temporalization of allegory shares significantly the historicizing function of typological hermeneutics. Meaning is not traced to another scene, to an atemporal world in which universal truths are universally enforced, but rather to a historically situated action. The locus of meaning is no longer elsewhere, but later. We might well say, inverting Empson's explanation, that the meaning of Sin and Death is sin and death, that the transforming effect of their advent is written at large in the subsequent history of the world.

Just as Satan is the original of the quest hero, Sin and Death are the originals of the dragons that harass the hero's approach to Paradise. The typical quest hero slays these guardians; his ironic negation spawns them. Just as the "vast abrupt" and "palpable obscure" that Satan must cross reflect the internal conditions of his "dismal situation," Sin and Death are concretions of Satan's "proud imaginations."[26] In a parody of the birth of Minerva, Sin is born from the head of Satan at the moment in which he enters into "bold conspiracy against Heav'n's King" (II.751).[27] She is the physical embodiment of the most vain of Satan's "proud imaginations." The creation of hell is implicit in the birth of Sin, whose language previews the infernal seat: "All on a sudden miserable pain / Surpris'd thee, dim thine eyes, and dizzy swum / In darkness, while thy head flames thick and fast / Threw forth" (II.752–5).

The birth of Sin is followed by a recognition scene that is effaced by Satan's repression of Lucifer's history when he fails to recognize her at Hell's gate:

> A Goddess arm'd
> Out of thy head I sprung: amazement seiz'd
> All th' Host of Heav'n; back they recoil'd afraid
> At first, and call'd me *Sin,* and for a Sign
> Portentious held me; but familiar grown,
> I pleas'd, and with attractive graces won
> The most averse, thee chiefly, who full oft
> Thyself in me thy perfect image viewing
> Becam'st enamor'd, and such joy thou took'st
> With me in secret, that my womb conceiv'd
> A growing burden. (II.757–67)[28]

The birth of Sin and the creation of hell figure the relationship of concept to act as that of conception to birth. The womb of Sin is the birthplace of unbeing. Hell, parodying the emergence of life from the fertilized womb, unfolds the *idea* of Sin as the gestated spawn of Satan's sterile conception. The iteration of the parodic birth of Death as it will be transposed into the history of the fallen world is represented by the incestuous second generation of the hellhounds and their cannibalistic return to the womb of Sin (II.775–803).[29] As Maureen Quilligan points out, Sin sits at the mouth of hell and "Satan's task is to talk her into opening the gate so that he may give birth to his grand design – which is to have the children of light come trooping back through the hellish maw, unmaking their creation in sin, tombing themselves in hell's womb."[30] The parody of the trinity provided by the Satanic family figures forth the entrapment of desire in the closed orbit of narcissism as the antithesis of the divine propagation of holy love in the emanation of desire for and through others. Satanic desire pulls affection from the orbit of God's propagating emanation and folds it in upon itself; like Sin it seems "woman to the waist, and fair, / But end[s] foul in many a scaly fold / Voluminous and vast" (II.650–3). Such self-enfolded desire is always exorbitant, both out of the orbit of creation and excessive, entrapping. Parthenogenesis and incest mark the inability of this desire to emerge in propagation, to sacrifice a part of itself to the desire of another and thus achieve true increase through multiplication. Such a contrasting and interpreting possibility will be given in Book VIII, when Adam donates a rib to the formation of one who will "partake" with him. But, before we are given Adam's account of the birth of Eve, the birth of Death and the proliferation of the hellhounds elegantly figures the narcissistic captivation of desire as the engendering of uncreation.[31]

The allegory of Sin and Death places Satan in a context less becoming to him than Pandemonium had been, and further discloses the advantage in knowledge that the Christian reader has over him. As Joseph Summers notes, "The sudden reduction of action from civil, military, and mythological to the domestic is essentially comic" and the intervention of Sin to prevent combat between Satan and Death is "wonderfully operatic."[32] The absurd narrative of Sin running through hell shouting the name Death while pursued by her lusty progeny who "overtook his mother all dismay'd" (II.792) completes the reduction of the decorum to low comedy. But what is actually diminished by the scene? Sin's narration of the generic tale of a woman seduced and abandoned by a soldier retells the story of Satan in the form in which it will be reiterated in mundane history. Satan's quest for self finally ends with his capture by his own allegorical text. The great originals of evil can only reiterate the patterns they produce. The reduction of the devils to folklore goblins at the end of Book I is recapitulated by the reduction of Satan to a character type in a low style genre. The general of hell becomes the miles gloriosus of postlapsarian comedy and the grand originals of Sin and Death are recognized in the sordid and furtive details of an earthly future.

The first two books of *Paradise Lost* present Satan in conference with a close colleague, performing an assigned task alone, and (grotesquely) engaged in the comic recollection of his family romance. From these encounters emerges a portrait of the satanic subject as disjoined from the universe of light – whose patterns are briefly suggested in the invocation – and limited by this disjuncture. When Adam loses his ability to author himself, he is "forfeit and enthrall'd / By sin to foul exorbitant desires" (III.176–7), that is, to desires that are outside the circle of emanation and return inscribed by divine love. Satan dwells in *bottomless* perdition. His exorbitant desires slip down an endless chain of displaced objects that turn out to be projections of a self in search of itself but unable to find itself reflected and creatively altered in a universe of others. The rhetorical figure through which the self-captivation of the satanic subject is portrayed is irony. Satan's attempt to conform the universe to his intentions ends with the reversal of that goal, as Satan's own lost subjectivity becomes the sole object of his desire, an object that necessarily recedes along an endless chain of metonymies: to reign in heaven, to reign in hell, to dominate and destroy the newly created race of men. The purely negative nature of these objectives attaches irrevocably to Satan himself when he proclaims in Book IV, "Evil be thou my Good" (110).

Before this confrontation between Satan and divine creation, however, Milton establishes the patterns of a counteruniverse to that of hell. If Milton's portrait of hell presents the thesis of difference, the disjunction of creature and creator, his portrait of heaven presents the antithesis of this disunion, the identity of creature and creator. This identity is based on a complex temporality as expressed in its accompanying rhetoric. The identity of creature and creator is achieved over time through the circulation of affection within the orbit of divine desire. This desire is never exorbitant because it is self-propagating and continuous. Book III quite literally sheds light on the structure of the universe from which Satan is excluded.

# 3

## EFFULGENT GLORY

### I

THE NARRATIVE LINE OF *PARADISE LOST* rises inexorably toward the dramatic climax of man's "first disobedience." The first two books explicate the immediate cause of the fatal act that is to come – the displaced resentment of Satan and his plan to attack God through his creation. A complex rhetoric of feeling participates in this exposition, sometimes reinforcing, sometimes challenging the narrator's interpretation of the action. This implicit development adds to the dramatic logic of the events leading up to the temptation – the background of Satan's fall and the beginning of his journey to Eden – a sensual apprehension of the "dismal Situation" of the damned. The force of the apocalyptic vision in Book III depends upon the contrast between its underlying rhetorical patterns and those of the first two books. The pattern of frustrated hypotheses that characterized the discourse of hell is familiar in man's fallen experience, a fact Milton implies when his proleptic similes project the devils into human history. The temporal sequence asserted is one in which the reader is expected to recognize what has become familiar in human history as descending from an infernal original. He or she is to know hell by its family resemblance to the fallen world and to understand the fallen world through its relationship to hell.

The presentation of human time in relation to an eternal heaven in Book III is a more difficult poetic problem, for eternity is static and therefore more suited to description than narration. Change is the hallmark of narrative, but how does one portray a *decisive event* in an unchanging world? This question leads beyond the immediate poetics of Book III to a consideration of Milton's theological presuppositions about the relationship of time to eternity.[1]

In Milton's story, the still perfection of heaven descends into our world directly only through and during the Incarnation of Christ. This descent is completed by the Passion, an event that takes place outside the time of Milton's narrative, yet informs it.[2] It is toward the absent center that Milton's narrative tends. To complete his narrative justification of God's ways to men, Milton presents the anticipated but excluded climax of the Passion as a logical result of the plot. To do so he must construct a causal series of interlocking episodes linking man's first disobedience to the appearance of "one greater man." By motivating the incarnation and creating an anticipation of it before the fall, Milton establishes the temporal perspective of a revealed future to revise and give meaning to the temptation before it occurs. The narrative of Satan's journey is suspended while Book III provides an anticipation of Christ's earthly career as a larger context in which Satan's adventure is to be interpreted. The meaning of a contingent historical event is deferred while its future consequences are examined.

To create the occasion for this revelation of the future, Milton takes the extraordinary step of dramatizing a dialogue within the Godhead, and thus creating a division of voices interior to the divine self. The Son's mediatory role within the Godhead thus ascribes to God the sense of action as issuing from an interior dialogue similar to that of the historical subject, who commits himself to action after an interior consideration of presently perceived need and anticipated consequences. The dialogue in heaven allows Milton to contrast the monological nature of Satan's discourse with a representation of the internal dialectic of the Godhead as it reconciles the conflicting demands of mercy and justice to determine a course of action in the world.[3]

For many readers, Milton's presentation of the Father in Book III brings the poem's narrative and emotional values into conflict. The Father elicits unease and irritation rather than adoration and love. The presentation of the Father is offered as evidence that Milton's theology is at war with his poetry, that the materials of the poem are intractable.[4] There is in this view a certain anachronistic identification of Milton's experience of theology with that of the modern reader. There is reason to believe that, as Frank Kermode suggests, the Father's speech in Book III as well as several other controversial theological points – the materiality of angels, mortalism, the rejection of creation ex nihilo – are in the poem because they are "related to [Milton's] feelings about life in general."[5] In view of this fact, Milton's apparent heterodoxies are more valuable as signposts to the innermost workings of his theology as it informed his world than as embarrassments to be explained away by criticism. They are specifically the points at which Milton's experience in the world put in question the orthodox views he rejects.

By focusing on the rhetoric of emotion in Book III, it is possible to recover some of the original intensity of a theology that is not dead but, on the contrary, is inextricably bound up with the poet's sense of his own being in the world. In Chapter 8 we will be able to specify more precisely the relationship between Milton's poetics and the speculative theology of his age. For now it will suffice to examine the theory of salvation through Christ that forms a part of the thematics of *Paradise Lost* III in relation to the experience of faith in that salvation – the unarguable intuition that Christ died for man – that theology sought to justify. In pursuit of that purpose it may be useful to enter into the assumption of God's goodness that presupposes Milton's theodicy, neglecting for the time being the resistance of Milton's language to such a presupposition. My focus, therefore, will be on the way in which Milton's presentation of the Godhead accounts for an alienating quality it cannot eliminate, the way it "saves the appearances."

Fallen readers should not expect to feel comfortable with the Father whom "brightest Seraphim / Approach not, but with both wings veil thir eyes" (III.381–2). The difficulty of accepting the Father is, as Stanley Fish points out, a measure of our "crookedness" or, in the terms of the present argument, the exorbitance of our desires.[6] It is not so much the Father who is characterized in book III as the reader's relationship to the Godhead.[7] The Father is not only the austere rhetorician of the dialogue with the Son, but also the "Fountain of Light" (III.375) that pours over all quarters of the universe. The image patterns of Book III dramatize the processes of emanation, mediation, and return that underlie and maintain a divine creation envisaged in dynamic terms as continually in motion, in the process of resisting a "natural" entropy toward uncreation. The assertion of this process within the Godhead links providential time to the personality of the Son and puts in motion an otherwise static Neoplatonic ontology.[8]

Book III leads the fallen reader into this dynamic creation, continuing to project and elaborate the dialectic of temporal perspectives established in the first two books through three major episodes: a renewed invocation, the dialogue in heaven, and the arrival of Satan at the frontier of the new creation. Each of these episodes sophisticates the reader's understanding of the narrated events and thus plays the role of historical revelation in his or her self-authorship. The three scenes depict three distinct subjects: the inspired poet, the omniscient God, and the fallen archangel. It is through these successive mediations that the view from the throne of God becomes intelligible.

## II

The new invocation, with which Book III begins, signals the end of the linear motives of the poetry of the damned and reasserts the dialectical pattern of difference recuperated as identity noted at the beginning of Book I:

> Hail holy Light, offspring of Heav'n first-born,
> Or of th' Eternal Coeternal beam
> May I express thee unblam'd? since God is Light,
> And never but in unapproached Light
> Dwelt from Eternity, dwelt then in thee,
> Bright effluence of bright essence increate.
> Or hear'st thou rather pure Ethereal stream,
> Whose Fountain who shall tell? before the Sun,
> Before the Heavens thou wert, and at the voice
> Of God, as with a Mantle didst invest
> The rising world of waters dark and deep,
> Won from the void and formless infinite. (III.1–12)

The precise nature and identity of the "light" invoked in this passage has been the subject of long and continuing debate.[9] Dogmatic considerations aside, there are good poetic reasons for identifying the Son with "holy Light," at first metaphorically and later literally.[10] The poem asks us to approach "holy Light" through a comparison to sensible light. The apparently inexhaustible source of sensible light is the sun, which is, therefore, a natural vehicle for a metaphor of which the tenor is the Father.[11] Patrides has explored the use of this metaphor by the church fathers to illustrate the nature of the Trinity.[12] He cites Athanasius:

> We see that the radiance from the sun is proper to it, and the sun's essence is not divided or impaired; but its essence is whole and its radiance perfect and whole, yet without impairing the essence of light, but yet as a true offspring from it. We understand in like manner that the Son is begotten not from without but from the Father.[13]

My point is not to argue that Athanasius influenced Milton but that the interpenetration of the languages of theology and poetry, apparent when Milton's passage is placed beside that of Athanasius, suggests the common ground of both in the use of metaphor to organize experience. Although Milton's opinions on the nature of the Son, expressed in the *Christian Doctrine,* are closer to (without coinciding with) those of Arius than those of Athanasius, both Milton's and Athanasius's *representations* of the Trinity necessarily return to the common ground of experience, the observation of the sun.[14]

Once formed, a metaphor of this sort (the ascription of family positions to the persons of the Trinity would be another example) moves back and forth between poetic and theological discourse. There is, however, an important distinction between the mimetic and the speculative uses of the trope: The speculative metaphor is "sublated" into a deductive discourse that effaces its sensible vehicle. It becomes a concept. When the speculative metaphor is reinserted into a narrative, the repressed vehicle returns to engage in the chain of causal events that forms the plot, and reestablishes the series of associations and analogies that allowed the metaphor to rise out of the language to begin with.[15]

The use of the sun as a vehicle for the unapproachable Father operates in the invocation ("God is Light") and throughout Book III. The metaphor, however, is not simply an implicit identification of divine and sensible light. Rather, it is the frame of a continuous analogy between two enfolded processes: the vitalization of our world by the sun and of the universe by God. Physical light emanates from the sun as spiritual light from the Father. In an especially significant passage, Uriel explains the conservation and distribution of sunlight to the disguised Satan, while both stand on the sun:

> Look downward on that Globe whose hither side
> With light from hence, though but reflected, shines;
> That place is Earth the seat of Man, that light
> His day, which else as th' other Hemisphere
> Night would invade, but there the neighboring Moon
> (So call that opposite fair Star) her aid
> Timely interposes, and her monthly round
> Still ending, still renewing through mid Heav'n,
> With borrow'd light her countenance triform
> Hence fills and empties to enlighten the Earth,
> And in her pale dominion checks the night. (III.722–32)

Unlike Pandemonium, where artificial stars must be "fed / with *Naphtha* and *Asphaltus*" (I.728–9), divine creation is lit by a co-operative and conservative system of emanation that draws light from and returns it to a never-empty fountain. This emanation and return of "holy Light" defines the orbit of creative desire and gives point to the exorbitance of Satan's ambitions – which are both outside the orbit defined by Uriel and excessive in their need of a supplementary, artificial light that is obtained by *consuming* fuel.

Physical light appears to be continuous with its source. Like God, the sun is light, is wrapped in light, and continuously radiates light. Should the sun's light fail, "night would invade." Uriel's description of the exchange of light between earth, sun, and moon suggests that creation is a continuing process in which night or uncreation is bounded but not abolished by the primal *fiat lux*. Night must be "checked" by the circulation of light within the orbit of created

53

things. Since light is God, this orbit is defined and unified by his presence.

The ambiguous continuity of "holy" and sensible light is to the point. The light we *see* is one aspect of the vivifying emanation of God that permeates the created world.[16] The metaphor "God is Light" provides a tangible correlative, common material light, to suggest the more elusive character of divine light. Yet the narrative goes on to insist that the association is not metaphoric but literal. This collapse of metaphor into repetition, frequent in Milton's mimetic presentation of theological discourse, is another aspect of the rhetoric of identity. In this case the metaphor links the two lights on the basis of common attributes, and the narrative dialectically sublates the sensible term by making it a synecdoche of the tenor – that is, by hierarchizing the two luminosities so that the one we see is understood to be the emanation of the one we seek to know. The narrative, in this way, performs and dramatizes what Thomas Aquinas deduces from precepts: that words are used "primarily of God and derivatively of creatures, for what the word means – the perfection it signifies – flows from God to the creature."[17] Thomas's doctrine and Milton's narrative strategically reverse the temporal ontology of the metaphor so that the sensible is understood as a partially emptied *figure* of the numinous. The meaning of sensible light is understood to inhere in its continuity with "holy Light."

This movement from the abstract to the particular provides the thematic structure as well as the underlying rhetoric of the invocation. In the invocation's personal passages, the narrator joins the reader in the epiphany his rhetoric has engineered. His apprehension that nature and nature's light in particular are permeated by and continuous with God's light enables his acceptance of blindness by assuring the recompense of an inward-shining "Celestial Light" (III.47–55). The poet interprets his experience as a confirmation of the promised pattern of providence, as good brought out of evil.

III

The invocation to Book III begins with an abstract statement of the creative pattern of emanation and return that defines the orbit of divine desire. The narrator then points to the inscription of this pattern in the historical events of his own life. He begins at the center of the universe and follows one ray of the "eternal coeternal beam," Until it "shine[s] inward, and the mind through all her powers / Irradiate[s]" (III.52–3). When the narrator completes the invocation and resumes the narrative of actions, he suddenly reverses his path along this inspiring beam. He enacts, verbally, the return cycle of the dialectic of illumination to "see and tell / Of things invisible to mortal sight" (III.54–5). By following the beam of celestial light back to its source (a spatial image of the reversed temporality of theological metaphor!), the poet moves from the perimeter of creation to the center and looks back at himself from the throne of God:

> Now had th' Almighty Father from above,
> From the pure Empyrean where he sits
> High Thron'd above all highth, bent down his eye,
> His own works and their works at once to view. (III.56–9)

Suddenly we are looking through the omniscient eye of the Father, and we see the concentric circles of creation from the center.

The words of the Father, issuing from this place, present a point of view alien to our own:

> Only begotten Son, seest thou what rage
> Transports our adversary, whom no bounds
> Prescrib'd, no bars of Hell, nor all the chains
> Heapt on him there, nor yet the main Abyss
> Wide interrupt can hold; so bent he seems
> On desperate revenge, that shall redound
> Upon his own rebellious head. (III.80–6)

Assuming that the Father refers ironically to the fact that Satan breaks his restraints only through divine forbearance, Empson calls this passage "the first of God's grisly jokes."[18] At the risk of adding the charge of equivocation to that of sour humor, I would observe that what the Father says is not ironic but literal. "No bounds / *Prescrib'd* . . . can hold" Satan. No divine "fore-writing" requires Satan to remain in hell. This is precisely the point. The prescribed bounds, sensible signs of Satan's "dismal Situation," are props that project the unboundedness into which Satan has fallen. The irony is not in the Father's abuse of language but in Satan's belated discovery that the self is defined by its limits. After the semicolon it becomes even more clear that the satanic transportation to which the Father refers is interior as well as physical. "So bent he seems" functions syntactically as a conditional clause turning the sentence into a comment on Satan's appearance: "He looks as though no restraint could hold him." Finally the passage sets up a "hyperliteral" explosion of "revenge" into its constituent parts: *re vin dicare,* to force to say again. Satanic revenge is desperate (that is, hopeless) because it necessarily takes the form of repetition. The prescribed bounds of hell will not prevent Satan's reiteration of hopeless rebellion. He is free to be what he is, or, more precisely, what he says he is.

The apparent knottiness of the Father's language in passages like this reflects the complexity of his atemporal or, rather, transtemporal perspective. Anthony Low suggests that *"Paradise Lost* has a double vision: divine comedy and human tragedy."[19] This double vision is defined thematically by doubled plots of the fall of man and its divine recuperation by Christ. Structurally the double vision requires the narrative union of two temporal perspectives, which we have identified as proleptic retrospection – looking forward to something as though it were a past event. The Father's transtemporal point of view incorporates both prospective and retrospective temporal frames. His language links specific event and apocalyptic closure in a single coherent design that will become available for human understanding only as an experience in time. The future, from this perspective, may be thought of as a crease concealing from man the part of providence God has folded under the present. In the process of unfolding events, narrative interprets sequence as consequence.[20] In effect it preserves the crease marks that reveal the way in which a seamless whole has been formed of infolded segments. The presentation of the Father required of Milton a language that would characterize in an implicit way this view of the future as a folded-under present.

The Father's subjectivity is not situated but diffuse. Omniscient and ubiquitous, the Father occupies the center of a creation figured as a vast set of concentric circles and his subjectivity ranges from center to circumference, holding the blind poet at the end of one eye-beam and the "seeming" adversary at the end of another. This instability of point of view, together with the temporal infolding of serial events, renders the Father as a determinate emptiness at the narrative center of the poem. The poem enacts the theological conception of a God who is everywhere and nowhere. It is this disorientation of the subject that accounts for the poetic alienation of the Father from the reader.

What alienates the reader from the Father's speech is the displacement of the reader's concerns. It is not so much what the Father says that is unsettling, but the fact that he speaks about man, not to man. The Father simultaneously perceives and expresses the emptiness of Satan's rage and its tragic implications for man. His speech takes into consideration Satan's "desperate revenge," the need for free will, and the exculpatory arguments Adam and Eve might offer after their fall. What affects the reader as testy and defensive may also be seen as omniscient. Fallen syntax is linear and the fallen creature moves compulsively from one postulate to another. Whatever he sees he sees in relation to himself; he is a situated subject. In contrast, the Father's point of view is inclusive. It is outside a created universe that it perceives as a unit in need of tuning. The dialogue in heaven takes on a different character when its audience within the narrative is recalled. It is not a sermon preached to man but rather something overheard. The design of the poem juxtaposes the council in heaven with Satan's councils in hell. Satan shares his thoughts with Beelzebub, then the two preeminent devils manipulate the discussion in Pandemonium. In contrast, the Father's speech is freely given to the angels. If one takes the speech as expository rather than hortatory, it may be seen as an act of sharing the benefits of omniscience.[21] Such a sharing increases understanding and understanding increases faith and love. Without understanding, the exercise of free will is impossible, for "reason also is choice" (III.108).

The Father concludes that to preserve the system of emanation and return of love, mercy and justice must be reconciled (III.132–5). If Adam and Eve are to be "authors to themselves in all / Both what they judge and what they choose," their judgments and choices must determine the twists and turns of the narrative they write and live. As we have seen, the dialectic of self-authorship is doubled. Judgments and choices both form and disclose moral character.[22] Unlike the nondialectical subjectivity of Satan, the self-authorship of Adam and Eve engages a prior set of external circumstances, in this case, God's law. Justice supplies the consequence that allows Adam and Eve to define themselves through interaction with the other, be it the material conditions of the created world or the will of God expressed in them. Reiterating the divine pattern of emanation and return, Adam and Eve express and form their characters through a sequence of judgment, choice, and action, and the consequences of their actions represent a mediation of human will and the laws of God expressed in nature. The divine ordering of the created world thus returns an individual's actions to him or her not as his or her image in a mirror but as recast by its confrontation with the will of another. Justice allows men and women to go beyond repetition to creative change. It is thus a necessary component of the economy in which free will can operate. Because it allows the effects of the creature's choices to be written in the history of the universe and in his or her own character, justice is a precondition of free self-authorship. The consequence of an act *in the world* is the creative limit or bound that enables self-definition to be realized as a dialectic of self and world, as opposed to the nondialectical relation of unbounded interior projection that characterizes the compulsive repetitions of the devils.

When the Father proclaims that in the reconciliation of justice and mercy, "Mercy first and last shall brightest *shine*" (III.134, my emphasis), we return to the metaphor of light with which Book III begins. Mercy will be extended to fallen man through the mediation of the Son, in whom "all his Father *shone* / Substantially express'd" (III.139–40, my emphasis). The mediation of the Son is, from the start, mimetic. He gives to the unsituated subjectivity of the Father the expressive location of the human face: "And in his face / Divine compassion visibly appear'd, / Love without end, and without measure Grace" (III.140–2).[23] The face of the Son visibly represents the Father's grace as visible light represents the Father's presence. The mediating function of locating and situating divine grace in time and space is also apparent in the Son's role as the efficient cause of divine creation. It is the Son who circumscribes space to define the boundaries of the created world and to extend God's presence into carefully delineated regions of chaos. If Satan expresses the rage that no "prescribed" bounds can restrain, the Son is the boundary that defines free will and saves fallen man by bringing him back within the defined orbit of divine creation.[24]

In the dialogue of the Godhead in Book III, the Son performs his mediatorial function by situating man within the orbit of God's concern. The Father's prime consideration is to keep the system working, to maintain and encourage the flow of faith and love. The Son speaks directly to the point:

> O Father, gracious was that word which clos'd
> Thy sovran sentence, that Man should find grace;
> For which both Heav'n and Earth shall high extol
> Thy praises, with th' innumerable sound
> Of Hymns and sacred Songs. (III.144–8)

Representing man in the Godhead, the Son argues that mercy to man will yield a profit in the net production of love.

The Son's arguments move man back into the center of consideration and, consequently, relieve the reader's alienation. The Son locates man as an integral part of the system of creation and links his rehabilitation to the providential design. When the Son refers to man as "thy creature late so lov'd, thy youngest Son" (III.151), he invokes the filial relationships implied by the name "father" and asks for a response that will make literal the metaphor of paternity under which humankind may approach deity. In other words, the Son performs – existentially – the speculative reversal of metaphor by which Aquinas attributed all names to God.[25]

Narrative demands that a name like Father or Son be translated into fatherly or filial actions. Once again it is this translation or enactment that distinguishes poetic from speculative theological metaphor, and it is precisely that sensible vehicle that the speculative theologian seeks to efface that allows living metaphor to enter into or to constitute a set of associations and to give the effect of interior meaning to a series of narrated events. Naming the creator "Father" implies not only that he is progenitor but that he also has a con-

tinuing commitment to his progeny; he who has given them life
will raise them to a kind of maturity. The Son, by sharing his title
with mankind, represents the interchange of love and faith
throughout creation under the figure of the family, and anticipates
the task he will accomplish when he perfects the brotherhood of
man in Christ.

Having determined to save mankind, the Father goes on to consider how salvation may be achieved. Since salvation must be freely
chosen, God will enable man to choose to be saved by setting out
a series of lights:

> And I will place within them as a guide
> My Umpire *Conscience,* whom if they will hear,
> Light after light well us'd they shall attain,
> And to the end persisting, safe arrive. (III.194–7)

Thus we return to the varied manifestations of light. The familiar
text of the Fourth Gospel supplies the gloss that makes the future
fulfillment of the dialogue explicit: "Then spoke Jesus again unto
them, saying, I am the light of the world; he that followeth me
shall not walk in darkness, but shall have the light of life" (John
8:12). By projecting the action from the Son to the incarnate Christ,
Milton moves again from heaven to history. The "light after light"
that leads man to salvation arrives with a historical event marked
by a light in the sky over Bethlehem, and the "Umpire Conscience"
makes its judgments in response to contingencies encountered in
historical situations. The translation of the Son into the human future
as Christ answers and explains the earlier translation of the devils
as pagan gods and folklore goblins.

The Father's demand for "rigid satisfaction, death for death"
(III.212), with what Empson aptly calls the "stage villain's hiss" of
"die hee or Justice must" (III.210), is not calculated to attract the
reader's affection.[26] Empson's explanation that "God is much at his
worst here, in his first appearance; but he needs to be, to make the
offer of the Son produce a dramatic change" has much to recommend it, but, at the risk of appearing to "save the appearances,"
one can see the Father's unpleasant tone as logically as well as dramatically appropriate.[27]

I have been arguing that the Father's voice is, somewhat paradoxically, that of an unsituated subject. Speaking from no distinct
point of view, he expresses the needs of a system, a creative machine.
He is, in the strongest sense, *im*personal. What this means in the
terms of Milton's discourse is that the Father is the God of the Jews,
and that his words express *the Law*. Thus Milton polarizes the "persons" of his Trinity according to the Old and New Covenants. The
Father, expressing the letter of the Law, speaks the logical requirements of communion. The demand of "death for death" is predicated on man's breaking of "fealty" (III.204). Given the mechanics
of the created universe – its dependence on an unbroken exchange
of love and faith – to break "fealty" is necessarily to fall into exorbitant desires, to substitute a reflection of the self for the substantial
and productive objects of a divine, and intersubjective creation. To
obviate this result by some direct and personal intervention would
be to subvert free will by depriving an act of its consequences. The
mediation offered by the Son, who acts to temper the administration
of the Law by subordinating the letter to the Spirit, is a historical
solution. It maintains the system by modifying the faulty component. The Son by becoming man – in time – re-creates the circumstances (the "Light after Light") in which man can experience
a historical development toward renewed communion:

> because in thee
> Love hath abounded more than Glory abounds,
> Therefore thy Humiliation shall exalt
> With thee thy Manhood also to this Throne. (III.311–14)

The actions that emerge from the Godhead result from the mediation of the Law, understood as the requirements of creation as
a whole, by the Son's representation of the specific needs of man.
The rhetoric of emotion is alienating with respect to the Father
because he speaks from the remote position of the universe known
*in itself*. The subjectivity that emerges from the Son's mediation represents this universe *for us*.[28] The orbit of the Spirit expressed in
the dialogue of the persons of the Godhead supplies the pattern of
exchange that links each creature to creation. This underlying process accomplishes the individuation and return of a unified substance.

An example of the rhetorical presentation of the mediation of the Son's empathic point of view, situating man as subject within the dialogue, may be seen in his restatement of the Father's "and so losing all, / To expiate his Treason hath naught left" (III.206–7), as

> he her [grace's] aid
> Can never seek, once dead in sins and lost;
> Atonement for himself or offering meet,
> Indebted and undone, hath nothing to bring. (III.232–5)

"Man" is the subject of the active verbs "seek" and "hath" and of the adjectives "lost," "indebted," and "undone." His pronoun, "he," is expressed, and even the negatives "never," "nothing," "in-," "un-," imply the positive that once was, is now lost, and will be restored through sublation to a higher spiritual level.

Like the disciples he will acquire when incarnate, the Son internalizes the principles made explicit by the Father's discourse. When all men are brothers in Christ, when all men internalize the law and follow the will of providence, "wrath shall be no more" (III.264). The dialogue in heaven can thus be seen as a dramatization of the temporal movement of the Christian covenant – from law to faith, from faith to understanding, from understanding to love. The Son's role as mediator is finally projected by the transformation of "light" to "breath":

> His words here ended, but his meek aspect
> Silent yet spake, and breath'd immortal love
> To mortal men, above which only shone
> Filial obedience. (III.266–9)

The blazing light of the Father, from which the seraphim hide their faces, now shines as "filial obedience" and, in this form, "breathes" "immortal love" into "mortal men."[29] The anticipated historical intervention of the Son as Christ promises to convert the metaphor of filiation to literal truth. It is the (rhetorical) pivot through which *figure* and *history,* general law and particular event, are made to co-incide. We shall later see the implications of this pivot elaborated as a historical revision of the word "death," from the end of self to the end of time.

The Father's concluding remarks (III.274–343) enlighten the heavenly host (and the overhearing reader) with a summary explanation of the process through which fallen man will be restored. The incarnation will be an intersection of eternal divinity and human time that reverses – as in a mirror – the intersection of human time and satanic timelessness. The eternity of God is the measured measurelessness of "effulgent glory," of the emanation and return of creative love. In contrast, the timelessness of hell is that of repetition, of action that undoes itself and returns always to the same circuit of exorbitant desire. Man's temporality lies between these two poles. He works and by working transforms the stuff of the world to his own form. His time is measured first by a promise of increase through propagation that matches the effulgent creativity of God and, after the fall, by the prospect of death and a decisive transformation from earthly to eternal life. This transformation is achieved by a reversal of direction similar to the one that ended the invocation to Book III. As Milton rode a ray of light from his dead eye to God's life-giving gaze, restored man passes through the gate of death to retrace, in the reverse direction, the Son's *via dolorosa*.

Unlike Satan, who seeks to appropriate the forms of others through imitation (of a cherub, a cormorant, a toad, a serpent, and finally a god), the incarnate Son assumes manhood by assuming the defining condition of mortality (III.281–9). In rhetorical terms, the Son forecloses the endless line of metonymies that constitute the "dismal Situation" of the damned – what J.B. Leishman has wittily referred to as "just one damned thing after another" – by converting them into a synecdoche that denies the substitution of imitation (or representation).[30] The Son makes flesh the living presence of God and not the dead inscription of the law – he is the inspiring breath of the Father's "effulgent glory."

The function of the alternately alienating and attractive aspects of the dialogue of the Godhead may now be clarified. The Father's distancing language, projected through a rhetoric of objective principles, is felt as difference from the divine. The Son's promised acceptance of mortality, however, situates him as a divine subject, occupying the same peculiar temporal position as the Christian in a fallen world. He knows his time is measured as the interval between now and a future end of time that will end and transcend the self situated in the determinate time and space of the body. The Son's mission is to descend into the created world and experience mortality, not by empty imitation but by material and empathic participation. Through this promise he returns man to the center of divine concern and converts difference into identity. Yet by the end of the dialogue the unity of the Godhead is reasserted: the Father's promise that "mercy first and last shall brightest shine" (III.134) is fulfilled by the exaltation of the Son, who becomes "Son both of God and Man" (III.316).

The ultimate resolution of the historical process is understood as the abolition of all difference:

> The World shall burn, and from her ashes spring
> New Heav'n and Earth, wherein the just shall dwell
> And after all thir tribulations long
> See golden days, fruitful of golden deeds,
> With Joy and Love triumphing, and fair Truth.
> Then thou thy regal Scepter shalt lay by,
> For regal Scepter then no more shall need,
> God shall be All in All. (III.334–41)

When the process of internalization is complete, rhetorically projected relationships, indeed, language itself, will collapse as the will of God establishes a homogeneous community of the Godly.[31] This community beyond the limits of language is also necessarily beyond the (common) horizon of narrative and of time. The promise of a time when God is "All in All," completes the displacement of the meaning of events from their origin in created essences to their terminus in a set of known consequences. Revelation itself is clearly a temporal process in which the relationship of contemporary events to an apocalyptic eschatology is progressively disclosed.

The dialogue in heaven raises the question of how mercy and justice can be reconciled after man breaks the Law. The answer, which comes jointly from the Son and the Father, is that justice may be served by reformation as well as punishment – the fallen subject is, in this case, capable of change. This change is achieved when fallen men, in imitation of the Son, internalize the Law and so extirpate (or repress) their own forbidden desires. Restored man will assent intuitively to the Law and thus experience its prohibition as his own affirmation.[32]

What is most interesting about Milton's poetic dramatization of these individuating events is the fact that he completes them with a return to a communal subject. The self-authored ego is always not only temporal but temporary. The dialogue of Father and Son ends with a reunification of the Godhead, envisaged as the reconciliation of justice and mercy. This reunion is quickly joined by the heavenly choir, which recapitulates the themes of the dialogue:

> Thee Father first they sung Omnipotent,
> Immutable, Immortal, Infinite,
> Eternal King; thee Author of all being,
> Fountain of Light, thyself invisible
> Amidst the glorious brightness where thou sit'st
> Thron'd inaccessible, but when thou shad'st
> The full blaze of thy beams, and through a cloud
> Drawn round about thee like a radiant Shrine,
> Dark with excessive bright thy skirts appear,
> Yet dazzle Heav'n, that brightest Seraphim
> Approach not, but with both wings veil thir eyes.
> Thee next they sang of all Creation first,
> Begotten Son, Divine Similitude,
> In whose conspicuous count'nance, without cloud
> Made visible, th' Almighty Father shines,
> Whom else no creature can behold; on thee
> Impresst th' effulgence of his Glory abides,
> Transfus'd on thee his ample Spirit rests. (III. 372–89)

The angels return to the light metaphor of the invocation and follow it with three images of mediation: The source of light is invisible as a situated point but known through its diffusion in a cloud; like the empirical sun, it appears as a dark corona; and it may be approached only with shielded eyes. The Son's "count'nance" makes "conspicuous" this darkness at the center of the light. As the carrier of the Father's "effulgent glory," the Son makes light visible without cloud and brings man within the orbit of the sun. The scene in heaven ends with the blending of the choir's many voices into one music; musical harmony thus provides a final, implicit metaphor for the dialectic of the individual and the community to which he or she is joined by the measured rule of an internal law ("Umpire Conscience") and the shared "light after light" in which that law is read.

This closure achieved, the narrator returns his attention to Satan. The great conceptual climax of *Paradise Lost* is the restorative movement of the apocalyptic vision. The dramatic climax is the fall of man in Book IX. The return to Satan is thus a return to the rising action of the dramatic narrative.

## IV

After the long parenthesis of the scene in heaven, we find Satan at the borders of creation (III.418–30), and the limitations of a situated point of view return with him. What seemed a globe from one perspective becomes a continent from another (III.423–5). In contrast to the Godhead, Satan is part of the landscape he inspects: "There lands the Fiend, a spot like which perhaps / Astronomer in the Sun's lucent Orb / Through his glaz'd Optic Tube yet never saw" (III.588–90). When Satan lands in the Paradise of Fools (III.440–97), we see again the narrative device of proleptic transposition. The scene in heaven looked forward to the end of history, but first as Satan appears, we look forward to the mediate future history of the fallen world.[33] The two contexts – temporal and eternal – function dialectically in the remainder of Book III. Satan's vision, egocentric and focused totally on the intention of his movements, is counterpointed by the narrator's continuing evocation of the inclusive, eternal vision that we now recognize as the pattern of providence.

When Satan deceives Uriel, the narrator tells us the angel is "the same whom *John* saw also in the Sun" (III.623). The allusion to Revelation (19:17) juxtaposes Satan's imminent success and ultimate defeat. The superimposition of John's time and Satan's creates a rhetorical pivot at which the two perspectives at work in Book III are joined. In the prospective or dramatic view, Satan's successful deception of Uriel is a logically necessary episode in the chain of events leading to the fall of man. In the retrospective or narrative view – now identified with the view from the throne of God – it is part of a pattern in which all events are design elements in an ultimate "conformity divine." A curious detail illuminates the temporal and temporary nature of Satan's successful deception:

> So spake the false dissembler unperceiv'd;
> For neither Man nor Angel can discern
> Hypocrisy, the only evil that walks
> Invisible, except to God alone,
> By his permissive will, through Heav'n and Earth:
> And oft though wisdom wake, suspicion sleeps
> At wisdom's Gate, and to simplicity
> Resigns her charge, while goodness thinks no ill
> Where no ill seems. (III.681–9)

We shall see in Chapter 5 that the ability to discern hypocrisy is reserved to God because the capacity for hypocrisy is an effect of dramatic time. It will suffice to note now that Satan's hypocrisy is effective – for a time – but that it will yield to truth when he confronts the new creation in Book IV.

The dialectic of suspicion and simplicity introduced in the narrator's comment on hypocrisy is, on one level, another reflection of the dialectic of dramatic and narrative time, of prospective and retrospective views. But, on another level, it considerably deepens this temporal dialectic by disclosing its relationship to the dialectic of self-authorship. In Book IV, Milton depicts the prelapsarian world of Adam and Eve, a world in which suspicion "to simplicity / Resigns her charge." Like everything else in *Paradise Lost*, Satan's entry into that world is achieved through God's "permissive will." The theodical intent of the epic is thus at issue here, at the portal of man's world. It will be my burden in the next two chapters to explore the entry of "ill" into this world "where no ill seems," to establish the relationship of self-authorship to what "goodness thinks," and to show how "ill seeming" is a necessary moment in a rhetorical dialectic that situates self-authorship at the intersection of anticipation and retrospection.

# 4

## "WITH ANSWERING LOOKS"

IF WE DEFINE the narrative of *Paradise Lost* as the chain of events that leads to "Man's first disobedience" and its consequences, the action of Book IV is slight. Only two events in it are directly related to the fall of man: Satan, overhearing Adam discuss with Eve the single prohibition, obtains the means of their downfall (IV.411–535), and he begins to act upon this new intelligence by inspiring Eve with a dream (IV.800–11). The expression of specific sensibilities rather than the relation of connected actions accounts for the greater part of the book. The lyric interlude in the garden provides a moral context for the ensuing narrative action by further establishing the patterns according to which temporally unfolding events are to be understood. The lyric form itself suggests the prelapsarian experience of human time as pleasant and varied repetition in contradistinction to the more urgent time of irreversible historical events represented by narrative. Satan's entry into Paradise is presented as the intrusion of narrative (as opposed to lyric) time into the world of men and women. The rhetorical projection of Satan's experience and Eve's innocence thus becomes an opportunity for the mimesis of two polar experiences of time.

The principal speeches in Book IV reveal a densely textured development evocative of both these temporal experiences and the relationships between them. The experience of time in the Garden of Eden is projected through and by the situating of a specifically prelapsarian and human subject, distinct from the self-entrapped subject of Satan at the one extreme and the unsituated subject of God at the other. Against the pastoral serenity of Eden, we see

Adam and Eve not simply acting in accordance with their natures but rather continually creating those natures through actions that both reflect and determine the character of their being. At their polar extremes, God and Satan are, or seek to be, self-generating. In contrast, the subjectivity of Adam and Eve is mediated by the earthly creation they inhabit. Adam and Eve are created without antecedent, given an exceedingly brief history, and set to the task of defining themselves within the world in which they have been placed. Their condition in this world involves a relation to their origin in the creator and to the future in the forms of work – the shaping of the garden – and procreation, the execution of the creator's image in the propagation of their own race.[1] Both activities propel Adam and Eve toward a concern with the future. The care of the garden is a task of maintenance. Pruning and weeding prevent a future uncreation from overtaking the garden, just as moonlight prevents Old Night from repossessing the earth. Procreation is, as we shall see in Chapter 5, essential to the return of love owed to the creator. Concern for the future, realized as the anticipated transformation of the environment, distinguishes Adam and Eve as human subjects.[2]

Like the fallen reader, Adam and Eve situate their concern for the future through the narrative processes of anticipation and retrospection; thus they situate themselves as actors within time, choosing to do certain things in the expectation of certain results. But, until the fall, the role of contingency does not loom large in their predictions. "Goodness thinks no ill / Where no ill seems" (III.688–9). Contingency and occasion for error enter the Garden with Satan. The fallen reader understands this threat in a way that Adam and Eve do not, and the dramatic irony the reader thus imposes on the plot defines his or her distance from the prelapsarian pair. The distance between appearance and being is manifested *in time* as a difference between expectation and result. Irony is the inscription in language of the inadequacy of appearance. It announces that things are not what they seem and that truth may not be reliably represented. The reader, concerned for the fate of Adam and Eve (and, a fortiori, his or her own), experiences a desire to enlighten them. But to do so would be to breach the space of "goodness" in which "no ill seems" and thus transform the quality of Adam and

Eve's concern with the future from hope to suspicion. It is my purpose in this chapter to elucidate the rhetorical patterns of Milton's presentation of Eden and to relate the irony of postlapsarian nostalgia to the tension between lyric and narrative form in Book IV.

## I

The latter part of Book III presents the conclusion of Satan's journey through chaos. As he describes the completion of the journey, the narrator questions the Devil's apparent success by placing it in the context of his ultimate defeat. Thus, when Satan sees Uriel in the sun, we are reminded that this angel is "the same whom *John* saw also in the Sun" (III.621–3). The beginning of human history anticipates its end. When the poem focuses on the earth, the stage upon which that history will be played, the inclusion of the beginning in the end is reasserted:

> O for that warning voice, which he who saw
> Th' *Apocalypse,* heard cry in Heav'n aloud,
> Then when the Dragon, put to second rout,
> Came furious down to be reveng'd on men,
> *Woe to the inhabitants on Earth!* that now,
> While time was, our first Parents had been warn'd
> The coming of their secret foe, and scap'd
> Haply so scap'd his mortal snare. (IV.1–8)

The first sensibility expressed is that of the narrator, who speaks from the complex and reflexive vantage point of fallen, yet redeemed, man. Although he knows that the dragon will be put to "second rout," he also knows that a history full of pain and betrayal stands between him and that final victory. The narrator speaks with the voice of experience, from within the "mortal snare." His ability to invoke at once the immediate dramatic context – to call for a warning voice – and the anticipated narrative recuperation of the unfolding tragedy marks his regenerate condition and defines the paradoxical temporality of the Christian subject who lives in time by employing a frame of reference beyond time.

When the narrator turns his attention to the tempter, he makes

it clear that Satan's journey is real for man, yet illusory for the
Devil. Satan is "to wreck on innocent frail man his loss / Of that
first Battle, and his flight to Hell" (IV.11–12); that is, to extend
the "dismal Situation" of the damned to Adam and Eve. His mission
to escape hell is also a mission to extend it and is thus ineffective
precisely to the degree of his success. Nostalgia, as the motion of
memory that continually defines the present as a loss of the past,
is a prime element of the situation of the damned:

> Now conscience wakes despair
> That slumber'd, wakes the bitter memory
> Of what he was, what is, and what must be
> Worse; of worse deeds worse sufferings must ensue. (IV.23–6)

The memories of paradise invited by the lyric description of the
garden in Book IV are similarly painful to fallen man. The poem,
by evoking parallel nostalgias, opens the opportunity to suggest
alternative responses.

Having landed on Earth, Satan is situated between the heaven he
has lost and a world he can win only by ruining (IV.27–30). In
the "darkness visible" of hell, Satan's gaze "with obdurate pride
and stedfast hate" (I.58) projects the landscape of his exorbitant
desires into an external emptiness. On Earth, sunlight illuminates
Satan's inner darkness and starts the introspection of his great soliloquy. Satan responds not only to the brightness of the sun, but
also to the imprint of divine order that renders the sun "like the
God / Of this new World" (IV.33–4). His correct reading of the
presence of the creator in the created calls forth a process of rationalization that will, for a time, arrest action and consume his
energy and attention.

Soliloquy is the form of the discourse of the divided self, and
Satan's monological conversation represents the turning of the subject away from the world of others to seek the other in the self.[3]
As such it is not simply a debate between the "bad angel" he is
now and some memorial vestige of the "good angel" he once was.
It is rather an energetic effort to preserve his fantasy self against
the implosive force of the substantial reality of God's creation. The
rationalizing process gives the soliloquy its characteristic rhetoric

and transmits to the reader not only Satan's thoughts but the psychic pressures that breed them.

The sight of the sun, which Satan recognizes as a divine surrogate, arouses his memory of heaven and forces him for the first time in the epic to admit his essential (and therefore irreducible) difference from God. He realizes that his powers were and are derivative, "he created what I was / In that bright eminence" (IV.43–4).[4] While satanic power is relative to the numbers he subjects, God "with his good / Upbraided none" (IV.44–5). Confronted with these insights, Satan evades the responsibility for his self-defining actions by eliding the subject in passive constructions, "Pride and worse Ambition threw me down" (IV.40). Satan is prepared, at the beginning of his soliloquy, to absolve God of responsibility for his fall but not to accept that responsibility himself. By attributing the fall to his attributes of "Pride and worse Ambition," Satan silently reassigns blame to his creator and portrays himself as subject to passions that were formerly offered as glorious signs of his distinction. He perceives that he is subject to the other in himself, that is, to his exorbitant and uncontrollable desires, but he quickly projects these desires onto God, who is absolutely other than Satan. The distorted image of the Father is thus appropriated as an exterior location for Satan's destructive passions.

"Pride" and "Ambition" are expelled from the self and represented as external forces brought about by God's having placed Satan in an impossible situation:

> yet all his good prov'd ill in me,
> And wrought but malice, lifted up so high
> I sdein'd subjection, and thought one step higher
> Would set me highest. (IV.48–51)

In rejecting limitation Satan fails to realize that the self is born of limitation, the confining of matter by form; therefore, the ontological link between subjection and subjectivity escapes him. The contention that God's very goodness has situated Satan in a position from which he had to fall – an argument he will manifest in ironic action when he places Christ on the pinnacle in *Paradise Regained* – signals the limitation of introspection by his psychic defenses. Satan's

72

conception of heaven as an incremental hierarchy ("one step higher would set me highest") reiterates the fundamental failure of understanding that had caused his fall: his failure to distinguish absolute from derivative power and glory.

The rhetoric of the soliloquy gives the impression of memory rather than logical discourse. Each fragment of recollection draws other, related memories after it. Satan remembers "the debt immense of endless gratitude" (IV.52) that he had resented in heaven though he is now ready to assign his "sense of injur'd merit" to a misunderstanding. He controls and limits the emotions and insights released by memory with the revisionist theory that God's overgenerosity had inadvertently provoked his fall:

> O had his powerful Destiny ordain'd
> Me some inferior Angel, I had stood
> Then happy; no unbounded hope had rais'd
> Ambition. (IV.58–61)

Satan presents his fall to himself as at once contingent – if God had not raised him so high, the fall would not have occurred and necessary – "unbounded hope," a necessary concommitent of high position, could not do otherwise than raise his nemesis, ambition. In the view Satan expresses, it is the responsibility of God, not reason, to limit the passions of his creatures. Thus Satan argues precisely for the restriction of freedom of which he accuses God.

Reason, though subjected to passion, is revived by the sunlight to the point at which Satan can see the fallacies in his arguments but not draw the necessary conclusions from them:

> Yet why not? some other Power
> As great might have aspir'd, and me though mean
> Drawn to his part; but other Powers as great
> Fell not, but stand unshak'n, from within
> Or from without, to all temptations arm'd.
> Hadst thou the same free Will and Power to stand?
> Thou hadst: whom hast thou then or what to accuse,
> But Heav'n's free Love dealt equally to all? (IV.61–8)

Satan's reasoning should lead to the conclusion that "Heav'n's free Love [is] dealt equally to all"; however, his personality cannot accept this conclusion. As always, he responds to conflict by making himself the arbiter of existence; he rejects the truth to preserve the self he cherishes as immutable:[5]

> Be then his Love accurst, since love or hate,
> To me alike, it deals eternal woe.
> Nay curs'd be thou; since against his thy will
> Chose freely what it now so justly rues. (IV.69–72)

Satan first curses heavenly love and then, more logically, himself. The pronoun shifts in these lines are indicative of his state of mind. The soliloquy begins with an address to the sun, "O thou that with surpassing Glory crown'd" (IV.32). When the pronoun "thou" next appears, it is an imperative, "Nay curs'd be thou," parallel to, "Be then his love accurst." "Thou" now refers not to the sun but to Satan himself. The two curses – one a final effort at self-assertion, the other a despairing attack on the self – disclose the characteristic pattern of Satan's thought. The soliloquy begins as an address to the sun, but recognition of the sun brings recognition of an external reality that conflicts with his fantasy of monarchy. He recoils from this reality into the defended fortress of an ego that views itself as autonomous and omnipotent. Ironically, this retreat into the self sparks a lucid introspection. Unlike God, Satan cannot be in two places at once, and his retreat inward is realized as a compulsive flight from light to darkness:

> Me miserable! which way shall I fly
> Infinite wrath, and infinite despair?
> Which way I fly is Hell; myself am Hell;
> And in the lowest deep a lower deep
> Still threat'ning to devour me opens wide,
> To which the Hell I suffer seems a Heav'n. (IV.73–8)

These lines rewrite the boast of Book II, that the mind is its own place, and reveal a truth deeper than Satan had expected. The pattern of statement and discovery is important. The truth of Satan's words and the meaning of his actions are revealed to him in the course of time. The subject discovers itself as the presence of its own past.

Satan's discovery of the dimensions of his "dismal Situation" brings him to a consideration of repentance (IV.79–80), but self-knowledge falls short of enlightenment because he cannot surmount the relativism of the universe his mind has constituted. The inexhaustible effulgence of divine glory that powers the universe of *Paradise Lost* remains a determinate absence at the center of Satan's understanding. Because he measures "merit" according to social status rather than inherent goodness, he confuses self and reputation; he identifies himself with his followers' image of him. The "disdain" that prevents his submission is not only his scorn of God but also his fear that his followers will scorn him (IV.81–7) – he fears that they will disdain him and he will thus disdain himself. Standing alone in the sunlight, Satan appears deflated because he misses the regard of his subordinate devils to puff him up. When his self-love is deprived of this fuel, he undergoes a self-recognition that quickly turns to self-pity. Repentance would necessarily end his fantasy of omnipotence.

Satan's relationship to his reflection in the infernal host bears the same parodic relationship to God's image in man as the monarchy of hell does to that of heaven. God's passing, or effulgence, of his image to his creatures disseminates the substance of creation itself.[6] Creatures are *formed* out of this extension of deity. Satan's self-image, however, crafted for the devils and returned to him by them, is an exchange of empty illusions, the passage of an image between two mirrors. Later we will see a third alternative in the procreative production of the image between Adam and Eve. If the argument of self-authorship is correct, we should expect to find the human subject constituted in a specifically narrative form. Narrative, as we have seen, exists in the tension between the poles of difference and resemblance.[7] Satan offers his followers absolute resemblance in the form of an image that can only repeat or reinscribe itself regardless of context. The unsituated divine self is constituted as the absolute difference between God's ever-emanating substance and his image reflected in material form. In the case of Adam and Eve, we will see the dialectic of resemblance and difference realized and resolved in the family resemblance of their descendents.

Submission for Satan would require his surrender of that false
self on which he has constructed the polity of hell. The intimate
connection of Satan's identity and his sin is indicated by the ban-
ishment of the name Lucifer from heaven. When he allowed exorbitant desires to obscure the light he once bore, Lucifer ceased
to exist. Satan's role as adversary is thus the limit of his being. The
peroration of his soliloquy reaffirms his determination to subsist in
the role indicated by his new name:

So farewell Hope, and with Hope farewell Fear,
Farewell Remorse: all Good to me is lost;
Evil be thou my Good; by thee at least
Divided Empire with Heav'n's King I hold,
By thee, and more than half perhaps will reign;
As Man ere long, and this new World shall know. (IV.108–13)

The rhetoric of the soliloquy achieves a moment of self-persuasion
when Satan is able to reaffirm his identity as negation, as he who
opposes. Until the next eruption of truth, his process of rationalization is completed and he can return to the matter at hand, the
corruption of man.

## II

Although the reader enters the garden with Satan, his or her perceptions differ from Satan's. The Christian reader, benefitting from
the revealed history of the future, enjoys a broader perspective.
Satan's myopia is specified by the narrator's ironic comment that
the devil, seated like a cormorant on the Tree of Life,

yet not true Life
Thereby regain'd, but sat devising Death
To them who liv'd; nor on the virtue thought
Of that life-giving Plant, but only us'd
For prospect, what well us'd had been the pledge
Of immortality. So little knows
Any, but God alone, to value right
The good before him, but perverts best things
To worst abuse, or to thir meanest use. (IV.196–204)

Satan becomes absorbed in the demands of a particular moment and reduces an eternal meaning to an instrumental and immediate one. He takes the tree, which is properly a symbol, and makes it a tool. The tension between present need and atemporal meaning places Satan at an intersection of what I have called dramatic and narrative time. Standing at the beginning of a temporal action, Satan does not see the ironic significance that will be conferred on his present position by the configuration of the whole. Men, who become similarly absorbed in the immediate demands of temporally unfolding situations, likewise lose the *prospect* of immortal happiness by forgetting that the contingent becomes meaningful only in prospect of revealed truth, for it is only from this divine prospect that one can learn "to value right / The good before him." In this sense, it is perhaps not stretching the language too far to suggest that the Tree of Life has a function analogous to that of scripture in the fallen world.[8]

Thus to read the Tree of Life as a synecdoche of the whole of biblical revelation is to join the temporal and spatial senses of "prospect," to see what is to come by seeing what is placed before the eye. To read it, as Satan does, as a means to an immediate end, "perverts best things / To worst abuse." Satan reduces the *prospect* of life to the "sighting" of death, anticipating in perverse inversion the transumption of death into "the gate of Life" that will be effected by the incarnate Son, and lending prospective point to Adam's remark on the proximity of the trees, "So near grows Death to Life" (IV.424). Knowledge of the last things, provided by the cosmic perspective of Book III, in effect, embodies the warning voice the narrator calls for at the beginning of Book IV. The presence of the Trees of Life and Knowledge in the garden provides a text, which Adam could interpret to gain access to a portion of what can be seen from that privileged vantage point.

Satan, attentive only to the logistics of his mission, fails to grasp the significance of the tree on which he sits. The play on "prospect," which for Satan is the "space before" rather than "the time after," indicates a major pattern for the remainder of the poem. The new creation is one in which "prospect" is better understood in a temporal than a spatial sense. The dialogue of Adam and Eve in the garden contrasts specifically with Satan's monologue in respect to this shift from space to time. In fact, the tension between the two senses of "prospect" defines the locus in which the human subject is constituted, the intersection of time and place.

Not only the Tree of Life, but the general appearance of the garden, reflects a larger perspective to which Satan is blind. Satan stands apart, a creature for whom there is no place, no connection beyond the confines of the self, and for whom time is the measure of an endless repetition of the same. In contrast, the description of the garden is replete with emblems of cooperation and interdependence. The divine irrigation system (IV.223–35) is one example out of many. Water flows downward but is also "up-drawn," rivers mingle, separate, and reunite. The dialectic of individuation and reunion, played out among the persons of the Godhead in Book III and offered as the shape of an anticipated future in which man falls off from but subsequently rejoins a God who "shall be All in All," are written into the landscape of paradise, a landscape in which each detail functions both in an immediate context – here the need to irrigate the garden – and as a clue to the shape of "conformity divine."[9]

Adam and Eve preside over this garden as the sun presides over the world, "for in thir looks Divine / The image of thir glorious Maker shone" (IV.291–2). Though the reader need not see "undelighted all delight" (IV.286), as Satan does, nevertheless his delight in these creatures is mixed with a similar sense of loss – by nostalgia. Unfallen Adam and Eve, in their precisely tuned pastoral world, are recognized as man and woman but not as fully like us. They are presented rather as the logical construct of what man and woman might have been, just as the Garden of Eden represents a human past that inhabits the present as a memory of what has been lost.[10]

When Satan reminds us again of his presence, the meaning of his words is available only to fallen man:

> League with you I seek,
> And mutual amity so strait, so close,
> That I with you must dwell, or you with me
> Henceforth. (IV.375–8)

The very intelligibility of Satan's ironic "amity" to the reader attests to the later effects of the "League" he proposes. This "prehistoric" time in the garden, during which Satan seeks and finds a method to achieve his league, becomes "historical" in the moment of Satan's success. For the moment of the fall will transform time and become the founding instant of history. As he did in Book II, the reader looks back at Satan's acts as past events that are the ground of the postlapsarian present, the negation of which is anticipated according to the revealed history of the future. The reader's relation to knowledge is unique in that he or she superimposes on the scene in Eden knowledge both of Satan's proposed "League" and the Father's promise to provide "Light after light" to guide the Christian "home."

The experience of reading the poem, about which so much has been written, imitates the temporal experience of life at the intersection of these two kinds of knowledge.[11] To live in this way is to live the present as a conjunction of retrospection and expectation and to experience the contingent event as a foreshadowing type, the significance of which will be revealed at a future time. It is at once to anticipate and defer meaning. Empirical knowledge of worldly (fallen) experience and intelligence of "conformity divine" are not simply antithetical in Milton's presentation, for in the design of *Paradise Lost* the concept of the *felix culpa* is realized as the dialectical dependence of one upon the other. Knowledge of evil counterpoints and elicits knowledge of restored good; humiliation exalts. More striking is the way in which the narrative structure of the poem projects this theological commonplace through a dialectic that unfolds in time. Man, as the hero of this story, goes from innocence to experience to a renewed innocence that revises and subsumes both earlier constitutions through a series of negations and preservations that transform loss to gain, death to life, anticipation to memory.

The complexity of this perspective may be seen in two views of the animals sporting in the garden:

> About them [Adam and Eve] frisking play'd
> All Beasts of th' Earth, since wild, and of all chase
> In Wood or Wilderness, Forest or Den;
> Sporting the Lion ramp'd, and in his paw
> Dandl'd the Kid; Bears, Tigers, Ounces, Pards

Gamboll'd before them, th' unwieldy Elephant
To make them mirth us'd all his might, and wreath'd
His Lithe Proboscis; close the Serpent sly
Insinuating, wove with Gordian twine
His braided train, and to his fatal guile
Gave proof unheeded. (IV. 340–50)

Down he [Satan] alights among the sportful Herd
Of those fourfooted kinds, himself now one,
Now other, as thir shape serv'd best his end
Nearer to view his prey, and unespi'd
To mark what of thir state he more might learn
By word or action markt: about them round
A Lion now he stalks with fiery glare,
Then as a Tiger, who by chance hath spi'd
In some Purlieu two gentle Fawns at play,
Straight couches close, then rising changes oft
His couchant watch, as one who chose his ground
Whence rushing he might surest seize them both
Gript in each paw. (IV. 396–408)

In the first passage, the narrator presents the scene from the prelapsarian point of view until he reaches the serpent, which he invests
with a significance that it could not have had for Adam and Eve.
Thus the narrator may be said to occupy a prelapsarian point of
view until the symbolically charged serpent comes into view, at
which point he cannot refrain from reading his fallen knowledge
into the innocent world. The narrator's experienced eye sees a potential ill Adam and Eve's goodness cannot. According to this pattern the narrator's foreknowledge of the postlapsarian serpent me-
diates his perception of it, even in its final moments of innocence.[12]
This description of the animals articulates the forward and the
backward glance so as to project, first an awe at the prelapsarian
lion dandling the kid that depends on knowledge of the later relationship between these animals, and then disillusionment (literally,
since the narrator lets the illusion of innocence lapse to insert his
retrospective comment) at the sight of the snake and the memories
it evokes. In the second passage, Satan takes the form of various

animals, and causes each to behave in ways that will become characteristic after the fall.[13] Thus all predatory behavior is traced to
Satan's originary predation of Adam and Eve. While the narrator
apprehends these traces as history, Adam and Eve remain as innocent
as the "two gentle Fawns at play."

Together, the two passages form a dyptych, in which evil is proleptically imputed to innocence "while goodness thinks no ill /
Where no ill seems" (III.688–9). In the moment that Satan seems
about to grip one in each paw, the attention of Adam and Eve is
focused not on the landscape they believe to be harmless but toward
each other: "*Adam* first of men / To first of women *Eve* thus moving
speech, / Turn'd him *all ear* to hear new utterance flow" (IV.408–
10, my emphasis). This turn away from the external world in favor
of their mutual conversation defines the moment of human innocence in Milton's dialectic of the self. Satan too turns from the world,
and it becomes necessary to distinguish the turn of Adam and Eve
to conversation from Satan's turn to soliloquy.

## III

When Adam and Eve speak, their language differs markedly from
that of the narrator. Thus the tension between the temporally complex and reflexive voice of the narrator and the edenically situated
voices of the prelapsarian pair forms the poles within which the
reader's resemblance to and difference from his innocent progenitors
can be read. In the conversation of Adam and Eve, Milton presents
the rhetoric of innocence in its least mediated form. The language
of Adam's address to Eve (IV.411–39) differs from both the obsessive rationalization of Satan and the retrospective reflection of
the narrator. Its organization represents a model of reason applied
to experience. Adam begins with the fact of God's bounty, recognizes that since he has nothing to offer God in return this bounty
is freely bestowed as an expression of God's goodness, and concludes: "Then let us not think hard / One easy prohibition" (IV.432–
3). Obedience is the result of reason acting on a reasonable presupposition of God's goodness. Faith and reason are, at this stage,
nearly indistinguishable; each supports the other.

Adam does not use the threat of punishment as a premise in the

argument of obedience, but he does bring it up as an item of speculative interest. His ignorance of death is a touching reminder of
his innocence, and his vague characterization of it as "some dreadful
thing no doubt" (IV.426) contrasts with the spectral presence of
death experienced by his descendents. Adam's brief meditation on
death is occasioned by the proximity of the Trees of Life and
Knowledge, "So near grows Death to Life" (IV.425), and he catches
from this spatial contiguity a hint of the significance he cannot fully
know – the dialectical antithesis of death and life. His reading of
the book of nature on this point brings him to the brink at which
he must be wise enough to "know to know no more" (IV.775).
For to grasp the meaning of the trees' proximity would be to enter
prematurely the symbolic of death and the revision of time it implies.
Adam's reflection on the trees is not halted by rationalization, as
Satan's reflections are, but by an understanding of and up to the
boundary of faith. He applies what God has revealed to him
(VIII.321–30) to correctly interpret the Tree of Knowledge as "the
only sign of our obedience left / Among so many signs of power
and rule / Conferr'd upon us" (IV.428–30). As part of that obedience
the juxtaposition of the Trees of Life and Knowledge is allowed to
remain a latent sign, read by the reader as an index of a severe
revision in Adam's future and the reader's past. That the question
of the meaning of death is posed for Adam by the juxtaposition of
the trees and posed by him to Eve establishes the fact that obedience
is not passive; rather, even in Eden, it is the active and continual
acceptance of limitation, of the subordination of curiosity to faith
in the validity of God's as yet undisclosed intention, and it requires
the exercise of reason, using revelation to understand the eternal
significance of choices made in temporal contexts.[14]

The reader's experience of Adam's remarks on death involves
something Adam does not know – that Satan overhears Adam's
words and thus obtains the means with which to ruin mankind. It
is thus the devil who supplies the interpretation foregone by Adam.
While Adam's "reading" of the trees is theocentric and constrained
by presuppositions about God, Satan's "reading" is characteristically
"exorbitant." Satan removes the Tree of Knowledge completely
from its symbolic juxtaposition to that of life (a juxtaposition he is

better equipped than Adam to read) and appropriates it to the dramatic context of his mission. As he had earlier appropriated the Tree of Life for "prospect" and so missed the prospect of renewed life it held, he now dismisses Adam's explicit revelation of the identity of the Tree of Life and turns to the Tree of Knowledge, which he appreciates only as an instrument with which to accomplish his immediate intention. The Tree of Knowledge becomes the knowledge he needs to gain power over mankind; it is reduced from its symbolic function to a "fair foundation laid whereon to build / Thir ruin!" (IV.521–2).

Adam speculates on death, and Satan opportunistically finds, in that speculation, the clue he needs to complete his mission. Satan's receipt of this intelligence is the crucial narrative action of Book IV. Now he possesses the object with which to ruin man, and he initiates his temptation by inspiring a dream in Eve, "assaying by his Devilish art to reach / The Organs of her Fancy, and with them forge / Illusions as he list" (IV.801–3).

## IV

Between Adam's unwitting betrayal of the prohibition to Satan and the fiend's resolve to build the temptation on it, Eve recounts the story of her creation. This story reveals the divine origin of an interpersonal dialectic that gives rise to a process of self-definition distinct from that of Satan. Eve recalls that on the day of her creation, she found herself reposed in flowery shade, and that wondering where and what she was, she followed the sound of running water to a quiet pool (IV.456–76). Eve's interaction with her own image in the water, although it raises the specter of narcissism, also emphasizes the dialectical nature of God's creation.[15] Eve is initially attracted specifically by the responsiveness of her image in the pool:

> I started back,
> It started back, but pleas'd I soon return'd,
> Pleas'd it return'd as soon with answering looks
> Of sympathy and love. (IV.462–5)

When a disembodied voice tells her that what she sees is her own image, and explains the limitations of such self-admiration – "with thee it came and goes" (IV.469) – she abandons the image to follow the voice, which in turn leads her to Adam:

> fair indeed and tall,
> Under a Platan, yet methought less fair,
> Less winning soft, less amiably mild,
> Than that smooth wat'ry image; back I turn'd,
> Thou following cri'd'st aloud, Return fair *Eve*,
> Whom fli'st thou? whom thou fli'st, of him thou art,
> His flesh, his bone; to give thee being I lent
> Out of my side to thee, nearest my heart
> Substantial Life, to have thee by my side
> Henceforth an individual solace dear;
> Part of my Soul I seek thee, and thee claim
> My other half: with that thy gentle hand
> Seiz'd mine, I yielded, and from that time see
> How beauty is excell'd by manly grace
> And wisdom, which alone is truly fair. (IV.477–91)

The voice, presumably of God, first disengages Eve from her reflection; it is Adam's voice and the gesture of his hand that prevents her return to the image in the pool and persuades her to invest her affection not in the image of herself but in another like herself – like her to the extent of being consubstantial.[16] Consideration of Eve's progress from love of her own image written in water through verbal instruction to love of her substantial origin embodied in Adam leads to a revised and expanded view of a key passage quoted earlier: Uriel's description of the created universe. The heavenly patterns are thus brought to earth and rewritten in human terms. Just as Eve passes through two temporally distinct phases of self-definition, mediated by divine and human words, the reader passes through two successive reconstitutions of the text. Structure and theme merge in a performative mimesis of temporal revelation – by which I mean the investment and reinvestment of the sensible world with progressively more powerful intelligible meanings.

The sequence of events following Eve's creation proceeds through a dialectic of identity and difference antithetical to that illustrated by Satan's exorbitant fantasies. When Eve mistakes her image in the pool for another like herself, she is attracted by "answering looks / Of sympathy and love." The intervention of the divine voice distinguishes the image in the pool, which is a reflection of Eve's reflected light, from "hee / Whose image thou art" (IV.471–2). What distinguishes the two images of Eve – the first a reflection of her bodily self, the second her substantial original (and the sense in which we use "original" here will require further discussion) – is the future consequence of the exchange of love:

> him thou shalt enjoy
> Inseparably thine, to him shalt bear
> Multitudes like thyself, and thence be call'd
> Mother of human Race. (IV.472–5)

The infinite regress of the mirror image, in which love is captured in the abyss of the self – an abyss given concrete form by the portrait of hell in Books I and II – is superseded by the infinite dissemination of love through the propagation of a loving race. It is from this propagation that Eve will receive the defining epithet of "Mother." To escape self-constitution as Narcissus, Eve may anticipate the constitution of herself as "Mother of human Race" that will follow her insemination by Adam.[17]

It is at this point that I wish to recall Uriel's description of the created universe near the end of Book III. In Uriel's account, the intervention of the divine Word reduces the "hateful seige of contraries" of formless matter, to an ordered system permeated and unified by divine light. Uriel, standing on the sun, explains the flow of light within this creation:

> Look downward on that Globe whose hither side
> With light from hence, though but reflected, shines;
> That place is Earth the seat of Man, that light
> His day, which else as th' other Hemisphere
> Night would invade, but there the neighboring Moon
> (So call that opposite fair Star) her aid
> Timely interposes, and her monthly round

Still ending, still renewing through mid Heav'n,
With borrow'd light her countenance triform
Hence fills and empties to enlighten the Earth,
And in her pale dominion checks the night. (III.722–32)

Uriel depicts creation as a sophisticated fountain (rather like the array of gravity-driven fountains Milton may have seen at the Villa d'Este) in which light emanating from heaven flows through a system of exchanging couples or pairs that fill and empty according to a repeating cycle. The role of the moon in this feat of divine engineering, collecting and dispersing "borrow'd light" to "enlighten the Earth" and "check the night," anticipates, on the cosmic level, the role of Eve in the garden. For Eve will capture and conserve the light reflected to her by Adam, filling and emptying according to *her* "monthly round." Milton thus provides an ontology for the traditional association of the moon and the character of woman, one that emphasizes not her "lunatic" mutability but the conserving circularity of her changes and their connection to her reproductive function.

The intervention of the voice that draws Eve from the contemplation of her image in the pool in Book IV thus completes the intervention of the Word witnessed by Uriel when the Son effected the creation of the world:

> when at his Word the formless Mass,
> This world's material mould, came to a heap:
> Confusion heard his voice, and wild uproar
> Stood rul'd, stood vast infinitude confin'd;
> Till at his second bidding darkness fled,
> Light shone, and order from disorder sprung:
> Swift to thir several Quarters hasted then
> The cumbrous Elements, Earth, Flood, Air, Fire,
> And the Ethereal quintessence of Heav'n
> Flew upward, spirited with various forms,
> That roll'd orbicular, and turn'd to Stars
> Numberless, as thou seest, and how they move;
> Each had his place appointed, each his course,
> The rest in circuit walls this Universe. (III.708–21)

Uriel's description begins broadly with the "formless Mass" of preexistent matter, then proceeds, according to the hexameral account, to a division of light from darkness, the distinguishing of the four elements, the organization of the spheres, the sun and the moon, and finally "that spot to which I point is *Paradise, / Adam's* abode, those lofty shades his Bow'r" (III.733–4).

At each step, Uriel's narrowing focus describes a system of interlocking systems in which each unit replicates on a smaller scale the larger unit of which it is a part. (Modern physicists call this a "scaling effect" but, of course, Milton's contemporaries understood it under the rhetoric of analogy, or of the macrocosm replicated in the microcosm.) At each step, heavenly light enters, flows through a particular level of the system, and is passed on to the next smaller unit. Eve is the pivotol link in this dynamic "great chain of being."[18] Ultimately, Eve's progeny will provide the "answering looks / Of sympathy and love" that return – in the form of verbal prayer – the light instituted by the Word.[19] Eve is pivotal not only because her reproductive function will serve to multiply the Word's reflected and reflecting image, but because she is the point at which the spatial images of Uriel are converted into temporal images. The visual "prospect" from the sun is elaborated, in Book IV, as a prospect of the future. This future may even be extended from Eve to second Eve, when "vast infinitude" will once more be "confined" at the behest of the intervening Word. Thus the transformation from creation to procreation establishes the glance to the future that defines human time.

What I am suggesting in joining Uriel's description of the design of the world to Eve's account of her creation is that Milton has built into the architecture of the poem an eyebeam connecting the two episodes, rather like the eyebeam connecting the narrator on Earth to God above the universe at the beginning of Book III. But in this case the direct line between Uriel's discourse and the scene in the garden is disrupted by the intervention of several other narrative episodes or, in other terms, by the intervention of Satan and the satanic viewpoint. According to the logic of narrative, these intervening episodes signify duration, the passing of time, and so perform the deferral of meaning that characterizes the narrative of historical consciousness. The fulfillment of Uriel's text comes, after a time, when the glance that anticipates the future is able to rewrite the past.

The head and loin births of Satan, Sin, and Death are the antithesis of the exchange of light realized as an exchange of seed that is represented by the reproductive future of Adam and Eve.[20] Satan loves precisely the image of himself in Sin, to whom he cannot lend "substantial life" because she is his self-conception and not a *coupling* at all. Together, Sin and Satan give birth to nothingness, that is, Death. The voice in Book IV educates Eve to the importance of difference, to the recognition of an exterior voice that connects the procreation of man and woman to the creation of God. The temporal opening of creation into the expectation of future generations once again reiterates the fact that God's design is to be realized in history.

Providence encourages the development of a self that realizes its integrity only by participating with another in the creation of images, which are themselves possessed of "substantial life." Adam and Eve thus realize themselves when they join to reembody the substance God extended to Adam. This conception gives point to Milton's argument in the *Christian Doctrine* for what amounts to *creatio ex deo,* an argument everywhere implicit in the architecture of *Paradise Lost.*[21] The Father's "impression" of "th' effulgence of his Glory" on the Son in Book III (388) can now be recognized as the foundation and template for the creation that proceeds from the Godhead. The (pro)creative interaction and its effects are reproduced in the great love song of Eve to Adam in Book IV:

> My Author and Disposer, what thou bidd'st
> Unargu'd I obey; so God ordains,
> God is thy Law, thou mine: to know no more
> Is woman's happiest knowledge and her praise.
> With thee conversing I forget all time,
> All seasons and thir change, all please alike.
> Sweet is the breath of morn, her rising sweet,
> With charm of earliest Birds; pleasant the Sun
> When first on this deligtful Land he spreads
> His orient Beams, on herb, tree, fruit, and flow'r,
> Glist'ring with dew; fragrant the fertile earth
> After soft showers; and sweet the coming on

Of grateful Ev'ning mild, then silent Night
With this her solemn Bird and this fair Moon,
And these the Gems of Heav'n, her starry train:
But neither breath of Morn when she ascends
With charm of earliest Birds, nor rising Sun
On this delightful land, nor herb, fruit, flow'r,
Glist'ring with dew, nor fragrance after showers,
Nor greatful Ev'ning mild, nor silent Night
With this her solemn Bird, nor walk by Moon,
Or glittering Star-light without thee is sweet. (IV.635–56)

Eve uses language both to perform and to represent the round of
pleasant and varied repetitions that denotes the passing of time in
Eden, and she suggests that even this benign temporality is transcended by the eternal conversation of man and woman, a conversation Adam and Eve begin in their love and extend indefinitely
through the race that love is to found. When Adam retells the story
of Eve's birth in Book VIII, the relationship of this conversation
to the founding of human time will be further revealed. The pattern
of pleasant repetition will be extended to the narrative pattern of
retelling with a difference, which is in turn the formal representation
of the revelations of history.

Eve's intuitive performance of the providential pattern ends with
a request for discursive understanding of the harmony she has just
invoked: "But wherefore all night long shine these, for whom /
This glorious sight, when sleep hath shut all eyes?" (IV.657–8).
Adam's reply recapitulates Uriel's description of the creation and
thus makes more explicit the connection between the passages in
Book III and Book IV by bracketing Eve's discourse between two
parallel descriptions:

Those have thir course to finish, round the Earth,
By morrow Ev'ning, and from Land to Land
In order, though to Nations yet unborn,
Minist'ring light prepar'd, they set and rise;
Lest total darkness should by Night regain
Her old possession, and extinguish life
In Nature and all things, which these soft fires

Not only enlighten, but with kindly heat
Of various influence foment and warm,
Temper or nourish, or in part shed down
Thir stellar virtue on all kinds that grow
On Earth, made hereby apter to receive
Perfection from the Sun's more potent Ray. (IV.661–73)

Thanks to the gloss of the Word, supplied to Eve at the crucial moment, the "answering looks," which first attracted Eve to her image in the pool, are superseded by the more varied responses she receives from her image in Adam, who is himself the image of God. They are to be extended indefinitely in time by the children who will be the image of Eve, issuing from the "kindly heat" of her womb to "enlighten" the earth and affirm life over death, and prevent the return of "Night" when death inherits the fallen world.[22] This extension of the image of God into the future of human time receives perfection from the "sun's [and the Son's] more potent Ray."

Book IV ends with Satan's opening of the narrative sequence of the temptation. Before this sequence is resumed, the bulk of the next four books is given over to Raphael's narrative. The angelic discourse will provide Adam and Eve with a "historical" context for the narrative action of Book IX. Raphael's backward glance at the history that precedes the edenic prehistory of the human race will serve to mediate the breach between the spatial "prospect" of heaven and the temporal "prospect" of Earth by presenting a narrative pattern in which what appears to the eye is shown to be subject to the temporal location of the viewer.

# 5

## "DIVINE HISTORIAN"

S ATAN'S INSPIRATION OF EVE'S DREAM near the
end of Book IV begins the temptation and moves the narrative
toward the poem's central tragic action: the fall of man. Before
this narrative thread is again picked up in Book IX, a long, expository section intervenes. Raphael's visit to Eden, comprising
Books V–VIII, relates the events that precede the opening of the
epic in medias res. The content of Raphael's discourse sets the scene
for what Broadbent has called "the decline into history," by supplying a (pre)history that situates Adam and Eve as part of a providential design, extending into time as well as space.[1] Although
Milton's audience benefits from history and revelation, knowledge
of past and future events, Adam and Eve enjoy ample revelation
but meager history until Raphael's narration portrays their creation
as part of a chain of past events. Adam and Eve mark their need
for a personal past by curiously returning in their conversations to
the sparse events of their brief tenure in paradise: the prohibition
and their respective creations. As a narrative historian, Raphael describes events in the heavenly past by looking forward to the human
history that Adam and Eve will soon enter.[2] He thus defines the
present moment of their danger as the intersection of an irreversible
past and an anticipated future continuous with it; that is to say, he
introduces them to the modern historical consciousness implicit in
their creation as "authors to themselves." Raphael's account of the
war in heaven and the creation of the world is meant to be interpreted by Adam and applied to his own situation, to provide a
historical context for Adam's moral choice in Book IX. Adam will

then be able to use Raphael's narrative in much the same way that seventeenth-century Protestants were to use biblical narrative; that is, by abstracting from the narrated events a structural pattern that illustrates the historical manifestation of God's eternal decrees and creates a context for moral choice in analogously structured contemporary situations.

## I

The first note struck in Book V is that of the intimate connection of heaven and Earth before the fall. Adam and Eve, concerned about Eve's dream, refer their safety to God in their morning prayer:

> Hail universal Lord, be bounteous still
> To give us only good; and if the night
> Have gather'd aught of evil or conceal'd,
> Disperse it, as now light dispels the dark. (V.205–8)

In response, the Father sends Raphael to be the warning voice the narrator had wished for at the opening of Book IV.

When Raphael arrives in Eden, Adam's greeting situates the relationship of man and angel within Adam's knowledge of God's cosmic architecture:

> Heav'nly stranger, please to taste
> These bounties which our Nourisher, from whom
> All perfet good unmeasur'd out, descends,
> To us for food and for delight hath caus'd
> The Earth to yield; unsavory food perhaps
> To spiritual Natures; only this I know,
> That one Celestial Father gives to all. (V.397–403)

The epithet, "Heav'nly stranger" and the remark upon "spiritual Natures" indicate Adam's awareness of the differences between man and angel as his reference to their brotherhood as sons of "one Celestial Father" indicates his perception of their resemblances. The joining of different sorts of creatures and of individuals of one species under the unifying head of a divine provider anticipates one of the principal themes of Raphael's discourse and provides the angel with an occasion to establish the expanding dialectic of differentiation and inclusion that controls the rhetoric of the conversation of man and angel (V.496–503).[3] Raphael introduces temporal movement into Adam's vision of identity with and difference from the angels by suggesting that the difference between man and angel is one of degree, not kind, and that it may be narrowed or eliminated over time. By invoking the possibility of improvement "by tract of time," Raphael turns obedience to the single command into a dynamic action. Continued obedience, in itself, refines the body toward the condition of spirit.

Raphael's narration of the war in heaven illustrates the converse of the principle of improvement by continued obedience. If obedience leads to ascent, disobedience leads to a fall. The introduction of mobility, upward and downward, into the spatial architecture of providence unsettles Adam, who questions the notion of a character change from obedience to disobedience:

> But say,
> What meant that caution join'd, *if ye be found
> Obedient?* can we want obedience then
> To him, or possibly his love desert
> Who form'd us from the dust, and plac'd us here
> Full to the utmost measure of what bliss
> Human desires can seek or apprehend? (V.512–18)

To truly be an author to himself, Adam must recognize his ability to change the course of his existence by his acts, and he must be able to envision alternative futures as the putative consequences of alternative choices. Raphael's promise of improvement through continued obedience and punishment for disobedience introduces more sophisticated notions of moral responsibility and consequence into Adam's mind. Adam now knows that he can either improve or fall. His task is to effect improvement by perseverence in obedience: "God made thee perfet, not immutable; / And good he made thee, but to persevere / He left it in thy power" (V.524–6). To appreciate the force of "persevere" here, it is only necessary to meditate on the fact that Satan's temptation could have been ex-

tended indefinitely, had the first attempt failed.[4] It is one thing to
remain obedient in the *hortus conclusus* of Eden, another when confronted by the tempting promises of Satan, and still another in the
shifting contexts of a fallen world. To make this difficult lesson
clear to Adam (and to the reader), Raphael illustrates the possibility
of disobedience and its consequences by recounting the war in
heaven. Narrative, with its necessary extension of events in time,
allows him to elaborate the *doctrine* of obedience by representing
its *practice* in a complex, developing situation.

Raphael's presentation of the war in heaven uses metaphor to
dramatize the way in which, unlike the foreseeing deity, "consulting
on the sum of things" (VI.673), men and angels act on moral judgments made within a temporally unfolding situation. Like fallen
men, Milton's warring angels are involved in a historical drama in
which they must act on the basis of expectations that may or may
not be fulfilled. Judgment in such a predicament entails a continual
reassessment of past decisions and present situations in the light of
newly available information. It is my purpose in this section to
suggest the specific ways in which Milton's narrative represents
revelation as a temporal process and to relate the form of the narrative to its theological and experiential contexts.

As we have seen, one use of typological hermeneutics among
seventeenth-century Protestants is to create stabilized contexts of
moral choice by assimilating mundane experience to scriptural patterns.[5] Through typology, open-ended, contingent experience in
the world may be evaluated within the semantically and ethically
more stable context of the biblical narrative of revealed truth. The
closure of these written texts is thus extended to the more fluid
context of an individual's life, and the present is understood by
comparison with the past of biblical history and the prophesied future of revelation. Since individual experience is continually assimilated to a revealed narrative pattern, revelation is understood as a
progressive development within the life of the individual on the
one hand and within the history of the world on the other. As the
pattern of a situation is revealed in time, its analogous biblical pattern
may be perceived, and through it the meaning of the present situation discerned. The hermeneutic procedures of typology thus
utilize the narrative form of the Bible to supplement and extend its

doctrinal content. Milton's narration of the war in heaven similarly supplements its presentation of the doctrine of obedience to God with a dramatic example of the practice of obedience by the loyal angels during the crisis of the war.

Raphael recounts the story of the war in order to fulfill in part God's charge to advise Adam that continued happiness depends on continued obedience.[6] God instructs Raphael to bring on "such discourse" as to inform Adam of

> happiness in his power left free to will,
> Left to his own free Will, his Will though free,
> Yet mutable; whence warn him to beware
> He swerve not too secure. (V.235–8)

Raphael must himself determine the nature of the discourse that will best communicate to Adam the doctrine of free will in relation to the eternal decrees of providence. The purpose of the teaching is not to prevent the already foreseen fall, but rather to insure the fallen Adam's retrospective understanding of the choice he has made. Just as Raphael largely replaces the Miltonic narrator for Books VI and VII, he here accepts the charge with which Milton began, to "justify the ways of God to men." His justification will not save Adam from the fall, but it will be essential to the conviction of sin that will enable Adam's future repentance.[7]

Raphael must make clear to Adam not only the imminent danger, but the complex kinds of situations Adam's yet untested judgment may soon encounter. The presence of Satan means that wisdom can no longer be allowed to "resign her charge" to "simplicity," "while goodness thinks no ill / Where no ill seems" (III.686–90). Raphael must awaken Adam's suspicion and teach him to see what does not seem. The angel thus begins the story of the angelic discord by referring to Lucifer's hypocrisy during and after the exaltation of the Son: "So spake the Omnipotent, and with his words / All seem'd well pleas'd, all seem'd, but were not all" (V.616–17).

The disparity between Lucifer's private and public reactions to the exaltation of the Son unfolds *in time* as Lucifer's subsequent actions betray his previously secret intentions. Thus in the phrase "seem'd well pleas'd," the "seem'd" represents a retrospective view of the situation after the fact of the rebellion has disclosed Lucifer's formerly concealed displeasure. Raphael acts as a Thucydidian rhetor, recounting the private councils of Satan and Beelzebub, councils that we must assume he imaginatively reconstructs according to his moral purpose and his reflection on their subsequent outcomes.[8] By inventing these dialogues, Raphael discloses the dialectical moments of concealment, discovery, and revision that constitute Adam's induction into a sense of history as the irreversible progress of connected events that remains theoretical for him until his fall. By representing Satan as the arche-equivocator (V.683–93), Raphael emphasizes the temporal nature of deception as a concealed internal state that manifests itself externally *in time*.[9]

Christians have recourse to their knowledge of God in their efforts to interpret unfolding historical events. The Abdiel episode exemplifies for Adam the way in which appeal to revealed (and therefore eternal) truth can fortify one against the deceptions of merely temporal concealment.[10] Abdiel confronts his newly rebellious colleagues with what he has learned of God: "By experience taught we know how good, / And of our good, and of our dignity / How provident he is . . ." (V.826–8), but he places his most irreducible argument first: "Shalt thou give Law to God, shalt thou dispute / With him the points of liberty, who made / Thee what thou art. . . ?" (V.822–4). Although the argument from experience is inductive, open to revision on the basis of subsequent evidence, the argument from origins is deductive and timeless. Abdiel argues that if God is the creator, then God's designs and decrees are foundational. They are the rules of the game. In Abdiel's logic, experience of God's goodness is important but subordinate to knowledge of God's eternal nature and of the creator – creature relationship. Knowledge of eternal truth then becomes prerequisite to the correct interpretation of the accumulating data of experience.[11] Satan recognizes the foundational nature of Abdiel's argument when he tries with one double stroke to deny his premise and to subsume it within his own relativistic empiricism: "We know no time when we were not as now; / Know none before us, self-begot, self rais'd / By our own quick'ning power" (V.859–61).

Abdiel's integration of new data and universal and eternal truth renders his reason "right." He understands what he comes to know through experience by seeing it in relation to precepts derived from what he has been given to know of an unchanging God and his eternal decrees. Experience is respected in so far as it can be made consistent with what has been divinely ordained. We can also see in Abdiel's reasoning the foundation of a type. Abdiel joins (or, in Milton's chronology, anticipates) the Old Testament succession of single just men, defenders of God against a corrupt multitude. The Christian reader is encouraged to place his or her spiritual experience in this narrative context, to conform his or her spiritual history to that which exemplifies the practice of obedience.

Thus the combat between rebel and loyal angels is in an important sense epistemological. One side fights to take destiny into its own hands, to be self-begotten; the other fights to affirm and uphold its conviction that destiny is the inalienable province of divine decree. The rebels seek advantage in "more valid arms," but the loyalists rely on the unalterable nature of things: "Wherefore should not strength and might / There fail where Virtue fails . . . ?" (VI.116–17). The effect of the foundational argument is to remove the dispute from its shifting temporal context and ground it in what is everywhere and always known to be true. By replacing the temporal process of discovery with the eternal truth of revelation, the foundational argument replaces an empirical epistemology with a hermeneutic one.

The war in heaven ends with the victory of Abdiel's foundational principle over Satan's situational logic, but not with the single quick victory that Abdiel and the loyalists expect. Instead the war episode illustrates the continuous operation of revealed truth within historical time and explores the epistemological limitations that validate free choice within a transcendent providence. Abdiel assumes that divinely ordered justice as apprehended by right reason will prevail over the illusions of satanic equivocation – and so it does. But by drawing the angels into a "brutish" and "foul" combat, the rebels, along the way to their defeat, approach an empirical validation of their position – they turn heaven into an image of hell. Raphael's account is so crafted as to offer Adam a context for choice in his impending temptation and to anticipate the pattern of life in the fallen world, where man must resist evil perpetually, as the moon's "pale dominion" "checks the night," until such time as evil is overcome by messianic intervention.[12]

That two days of inconclusive warfare precede the intervention of the Son suggests that action in history, even though sometimes appearing to be ineffective or indeterminate, is important, even while asserting that historical action is ultimately superseded by divine intervention. Raphael's handling of the heroic genre of the war narrative validates heroic action, while limiting its efficacy and assigning effective action to a divine agent. In effect, Raphael presents an analysis of the origins and limitations of the heroic genre itself.[13] The war in heaven teaches that the passions depicted in heroic poetry transcend human ontology and are rooted in temporality itself. The angels, when they enter battle, act like human heroes because they are absorbed into the dramatic context of armed conflict: "But the shout / Of Battle now began, and rushing sound / Of onset ended soon each milder thought" (VI.96–8). The memory of angelic harmony, present "at first" (VI.92), is quickly obscured by the exigencies of battle.[14] The representation of the angels drawn deeper and deeper into warfare, until the immediate situation obscures their own natures, illustrates for Adam the difficulty of perseverance and the potential complexity of the practice of obedience.

When the Son is about to end the war, he tells the loyal angels:

> Faithful hath been your Warfare, and of God
> Accepted, fearless in his righteous Cause,
> And as ye have receiv'd, so have ye done
> Invincibly: but of this cursed crew
> The punishment to other hand belongs;
> Vengeance is his, or whose he sole appoints. (VI.803–8)

Victory is achieved not by angelic works but by God's grace. As John Steadman argues, to reserve the victory for the Father, acting through the Son, is a way of reducing the *fortezza* ideal of epic heroism by emphasizing "the preponderance of divine might over the creature."[15] Milton thus invokes a familiar pattern in which biblical truth supersedes pagan fiction, but he also delineates the self-limiting factors that prevent action in time from effectively overcoming evil. The scriptural reservation of vengeance to the Lord limits the sphere of historical action, removing the execution of certain judgments from the unstable temporal contexts of human life to that of omniscient divinity. The Son's assertion that although the angels have fought "invincibly," punishment "to other hand belongs" ascribes the resolution of the crisis to a reassertion of divine decrees that originate beyond, but act within, historical time.

Calvin's commentary on the relevant scriptural verse (Rom. 12:19) emphasizes the *deferral* of action in favor of divine judgment:[16]

> To give place to wrath is to commit to the Lord the right of judging, which they take away from him who attempt revenge; Hence as it is not lawful to usurp the office of God, it is not lawful to revenge; for we thus *anticipate* the judgment of God, who will have this office reserved for himself. He at the same time intimates, that they shall have God as their defender, who patiently wait for his help; but that those who *anticipate* him leave no place for the help of God.[17]

The distinction drawn by Calvin and others between lawful resistance to evil and the divine right of punishment is elaborated in *Paradise Lost* by the depiction of the war as a necessary resistance whose end is to be anticipated together with the coming of the messiah. The loyal angels prefigure and dramatize the careful balance that Christians must achieve between their responsibility to act morally in the world and their affirmation of a power beyond time. The angels make war when necessary but defer judgment to the timing of the omniscient deity.

The warfare of the loyal angels puts into practice Calvin's interpretation of Romans 12:18 (the verse preceding the one paraphrased by the Son at VI.808):

> We are not to seek to be in such esteem as to refuse to undergo the hatred of any for Christ, whenever it may be necessary. And indeed we see that there are some who, though they render themselves amicable to all by the sweetness of their manners and peaceableness of their minds are yet hated even by their nearest connections on account of the gospel. . . . Cour-

teousness should not degenerate into compliance, so as to lead us to flatter the vices of men for the sake of preserving peace. . . . For we ought, for the sake of cherishing peace, to bear many things, to pardon offenses, and kindly remit the full rigour of the law; and yet in such a way, that we may be prepared, whenever necessity requires, to fight courageously: for it is impossible that the soldiers of Christ should have perpetual peace with the world, whose prince is Satan.[18]

If the moral probity of God's loyal angels does not grant them the victory Abdiel expected, it does enable them to withstand Satan's aggression. They are sufficient to stand, but not to overcome (invincible but not victorious). The ultimate defeat of evil is reserved for the eschata of history, which will remove the temporal contexts of deception. Until then upright men and angels will resist evil within history, drawing the ability to do so from knowledge of and faith in God's revealed truth. They will evaluate what they encounter *in time* in the light of their knowledge of how the story necessarily ends. The vision of the avenging Son in the chariot of paternal deity serves the angels and Adam as the vision of the transfiguration serves Peter, James, and John. It figures the power of eternity as a recourse from the confusions of time. In the Gospel accounts of the transfiguration and in Milton's war in heaven, the humiliation of the Passion is framed by the triumphant vision of the glorified Christ.[19] In both narratives a vision of the power of the last days provides the context for the acceptance of the hard tasks of life on the "subjected Plain." The vision of the transfiguration is granted to the chosen apostles following the temporary withdrawal of Christ and the failure of his disciples to expel demons and revive the dead in his absence. Thus the *historical* sequence of events narrated in the Gospel accounts of the transfiguration and the events that precede it may be taken as an analogue of the narrative of angelic failure and messianic triumph Raphael tells Adam. The biblical analogue at once guarantees the "truth" of a narrative that has no biblical warrant and embeds that account in a continuous history, the patterns of which contain the transhistorical truth of divine providence.[20]

The focus of the narrative of the war in heaven is the absorption of all efforts on both sides into the action of battle itself. The angels' behavior, with all its absurdities, is a credible attempt to cope with the specific situations in which they find themselves. Despite the burlesque of the disparity between angelic effervescence and military corporeality, the war in heaven demands to be taken seriously. War is ridiculed in *Paradise Lost,* but the ridicule, like that to which Satan is subjected, is hedged, circumspect, respectful of the power of military glory to corrupt if not actually to destroy.

The Son's mediating office is projected by his ability to understand a temporally unfolding situation by referring it to the divine decrees and the operation of final causes. He applies eternal principles to temporal action and thus rectifies time itself.[21] Through his mediation the perspective of eternity enters history – in the war in heaven, in Christ's experience of death on the cross, and in the final subjection of the Antichrist. This last victory will abolish history and raise the righteous from it into eternity. In each action, faith in the supremacy of providence to history supplies the eschatological perspective that transcends the temporally unfolding context by encompassing it within a larger, and always, already completed, design. Calvin assures his readers that "while the turbulent state of the world deprives us of our judgment, God, by the pure light of his own righteousness and wisdom, regulates all those commotions in the most exact order, and directs them to their proper end."[22] Raphael's narrative of the war in heaven superimposes the temporal and logical senses of "end" in this context. The (temporal) end reveals the (logical) end of the apparently adventitious events of history – both human and angelic.

The exaltation of the Son, which initiates the narrative sequence of the war in heaven, also initiates the expulsion of those who exclude themselves from history's ordained telos. Thus the beginning of the sequence implies its end in both logical and temporal senses. Those who proclaim themselves self-begotten are reborn as the orphans of time. The heroic conventions of the narrative are made to reflect not the limitations of heroic poetry, but the limitations of action within the temporal contexts heroic poetry celebrates. That even angels can lose their cosmic intuitions in the heat of battle reveals the power of a dramatically unfolding situation to overwhelm judgment when the urgency of response to violence precludes reflection. The full relevance of the narrative becomes apparent when, in Book IX, Adam finds himself faced with Abdiel's choice, isolated, an exile in his own domain. The reflection on "the sum of things" Adam will need at that moment will have been made available to him by Raphael's narrative of the war in heaven. The narration of the war, by emphasizing the dramatic difficulty of perseverence, makes concrete the heroism of "the better fortitude." By doing so, it will help keep Adam within the reader's sympathetic grasp at the moment of his greatest alienation.

Raphael's choice of a detailed and highly dramatic narrative to illustrate the doctrine of obedience and the vicissitudes of perseverence provides Adam with knowledge in a particularly useful form. Heaven before Satan's rebellion and Eden before the fall are both characterized as places of pleasant and varied repetition. The narrative of the war shows how this repetition is altered by the introduction of evil, which brings with it the irreversible historicity of the fallen world, a historicity in which nothing is fully known because everything is subject to revision. At the same time, the narrative asserts the firm control of providence over all historical developments and points the way toward the rectification of time by knowledge of and faith in what is always beyond and above it.

## II

As Book VII begins, the narrator's relief to be "standing on Earth, not rapt above the Pole" (VII.23) anticipates Adam's desire to know "what nearer might concern him" (VII.62). The information already given by Raphael must be placed in a mundane context so that Adam and Eve may apply its moral lesson. Adam's conversation with Raphael in Books VII and VIII helps him to discern his rightful concerns, to distinguish that which informs free will from that which appeals to idle curiosity.

Having heard much of heaven, Adam desires to learn of things closer to his own world (VII.84–97). His request signifies his desire for knowledge that will be useful to his exercise of free will by informing him further of his origins and God's expectations of him. The legitimacy of this request is judged by its purpose. Raphael interprets his "commission" as the free imparting of information "which best may serve / To glorify the Maker, and infer / Thee also happier" (VII.115–17). Significantly, Raphael says that it is the "heart" of man that comprehends such knowledge (VII.113). The proper response to "Almighty works" is twofold. Adam, if he understands Raphael's teaching, will come to a greater understanding of God's ways. Such understanding inevitably elicits love from a pure heart. After digesting the knowledge Raphael imparts, Adam's heart will comprehend and render freely to his Lord the adoration he deserves: Knowledge will be transmuted to love.

When Raphael elaborates this theme by comparing knowledge and food, he engages one of the major rhetorical structures of the poem and goes far beyond a simple warning against intellectual indigestion:

> But Knowledge is as food, and needs no less
> Her Temperance over Appetite, to know
> In measure what the mind may well contain,
> Oppresses else with Surfeit, and soon turns
> Wisdom to Folly, as Nourishment to Wind. (VII.126–30)

Earlier, Raphael tells Adam that eating is a refining process: "For know, whatever was created, needs / To be sustain'd and fed; of Elements / The grosser feeds the purer. . ." (V.414–16), after which the narrator tells us that, contrary to contemporary theological opinion, Raphael physically metabolizes his mundane meal:

> So down they sat,
> And to thir viands fell, nor seemingly
> The Angel, nor in mist, the common gloss
> Of Theologians, but with keen dispatch
> Of real hunger, and concoctive heat
> To transubstantiate; what redounds, transpires
> Through Spirits with ease; nor wonder; if by fire
> Of sooty coal the Empiric Alchemist
> Can turn, or holds it possible to turn
> Metals of drossiest Ore to perfet Gold
> As from the Mine. (V.433–43)

The converse is also true. Raphael explains that Adam, refined by continued obedience, may someday find angelic food "no inconvenient Diet, nor too light Fare" (V.495). Eating is a process in which the grosser food is transformed into the finer substance of the body that digests it. Food and eater may proceed up a scale of mutual refinement; Adam, becoming more and more ethereal, will be able to "transubstantiate" lighter and lighter food, until "from these corporal nutriments," he may "at last turn all to spirit" (V.496–7). To achieve this destiny Adam must remain obedient. To remain obedient he must exert "temperance over appetite," by refraining from eating a fruit that will give him indigestible knowledge. Thus the hermeneutic circle connecting knowledge and the fruit passes through Raphael's discourse on eating and knowing.[23] If Adam eats food that is inappropriate to the spiritual state he has thus far attained, he will not be able to refine its substance, and it will escape as noxious "wind." Similarly, undigested knowledge will turn "wisdom to folly."

It is curious that Milton, choosing the occasion of Raphael's meal to urge his views on angelic alimentation, also chooses to designate Raphael's metabolic processes with the word for the Roman Catholic doctrine of the eucharistic presence. Both context and language invite the reader to contrast the notion of spiritual transformation referred to by Raphael and demonstrated throughout the epic with the Roman Catholic doctrine of the sacrament of the Eucharist that Milton vehemently rejects, often with language that recalls the "concoctive heat" of digestion. A passage from the *Christian Doctrine* will serve as an example:

> The Mass brings down Christ's holy body from its supreme exaltation at the right hand of God. It drags it back to earth, though it has suffered every pain and hardship already, to a state of humiliation even more wretched and degrading than before: to be broken once more and crushed and ground, even by the fangs of brutes. Then, when it has been driven through all the stomach's filthy channels, it shoots it out – one shudders even to mention it – into the latrine. (*CP*.VI.560)

To further explore Milton's use of "transubstantiate" here and his use of knowledge and food as the terms of a metaphor that projects a monistic resolution of the Platonic dualism of soul and body, it will be useful to pause at this point in our reading to consider Milton's notion of the Lord's Supper in general and his presentation of the sacrament in *Paradise Lost* in particular. Focusing on the choice of a technical word so generally and closely associated with what Milton held to be a contemptible misreading of communion to represent an angelic practice, we can divine a major pattern in the poem and relate that pattern to the contemporary practices on which it commented.[24] We shall then be able to see how the notion of intellectual transubstantiation remedies the radical indeterminacy of temporal experience by relating faith and knowledge through a transcendent and interior affective experience that secures both.

When Adam expresses reservations at offering mundane food to his angelic guest, Raphael replies:

> Food alike those pure
> Intelligential substances require
> As doth your Rational; and both contain
> Within them every lower faculty
> Of sense, whereby they hear, see, smell, touch, taste,
> Tasting concoct, digest, assimilate,
> And corporeal to incorporeal turn. (V.407–13)

Clearly a connection is made between eating and knowing, a connection that places this passage within one of the large thematic units of the poem and allows us to contrast two ways in which humankind may seek to *know* God, one typified by the discourse of man and angel in the garden and associated with the Protestant understanding of the sacraments, the other exemplified by Eve's fall and associated with the Roman Catholic doctrine of the Eucharist. The distinction that Milton draws between the two provides his readers with an interpretive guide to a sacramental reading of the poem and of mundane experience. This distinction, like the one at stake in the use of family roles to designate the members of the Godhead, concerns the orientation of a metaphor that relates analogous perceptions as referents and signs.[25] The "transubstantiation" asserted by Raphael and urged by Milton moves always from corporeal to incorporeal, "the grosser feeds the purer." This spiritual eating is part of an interactive process through which "corporal nutriments" are assimilated to a spiritual nature already prepared to receive them. Thus Raphael instructs Adam and Eve:

> Wonder not then, what God for you saw good
> If I refuse not, but convert, as you,
> To proper substance; time may come when men
> With Angels may participate, and find
> No incovenient Diet, nor too light Fare:
> And from these corporal nutriments perhaps
> Your bodies may at last turn all to spirit,
> Improv'd by tract of time, and wing'd ascend
> Ethereal, as wee, or may at choice
> Here or in Heav'nly Paradises dwell;
> If ye be found obedient, and retain
> Unalterably firm his love entire
> Whose progeny you are. (V.491–503)

The Roman doctrine of the transubstantiation of the Eucharist precisely reverses the relation of referents and signs in Raphael's explanation. The spiritual effects of Christ's presence in the heart of regenerate man are "made corporal" in the consecrated host. "The Papists are wrong," writes Milton,

> when they attribute to the outward sign the power of conferring salvation or grace. They think that this power is released whenever the rite itself is performed. But the sacraments cannot impart salvation or grace of themselves. They are merely seals or symbols of salvation and grace for believers." (*CP*.VI.556)

Milton's position follows Calvin's teaching with respect to the sacrament in stressing the need to raise the mind *through* the physical sign *to* Christ's spiritual power, lest

when, not elevating our minds beyond the visible sign, we
transfer to the sacraments the praise of those benefits, which
are only conferred upon us by Christ alone, and that by the
agency of the Holy Spirit, who makes us partakers of Christ
himself, by the instrumentality of the external signs which
invite us to Christ, but which cannot be perverted to any other
use, without a shameful subversion of all their utility.[26]

Like most Puritans of his day, Milton treats the sacraments as
specific elements in a divine rhetoric. The sacrament is neither identical to the saving grace that may be communicated through it, as
the papists would have it, nor is it a *siglium nudum* or pneumonic
of Christ's sacrifice, as the memorialists would have it; rather, it is
a *siglium verbi*, a true communicating sign through which the receiver
is brought to the benefits of Christ's sacrifice.[27] In the words of the
*Savoy Declaration* of 1658,

Worthy Receivers outwardly partaking of the visible Elements
in this Sacrament do then also inwardly by Faith, really and
indeed, yet not causally and corporally, but spiritually, receive
and feed upon Christ crucified, and all the benefits of his
death.[28]

In the *Christian Doctrine*, Milton writes explicitly of the rhetoric of
the sacrament: "It is to be noted that a certain trope or figure of
speech was frequently employed . . . that a thing which in any way
illustrates or signifies another thing is mentioned not so much for
what it really is as for what it illustrates or signifies," and he warns
that "failure to recognize this figure of speech in the sacraments,
where the relationship between the symbol and the thing symbolized
is very close, has been a widespread source of error, and still is
today" (*CP.*VI.555). Milton's movement from visible sign to spiritual meaning once again recalls Calvin's analysis:

For we ought to understand the *word*, not of a murmur uttered
without meaning or faith, a mere whisper like a magical in-
cantation, supposed to possess the power of consecrating the

elements, but of the gospel preached, which instructs us in the signification of the visible sign.[29]

The sacrament thus must be understood as comprising both a *visible* sign and its *verbal* interpretation.[30]

In the matter of reading the sign of the Lord's Supper, William Ames provides a detailed explication of the gospel text, using strict Ramist rhetorical categories:

As touching the manner of opening the words of this phrase, "this is my body" according to art, . . . Most of our interpreters would have a trope in the words, that is, a metaphor or a metonymy.

But the trope is neither in the Article going before, nor in the proper *copula,* as in the word is; but in that which followes, that is, the word body, for body is put for a signe of the body, not that a true and proper body is excluded out of that sentence, but rather included by a relation which the sign has to the thing signified.

But there is not only one trope, but threefold is the word, the first is a metaphor, whereby one thing like is put for another unto which a metonymie of the adjunct adheres and is signified. For the bread is not onley like the body of Christ, but also by Gods institution it is made an adjunct of it: the second is a Synecdoche of the part for the whole, whereby the body of Christ is put for the adjuncts, in that Christ is put for all those benefits also which are derived from Christ to us.[31]

If I may presume to unpack this analysis: The troped word, "body," referring to the bread Christ is about to distribute to the apostles, metaphorically compares the bread to Christ's body, which is also about to be broken and disseminated to the faithful. (We should notice here the importance of the historical situation of the Last Supper as the single original to be reenacted in the sacrament.) The breaking of Christ's body on the cross will nourish the Christians spiritually, as the breaking of the bread at the supper promises physical nourishment.[32] The trope is then troped again; "body," as an adjunct of Christ, stands metonymically for its subject.[33] Finally, by synecdoche, the subject, Christ, is taken to include all its adjuncts, notably the efficacy of saving grace. Thus the value of the sacrament is not in eating the host but in following through the exercise of understanding that leads to a comprehension of God's grace and the *prospect* of salvation. Retracing the tropings of the Lord's Word unfolds its meaning as a history of its rhetoric and so refines discursive knowledge to a self-certain experience of saving grace.

Milton takes this rhetoric further by making it clear that the sacrament is literally not the bread but Christ's words. Like Calvin, he sees the physical presence of the bread as an illustrative adjunct of the "gospel preached," the visible sign that is the occasion of a verbal interpretation:

> That living bread which, Christ says, is his flesh, and the true drink which, he says, is his blood, can only be the doctrine which teaches us that Christ was made man in order to pour out his blood for us. The man who accepts this doctrine with true faith will live for ever. This is as certain as that the actual eating and drinking sustain this mortal life of ours for a little while – indeed, much more certain. (*CP*.VI.553–4)

In the light of this theory of the sacrament, we can see Eve's fall in *Paradise Lost* as a misreading of God's sign that has something in common with the Roman Catholic interpretation of the institution of the Lord's Supper, for Eve invests the fruit – which is properly the visible sign of her relationship of obedience to God – with transformative power *in itself.* Whereas Raphael suggests to Adam that mortals might learn to assimilate angelic fare by a process of self-refinement, Eve will propose to assimilate herself to what she takes to be the divine substance of the forbidden fruit. If we apply the mode of interpreting the sacraments given by Calvin and followed by Milton, we may say that the Trees of Life and Knowledge were visible signs, and the "gospel preached" was Raphael's explication of the single prohibition.[34] The sign of the trees recalls to Adam and Eve their covenant of obedience with God and seals to them the good effects to be obtained by its continued practice – refinement of knowledge and ultimate immortality.[35] When she falls,

Eve will miss the word and invest the sign with magic powers; she will take the sign literally, thinking that knowledge is invested in the fruit rather than the practice of disobedience entailed in eating. She will be offered this unholy communion by Satan, clothed in the obscure garment of the snake, whose tempting words will obfuscate the clear word of God's command, as the Roman priest's Latin murmur obfuscates the clear word of the gospel.[36]

Raphael's doctrine of transubstantiation through refinement contrasts with this negative transubstantiation that sacrifices spiritual truth to a trivial, material sign. The angel's claim, of course, has literal value: He means to say he can digest edenic food. But the analogy of knowledge to food with which the claim is advanced also serves as a complex gloss on Adam's prospects of improvement "by tract of time."

If we shift from the digestion of food to that of knowledge, we find that the angel defines as nutritious that knowledge that informs Adam of his personal happiness. Recalling that "the heart of man" is the faculty that comprehends divine creation (VII.114), we recognize that the proper response to "Almighty works" is double: Adam, if he interprets correctly, will come to understand more of God's ways. Such understanding will elicit love from his pure heart. Insofar as God is identified with love, he is known whenever his *visible* signs, *understood according to his Word*, evoke this emotion:

> Love refines
> The thoughts, and heart enlarges, hath his seat
> In Reason, and is judicious, is the scale
> By which to heav'nly Love thou may'st ascend. (VIII.589–92)

Thus the legitimate transubstantiation available to Adam is that which transforms visible creation into divine affection through the mediation of the Word. Such transubstantiation dwells not in the sign of the creator, but ascends the scale of nature to "heav'nly Love." If we recall Ames's threefold tropical analysis terminating in the benefits of Christ – that is, grace for man – we may now extract from Raphael's remarks a similar hermeneutic.

We may further note that the breaking of the bread in the institution of the Lord's Supper anticipates the breaking of its metaphoric tenor in the Passion. Thus what is revealed is strictly the future; the temporal consequence of Christ's earthly ministry is foreshadowed and explained at the Last Supper and reenacted at the communion table. Temporal origin and terminus are united and interpreted through a temporal practice. The meaning of the earlier event is revealed in the later one. I suggested earlier that the war in heaven follows a pattern derived from that section of the Gospels that begins with Christ's withdrawal from his disciples and ends with the transfiguration, and I argued that the glorifications of the Son at the end of the war and in the transfiguration were both offered as aids to carry faith past the humiliation of the Passion. I would now add that the institution of the Lord's Supper both in the Gospels and as it is anticipated by Raphael's mundane meal in *Paradise Lost* continues this analogy and imparts to Milton's text a putative scriptural warrant.

Adam and Milton's readers are asked to understand their mundane experiences as signs to be interpreted in terms of the scriptural revelation. By doing so they will extend faith, which will increase understanding and elicit love and further faith. This transformation of experience into love and love into faith is, for Milton, the true miracle of transubstantiation. Extending the "scaling phenomenon" we encountered in our discussion of Eve's encounter with her image in the pool in Book IV, we can now see the devolution and conservation of divine light subsumed within the dialectic of knowledge and food that relates human and divine love on a continuum of transformed desire.[37] Love, associated with light by its generative and "concoctive" heat, devolves from the Father to his creatures, where through the medium of verbal understanding, it is transubstantiated and (re)turned to the substance of God in the form of adoration.

Having defined useful knowledge as that which can be "transubstantiated," Raphael agrees to answer Adam's question about creation and explains that God decided to create a world out of chaos in which to cultivate creatures who will eventually replace the fallen angels. The Father's announcement of this plan (VII. 152–61) recapitulates the pattern of refinement and ascension developed in Raphael's discourse. The first part of the angel's narrative deals with the fall of the rebel angels and their exile from heaven. The second part deals with ascension, the rise of Earth from chaos and Adam from Earth.

Raphael quotes the Father's instructions to the Son, a more ambitious charge than Raphael's mission to warn Adam, but parallel to it as a divine delegation to "bring on" a particular style of "discourse":

> And thou my Word, begotten Son, by thee
> This I perform, speak thou, and be it done:
> My overshadowing Spirit and might with thee
> I send along, ride forth, and bid the Deep
> Within appointed bounds be Heav'n and Earth,
> Boundless the Deep, because I am who fill
> Infinitude, nor vacuous the space.
> Though I uncircumscrib'd myself retire,
> And put not forth my goodness, which is free
> To act or not, Necessity and Chance
> Approach not mee, and what I will is Fate. (VII.163–73)

Book VII elaborates the relationships and conditions expressed in this passage.

Raphael's account of creation attempts to approach by "process of speech" the absolutely immediate creativity of God (VII.176–9). Adam is cautioned that what he will hear as a linear narrative only approximates the identity of divine concept and execution. "Process of speech," we learned from Book VI, is precisely the temporal arena in which words come to reliably reflect thoughts, only after having been confirmed (or disconfirmed) by the timely appearance of works. The dialectic of dissimulation and subsequent disclosure that defined the proximate success and ultimate failure of satanic hypocrisy is elided by the eternal unity of divine appearance and essence, concept and act. Milton, through Raphael, assigns himself the task of refining and making digestible this difficult and unhuman immediacy. The ability of the poetry to make the reader feel awe and love at the creation and to grasp its implicit immediacy is the measure of its usefulness and its permissibility. Successful accommodation implies transubstantiation in the specifically "licit" form we have derived from Raphael's use of the term.

When the Son comes forth from heaven to perform the creation, the heavenly host peer with him into the boiling cauldron of uncreated chaos (VII.210–15). The shore of heaven is the boundary between creation and uncreation; beyond it, in chaos, there are neither boundaries nor dimensions. Creation begins with circumscription:

> He took the golden Compasses, prepar'd
> In God's Eternal store, to circumscribe
> This Universe, and all created things:
> One foot he centred, and the other turn'd
> Round though the vast profundity obscure,
> And said, Thus far extend, thus far thy bounds,
> This be thy just Circumference, O World. (VII.225–31)

"One foot he centred"! Where? This primordial act of creating the center can only have meaning through an equally primordial relation, that of the fixed and turning compasses "prepar'd / In God's Eternal store." The center is center by virtue of the motion of the turning foot. The compasses, which are the instruments of a primal situating or placing, are also icons of the simultaneous – that is, dialectical – linkage of fixed and moving, of time and space. The two poles of the eternally "pre-paired" compasses iconographically embody the two terms of metaphor: the process of speech, which attempts to present as immediate a dual relation that is instituted only by rhetoric itself, and its reflection of a dialectical ontology of self and other, self for other, self in other. The fixed and turning feet, understood as the tenor and vehicle of an accommodated discourse, redefine, within language, the flight and reversal of the eyebeam that captures "his own works and their works" to begin the heavenly discourse in Book III (59) and moves through Uriel's directions to the disguised Satan to the "conversation" of Adam and Eve in the bower (III.722–34) – a conversation that propagates the works and image of God, ultimately to return his gaze to heaven.[38] The identity of divine concept and act is asserted and reasserted in the hexameron of Book VII as the poem recapitulates the hortatory subjunctives that comprise the biblical account of creation (VII.243–519).

In Milton's hexameron an animistic Earth answers the Word's call to be. In response to the divine command "Main Ocean" over-flowed the Earth "not idle, but with warm / Prolific humor soft'ning all her Globe, / Fermented the great Mother to con-ceive"(VII.279–82). Mountains "appear / Emergent, and thir broad bare backs upheave" (VII.285–6). It is as though the universe, in-spired by God's Word, creates and re-creates itself in a self-sustaining process. Two contexts, one eternal, one temporal, function para-doxically in the poetry. The decrees of God are instantaneously effected. Yet the response of matter inscribes those decrees in pro-cesses that take place in time. The reversed mirror image of the temporal disclosure of satanic hypocrisy is the temporal revelation of divine truth, written and read in the visible world much in the way that uttered language makes visible *in time* the atemporal struc-ture of linguistic competence or puts into a linear string of words a visually conceived idea. The six-day structure of the Genesis story brings this double context with it, and Milton's poetry expands the accommodation. The exploration of the paradox that God's decrees are eternal yet appear in time takes Adam to the limits of human understanding. Beyond this accommodation, knowledge becomes indigestible. The creation begins with the setting of boundaries, and the narrative sets boundaries of another sort; it teaches Adam the limits of human understanding and leaves him on the shore beyond which knowledge is chaos.

The assertion of the double context in which a single action exists in distinctly temporal and eternal aspects simultaneously, evokes man's closeness to and distance from heaven. On the one hand Adam cannot hope to comprehend the immediate identity of concept and act in divine creation; on the other he may find a clear symmetry between the mysterious acts of creation described by the angel and the temporal procreations he observes and performs on Earth. Thus by a roundabout route, the terms of Raphael's description return us to his suggestion concerning the relationship of the two contexts:

> And what surmounts the reach
> Of human sense, I shall delineate so,
> By lik'ning spiritual to corporal forms,
> As may express them best, though what if Earth

Be but the shadow of Heav'n, and things therein
Each to other like more than on Earth is thought? (V.571–6)

The conclusion of Book VII illustrates the dialectical transubstantiation of knowledge to love by depicting the transcendent
creativity of the deity, the limitations on human and angelic understanding of that creativity, and the appropriate responses of awe
and praise. Though the creation comprises acts of measurement,
delineation, and limitation, God's goodness is "unmeasur'd," his
works "unmeasurable," his power "infinite." No thought can
"measure" him, no tongue "relate" his works (VII.603–4).

The emphasis throughout the account is on the double context
of the temporal expressing the eternal, the bounded reflecting the
infinite, the individual including the unity of all creatures. Obliquely
and quietly, these paradoxical contradictions point inevitably to a
historical event: the incarnation of God in man, the eternal and the
temporal joined in one body, the metaphor become substantial truth.
This event is deferred to beyond the limits of the narrative, always
ahead, portending the time when "God shall be All in All," and
narrative, devoid of its temporal medium, shall end. Yet it is also
originary, conditioning the apprehension of all that leads up to it.
The absent incarnation becomes the ultimate focus of Milton's
theodicy, the pivot on which the justification of God's ways to men
must turn.

### III

The Angel ended, and in *Adam's* Ear
So Charming left his voice, that he a while
Thought him still speaking, still stood fixt to hear;
Then as new wak't thus gratefully repli'd. (VIII.1–4)

These lines, added when Milton divided Book VII of the 1667 edition to make Books VII and VIII of the second edition, signal a
turning point in Raphael's visit.[39] Adam has been abstracted from
his immediate context into the imaginative re-creation of creation
provided by the "Divine Historian." Recovering from this attentive

ecstasis, Adam begins to assert his mundane perspective and to dominate the dialogue.

Adam understands that although the revelation of the heavenly prehistory of mundane existence is invaluable, he must govern the daily round of his activities by applying his discursive and empirical human reason. Such application may include finding a use for this new revelation in judging and choosing on Earth. Knowing that Raphael's history lesson has increased his understanding of heavenly things and his own relation to them, Adam desires to recount the few events of his own life history – how he came to know his own creation, how Eve was created, the prohibition of the fruit of the Tree of Knowledge, and his discourse with the creator – as a way to make himself more comprehensible to Raphael in his human particularity. In this way he can repay Raphael for the insights into angelic life he has been granted and establish his own uniquely human perspective. Adam's autobiographical narration may thus be seen as a counterrevelation intended to provide Raphael with a fuller context in which to judge (that is, to understand) man.

Adam's question on the moral economy of the planets (VIII.15–38) signals that he has digested Raphael's account of creation and regained his sense of self sufficiently to seek new information, additional nourishment – and along the way, to seek angelic corroboration of the answer he gave to Eve's related question (IV.657–8). Anxious to demonstrate his own methods of knowing, Adam summarizes the evidence he has obtained through observation:

> When I behold this goodly Frame, this World
> Of Heav'n and Earth consisting, and compute
> Thir magnitudes, this Earth a spot, a grain,
> An Atom, with the Firmament compar'd
> And all her number'd Stars, that seem to roll
> Spaces incomprehensible (for such
> Thir distance argues and thir swift return
> Diurnal) merely to officiate light
> Round this opacous Earth, this punctual spot,
> One day and night; in all thir vast survey
> Useless besides. (VIII.15–25)

Adam then applies his reason to this data:

> Reasoning I oft admire,
> How Nature wise and frugal could commit
> Such disproportions, with superfluous hand
> So many nobler Bodies to create,
> Greater so manifold to this one use. (VIII.25–9)

Adam's next step is to construct a model that might accommodate his data. Envisaging from his observations what is essentially the Ptolemaic system, Adam opines that a Copernican arrangement would be more efficient (VIII.33–8). Thus his question demonstrates the range and method of human reason. In Book V, Raphael distinguishes angelic and human reason, "Discursive, or Intuitive; discourse / Is oftest yours, the latter most is ours, / Differing but in degree, of kind the same" (V.488–90). Adam's question demonstrates the practice of discursive reason: Its dependence on observation makes it vulnerable to deception by dissimulation of appearances. The question moves the perceiving center of the narrative to Adam and begins to construct a poetic presentation of the human perspective. The distinction in action between intuitive, angelic reason and discursive, mundane reason again glances forward to the historical moment in which the two will be ineluctably joined. Adam's realization of the limitations on discourse up and down the chain of being will condition his appreciation of the incarnation when it is sketched for him in Book XII. The pairing of Raphael's narrative and Adam's presented in Books VII and VIII presents this distinction to the reader but presents it as interior to the discourse as it arises from the efforts of Raphael and Adam to understand each other. At this point in the transition between the two narratives, Raphael's perceptions are still tutorial.

Rather than resolve Adam's astronomical quandary, Raphael criticizes Adam's application of discursive reason and reminds Adam that appearance and essence need not coincide:

> Consider first, that Great
> Or Bright infers not Excellence: the Earth

Though, in comparison of Heav'n, so small,
Nor glistering, may of solid good contain
More plenty than the Sun that barren shines,
Whose virtue on itself works no effect,
But in the fruitful Earth; there first receiv'd
His beams, unactive else, thir vigor find.
Yet not to Earth are those bright Luminaries
Officious, but to thee Earth's habitant. (VIII.90–9)

Adam's reasoning is only as sound as the evidence of the senses on which it is based, and that evidence is dubious. When Raphael says that the specific design of the cosmos is irrelevant so long as its moral economy is understood, he demonstrates his intuitive reason: In essence the Ptolemaic and Copernican paradigms represent different routes to the same moral end. Raphael's discourse, like the epic in which it is embedded, locates truth in a repeating pattern of relations rather than in the specific contents of any given description. The analogy of Sun and Earth to Adam and Eve in Raphael's statement implies that Adam's potency, like the Sun's, is barren in itself but fruitful in Eve, and thus conveys the digestible essence of divine cosmology of which the Copernican and Ptolemaic models are the disposable rinds. Raphael's explanation illustrates his advice to Adam and Eve to "be lowly wise" and confine their speculations to pragmatic contexts: to "think only what concerns thee and thy being" (VIII.173–4).

Adam's response to this lesson begins a turn in the discourse. The colloquy of man and angel, which began in Book V with mutual assertions of continuity, turns in Book VIII to the careful delineation of difference. Adam enforces this shift of emphasis when he insists on the dignity of his distinctively human sensibility. Rather than simply subordinate his discursive to Raphael's intuitive insight, Adam makes the case that the human point of view holds a particular validity within a human experience to which Raphael's access is necessarily incomplete. In other words, Adam subversively accepts the distinction between human and angelic knowledge but resists its hierarchization: "But apt the Mind or Fancy is to rove / Uncheckt, and of her roving is no end; / Till warn'd, or by experience

118

taught, she learn" (VIII.188–90). Adam accepts Raphael's warning, but he also advances experience as a teacher, and, for the first time, he presumes to instruct Raphael – in the workings of the human mind.

The impulse to self-assertion, the feeling that his human perspective is uniquely valid in human contexts, prompts Adam to offer his own creation story. Raphael has given Adam a heavenly history to facilitate his understanding of divine ways. Similarly, Adam offers his personal history to elucidate human ways for Raphael. His introduction of the creation story betrays an aggressive desire to make himself understood on this, as it were, subdiscursive level of sensibility:

> Therefore from this high pitch let us descend
> A lower flight, and speak of things at hand
> Useful, whence haply mention may arise
> Of something not unseasonable to ask
> By sufferance, and thy unwonted favor deign'd.
> Thee I have heard relating what was done
> Ere my remembrance: now hear mee relate
> My Story, which perhaps thou hast not heard. (VIII.198–205)

Adam's elaborate courtesy suggests assurance, determination, and something of a desire to show off, to display the self. Picking up Raphael's rhetoric of knowledge and food, Adam assures the angel that he has digested Raphael's instruction and made its key figure his own (VIII.210–16).

Still following Raphael's model, Adam prefaces his narrative with a caution that it is difficult to communicate experience to another, especially experience of divine works: "For Man to tell how human Life began / Is hard; for who himself beginning knew?" (VIII.250–1). The remark at once contrasts happily with Satan's presumptuous rejection of his creation story (V.859–61) and, in a way analogous to Raphael's appeal to accommodation (VII.112–14), asserts that the following story is a personal history that only approximates a truth beyond telling. Adam's history, like Raphael's, is structured to impart a moral context to the narrated events.

In it the newly created Adam turns his "won'dring Eyes" to heaven and is raised "by quick instinctive motion" (VIII.257–61). Examining his own body (VIII.267–70), he puts his faculties of observation and reason to immediate use. Discursive reason serves to explain the operation of his "supple joints" and to appreciate his "lively vigor," but his origin and purpose puzzle him. Discovering that he can name and know the things he sees, he poses the question of his origin to his surroundings (VIII.273–82).

Adam's thoughts in his first moments represent a series of observations and conclusions: He is alive and that is good; he is surrounded by a nature he somehow knows; he reasons that he is a creature and desires to know his creator. With the desire of the creator, whom he understands to be beyond comprehension, Adam's reason recognizes that reason's limit has been reached. After allowing him to confirm this fact by exhausting his resources, God reveals himself in a dream that Adam awakes to find a reality. Adam, now placed in Eden, continues his search for the creator until God presents himself as "whom thou sought'st" (VIII.316). Adam seeks God both before and after being placed in Eden, and God's appearance, when it comes, comes in response to prayer.

Adam soon notes the absence of a mate and uses petitionary prayer for a second time. This second interaction between God and man is more complex and more instructive. When the creator responds by suggesting that Adam "find pastime" among the beasts (VIII.375), Adam continues to argue, confident of his knowledge of his own nature:

> Of fellowship I speak
> Such as I seek, fit to participate
> All rational delight, wherein the brute
> Cannot be human consort. (VIII.389–92)

The horizons of "rational delight" emerge only after God sharpens the issue by answering Adam's request for "fellowship" by asserting that the creator endures a solitude more acute than Adam's (VIII.403–11).

Adam retorts that while God is self-sufficient, man is not:

> To attain
> The highth and depth of thy Eternal ways
> All human thoughts come short, Supreme of things;
> Thou in thyself art perfet, and in thee
> Is no deficience found; not so is Man,
> But in degree, the cause of his desire
> By conversation with his like to help,
> Or solace his defects. (VIII.412–19)

In the seventeenth century, the word "conversation" carried a stronger meaning than it does now and could include conjugal as well as verbal intercourse.[40] The remainder of Adam's answer makes clear that he uses the term in this wider sense:

> No need that thou
> Shouldst propagate, already infinite;
> And through all numbers absolute, though One;
> But Man by number is to manifest
> His single imperfection, and beget
> Like of his like, his Image multipli'd,
> In unity defective, which requires
> Collateral love, and dearest amity. (VIII.419–26)

God's response affirms that Adam's recognition of his "single imperfection" and self-definition as neither God nor brute is the required expression of the divine image (VIII.440–4). The words with which he promises Eve to Adam further indicate a divine response to Adam's placement of intercourse at the horizon of discourse: "What next I bring shall please thee, be assur'd, / Thy likeness, thy fit help, thy other self, / Thy wish exactly to thy heart's desire" (VIII.449–51). Eve is to be Adam's other self by being another like the self. Not a simple mirror (as Sin is to Satan) but an image that propagates images.

The centrality of "propagation" as the culmination of the "conversation" of man and woman (cf. IV.639ff) completes the definition of Eve's function begun in Book IV.[41] The multiplication of thoughts and words in conversation depends on and implies the multiplication of bodies through procreation, and the location of the self in relation to another, essential to the rendering of love to the creator, depends on an other like the self, that is, an embodied other. The bodily image Adam finds in Eve redirects his (otherwise narcissistic) appreciation of the Lord's image to the further mirroring of that image in Eve. The "collateral love" of Adam and Eve – that is, the exchange of adoration for the image of the lord at a particular level of the great chain of created being – will extend God's creation through the procreation of his image. Each endowed with "substantial life," Adam and Eve enter a dialogue in which heavenly love is received, multiplied, and conserved.

Milton's depiction of the vertical devolution of divine love, engendering a series of horizontal circuits of "collateral love," joins a bodily and historical process to the timeless "manifestation" (VIII.422–3) of the divine decrees. The production of discourse (including, of course, the poem we read) is joined to the production of bodies (of readers), and the fullness of human speech is projected into a procreated earthly future wherein revelation is embedded in a conversation whose end is beyond time.

Having concluded his singular history of man, Adam focuses on the peculiar intensity of the "collateral love" he feels for Eve, a love he seeks to distinguish from the vertical or hierarchical love that binds him to the angel and binds both to God. Adam reports that he enjoys all the "delicacies" of "Taste, Sight, Smell, Herbs, Fruits, and Flow'rs" without "vehement desire" but that his response to Eve is "far otherwise":

> Transported I behold,
> Transported touch; here passion first I felt,
> Commotion strange, in all enjoyments else
> Superior and unmov'd, here only weak
> Against the charm of Beauty's powerful glance.
> Or Nature fail'd in mee, and left some part
> Not proof enough such Object to sustain,
> Or from my side subducting, took perhaps
> More than enough. (VIII.529–37)

Adam's fear that nature took from him "more than enough," creating Eve with an excess of "substantial life," raises the issue of

Eve's self-sufficiency that will be central to Adam's reactions in the separation scene of Book IX. Adam's anxiety is aroused precisely by the possibility that Eve is complete in herself. The excess Adam fears is thus connected to the excess of "exorbitant desires," desires that do not follow the spiral path of collateral love and divine transubstantiation, but rather withdraw into an abyssal self. Eve's failure to return love to Adam would not only expel Eve from the orbit of divine love, it would also leave Adam – or so Adam fears – with a deficiency of "substantial life" precisely defined by the empty place in his side from which Nature "took perhaps / More than enough":

> So absolute she seems
> And in herself complete, so well to know
> Her own, that what she wills to do or say,
> Seems wisest, virtuousest, discreetest best;
> All higher knowledge in her presence falls
> Degraded, Wisdom in discourse with her
> Loses discount'nanc't, and like folly shows;
> Authority and Reason on her wait,
> As one intended first, not after made
> Occasionally; and to consummate all,
> Greatness of mind and nobleness thir seat
> Build in her loveliest, and create an awe
> About her, as a guard Angelic plac't. (VIII. 547–59)

Raphael fails to see that Adam's concern is directly with "collateral love." Adam depends on Eve to remain the rib he donated to her creation – to maintain a synecdochic relation to him – and to aid him in the manifestation of their "single imperfection"; he fears her withdrawal into the self-sufficiency she had thought to find in her image in the pool.[42] Raphael's rebuke (VIII. 561–70) asserts the hierarchy that Adam fears may be insupportable and does not engage the issues of desire and dependency that are, from Adam's point of view, existential rather than theoretical – raising questions not of doctrine but of practice. Adam's reaction to this angelic failure is an aggressive assertion of man's unique personal experience

(VIII.596–611). His inquiry whether angels experience passionate love in heaven (VIII.615–17) is an implicit suggestion that terrestrial life may be beyond angelic understanding. The reader may "know" that Raphael is "right" and that Adam's uxoriousness will be the key to Satan's success, but the presentation of Adam as a subject situated in time works against the doctrinal condemnation offered by Raphael and allows the text at once to reject and justify Adam's behavior. As we shall have occasion to observe in the next chapter, the imputation of responsibility that falls short of blame, characteristic of tragedy, mitigates while it enforces a sense that Adam falls by an erring moral choice.

Although the reader knows that Adam will fall "not deceiv'd / But fondly overcome with Female charm" (IX.998–9), Adam's thoughtful delineation of the power and circumstances of his desire and his rejection of Raphael's resort to doctrine in Book VIII illustrate the distinctive subjectivity of man and contrast the two pedagogical approaches of Raphael during his visit to Eden. While the narrative of the war in heaven and of the creation have provided Adam with an understanding of satanic deceit and divine creativity that is "simple, sensuous, and passionate," the assertion of the doctrine of subordination of desire to reason brings forth a demand for an illustration of its practical application that sends the angel blushing back to heaven (VIII.618–19).

The detailed narrative presentation of Adam's dependence on "collateral love" and the risk of passion it entails dramatizes the doctrinal point made in Book III when the Father proclaims Adam and Eve "authors to themselves in all / Both what they judge and what they choose" (122–3). By exercising choice from within his temporal predicament, Adam will author himself as a principal actor in a human history shaped according to his ability to dispose the visible creation according to the providential pattern revealed to him at the intersection of doctrine and experience.

The dialogue of man and angel defines the provinces and practices of mundane and heavenly understanding. The horizon of this exchange of histories moves the reader toward the unnarrated event around which the "histories" of eternal heaven and temporal world turn: the incarnation of the Son as man and the historical union of mortal and immortal sensibilities. The fall of man remains temporally and logically prior to that predestined and anticipated event. In Milton's presentation of the fall, the breach between doctrine and practice that appears at the conclusion of Raphael's visit to Eden is enacted in a dramatic realization of Adamic choice.

# 6

## "THE HOUR OF NOON DREW ON"

THE FIRST LINES OF PARADISE LOST IX warn that we have reached the tragic climax promised in the poem's opening proclamation of a tragic and restorative movement.[1] The "tragic notes" of the fall are projected in various ways. As we have seen, Books IV and VIII disclose the characteristic subjectivity of Adam and Eve. In Book IX the narrator's explicit comments and the events he recounts are complemented by the rhetorically controlled alteration of that subjectivity through the polarization of Adam and Eve's pre- and postlapsarian perceptions of Eden. The prelapsarian perception is one of fecund harmony, as expressed by Eve:

> *Adam,* well may we labor still to dress
> This Garden, still to tend Plant, Herb and Flow'r,
> Our pleasant task enjoin'd, but till more hands
> Aid us, the work under our labor grows,
> Luxurious by restraint; what we by day
> Lop overgrown, or prune, or prop, or bind,
> One night or two with wanton growth derides
> Tending to wild. (IX.205–12)

After the fall, Eden becomes what Adam calls "these wild Woods forlorn" (IX.910), a place in which to hide from the gaze of heaven:

> O might I here
> In solitude live savage, in some glade

126

Obscur'd, where highest Woods impenetrable
To Star or Sun-light, spread thir umbrage broad,
And brown as Evening: Cover me ye Pines,
Ye Cedars, with innumerable boughs
Hide me, where I may never see them more. (IX.1084–90)

The narrative of Book IX must mediate these opposed perceptions
of the world to articulate the continuity and change that ensure the
unity and the disjuncture of Adam and Eve before and after their
fall.

Focusing attention on several representative passages will make
it possible to trace this movement from happiness to sorrow, from
fertility to barrenness, and to examine the rhetoric of emotion that
makes these transformations credible. An understanding of the
emotive rhetoric employed in Book IX will in turn provide insight
into Milton's method of portraying the self-authorship of his characters. In this chapter, I shall be particularly concerned with the
moment of the fall as a division between the experience of time as
a succession of pleasant and varied repetitions (as in Book IV.639–
66) and the entry of Adam and Eve into the historicity of what
Heidegger calls "being toward death."[2]

I

The decorum of Book IX is distinctly dramatic. The action is confined to Eden from beginning to end. On this stage we find three
characters in four combinations: Satan alone, Adam with Eve, Satan
with Eve, and Eve alone. The narrative action comprises a narrator's
prologue (1–47), Satan's entrance and soliloquy (48–191), a domestic
agon between Adam and Eve (205–411), the temptation of Eve by
the serpent, her soliloquy (471–833), the temptation of Adam by
Eve (834–1045), and an open-ended agon between the now fallen
Adam and Eve (1046–1189). Throughout these scenes the narrator
provides choral comment and stage directions. The book can thus
be seen as a "closet drama" in which the "unities" are observed
and the action is presented in a prologue and five acts.[3] The restriction of the action to such well-defined segments in time, all
occuring in the same place and with the same Aeschylean limitation

on the number of characters on stage as in *Samson Agonistes,* differs markedly from Milton's practice elsewhere in the epic. The material of Book IX is disposed as a causal series of interdependent episodes to establish a tense atmosphere of "tragic inevitability." We might well characterize Milton's procedure here as "Aristotelian narration." The five-act, tragic structure operates in two specific ways: It associates itself with the reader's memory of classical drama, its heroes and themes, and it makes available to Milton the strategies and techniques of dramatic representation developed by the ancients. The specific details of this pattern and its interaction with the thematics of the poem will become apparent as representative passages from each act are examined.

Finally, it will be possible to raise the structural fact of "Aristotelian narration" to the level of theme by demonstrating the interrelationship of Milton's thought in Book IX to the particular mimetic mode that conveys it. One major theme of *Paradise Lost* is human limitation. The fall embodies the first parents' unfortunate attempt to transcend their merely human understanding. The poem is precise about the nature of human knowledge and its limitations. Lacking the intuitive intellection of the angels, Adam and Eve know only what they can deduce or infer from divine revelation and direct observation. Their happiness in the garden depends on their faith in revelation, and, to remain happy, they must refrain from any attempt to abridge the otherness of revelation by testing it empirically. Adam's empiricism and its limitations are made clear to him (and the reader) in Book VIII when Raphael rebukes him for his astronomical speculations. The angel warns Adam not to confuse appearance and essence, "that Great / Or Bright infers not Excellence" (VIII.90–1). Adam is to use his empirical wisdom, "for Heav'n / Is as the Book of God before thee set, / Wherein to read his wond'rous Works" (VIII.66–8), but he must remember that despite its efficacy when properly used to interpret man's earthly kingdom, it will prove ineffective in probing what "the great Architect / Did wisely to conceal" (VIII.72–3). Any attempt to constrain the divine will or its revelations to human conceptual capacity might well be answered with the argument Abdiel uses to answer Satan's arguments: "Shalt thou give Law to God, shalt thou dispute

/ With him the points of liberty, who made / Thee what thou art[?]"
(V.822–4).

When Adam and Eve eat the forbidden fruit, they expect to be
released from their temporal situation and to know good and evil
essentially, as the angels know them, although the vagueness of
Eve's understanding leads her to confuse the acquisition of knowledge with the acquisition of power – a gnostic confusion. Of course
the knowledge actually conferred on them by the fruit is empirical
and appropriate to the intellectual constitution God has chosen for
them. Thus the Father explains the irony of their attempt to rise
to a new knowledge by reducing revealed truth to mere experience:

> O Sons, like one of us Man is become
> To know both Good and Evil, since his taste
> Of that defended Fruit, but let him boast
> His knowledge of Good lost, and Evil got,
> Happier, had it sufficed him to have known
> Good by itself, and Evil not at all. (XI.84–9)

Adam and Eve fall because they momentarily "forget" the divine
world of essence that informs their world of temporal appearances.
The dramatic structure of Book IX invites the reader's participation
in a similar forgetting. We know that Adam and Eve will fall on
this day, just as we know that Oedipus will encounter his father
on the road to Thebes. Yet we wish for a warning voice as the
narrator did when Satan entered the garden (IV.1). We concentrate
our attention on the human act "that brought into this World a
world of Woe" (IX.11), and, perhaps, we forget that Adam and
Eve are not alone and helpless. In this way (and in Milton's terms),
we repeat the tragedy of man in the moment that we engage its
representation, just as Raphael's dramatic representation of the war
in heaven repeats the absorption of angelic knowledge in dramatic
time that he sought to convey. The key to this unity of repetition
and representation is the specific temporality of the drama, projected
here without the mediation of retrospective narration Raphael had
supplied.[4] By embedding this drama in the narrative of *Paradise
Lost,* Milton re-presents the embedding of the life self-authored by

judgments and choices made within historical time within the transcendent pretext of divine providence. The mastery of drama by an enclosing narrative has already been demonstrated and thematized in Raphael's account of the war in heaven. Recalling our discussion of that account, we can now say that in Book IX, Adam and Eve are confronted with an opportunity to *practice* Raphael's *doctrine,* an opportunity that is, typically, seized only in retrospect, from the position of the fall.

## II

The dramatic action begins when Satan emerges from a fountain near the Tree of Life, "involv'd in rising Mist" (IX.75), death entering life at its root. Seventeenth-century meanings of "involve" include "to wind a spiral form or in a series of curves, coils or folds; to wreathe, coil, entwine," and "to roll up within itself, to envelop and take in; to overwhelm and swallow up."[5] The word evokes images of the movement of the snake (see Satan's description of the snake climbing the Tree of Knowledge [IX.589–93]), self-absorption, and Satan's status as a villain destined to be swallowed up by a death that is his own progeny.

The sexual connotations of Satan's entrance at the root of the Tree of Life fit the conceptual scheme of pollution of the generative process and enable the reader to relate the devil's activity in the garden to the felt experiences of his life.[6] The emphasis on propagation as the primary mode of human historical action before the fall, which we found in the discussions of Eve in Books IV and VIII is structurally linked to the phallic description of Satan's entry into the garden as it is thematically linked to the doctrine of original sin. Satan's appearance anticipates the dissonance of the cleavage of erotic desire from a subsuming conception of providential design that will be thematically manifested in the postlapsarian intercourse of Adam and Eve at the end of the book. The erotics of Satan's "involvement" resituate his "exorbitant" desire adjacent to the issue of "collateral love" assured by the Tree of Life.

By representing Satan as an anachronistic repetition of the debased eroticism initiated by the fall, Milton extends the rhetoric of the allegory of Sin and Death to their infernal Father. One might well link this rhetoric to seventeenth-century hermeneutics by describing it as an inverted type. The peculiar temporal structure obtained by representing a putative original (of sin, of death, of aimless eroticism) as the repetition of its own effects is paradigmatic for the rhetoric of Book IX, where it is disclosed to be nothing other than the temporality of tragic "inevitability." While the narrative tendency of typology is to displace closure (that is, to defer the fixation of meaning) to an anticipated historical future, the structure of Milton's inverted typology of Satan, Sin, and Death is to foreclose the historical future by an obsessive return to a temporal original. In much the same way, Oedipus finds his future already foreclosed by a past whose origin is displaced to a time before the action and ascribed to the agency of an immutable fate. Milton's text, however, discloses this fate as the self-enthrallment of the subject to his own self-regard, the inane triumph of the fantasy of omnipotence over the realization of self inscribed in the material history of its intersubjective encounters.

Satan's presentation as the original of the negative phallus, the initiator of the erotics of nonpropagation, situates him as the antithesis of the first parents. In his peculiar way, Satan is careful to see Adam and Eve as synecdochic of a much broader investment, just as they see themselves as representing and authoring a collective human future:

> For only in destroying I find ease
> To my relentless thoughts; and him destroy'd,
> Or won to what may work his utter loss,
> For whom all this was made, all this will soon
> Follow, as to him linkt in weal and woe,
> In woe then: that destruction wide may range. (IX.129–34)

Adam and Eve frequently refer to their expectation of "more hands," and the narrator describes Satan, in the snake, seeking "where likeliest he might find / The only two of Mankind, but in them / The whole included Race, his purpos'd prey" (IX.414–16). The dysymmetry of the human couple confronting the single adventurer, Satan, suggests a triangular structure in which the poles of "collateral love" are joined by the fall to the vanishing point of "exorbitant desire," and Satan's entrance into the garden suggests the dialectical continuity that puts the former in perpetual risk to the latter.

Satan's antithetical relation to the erotics of propagation is explicitly linked to the solipsism of satanic rhetoric by the lines with which the narrator introduces Satan's first soliloquy in Book IX: "Thus he resolv'd, but first from inward grief / His bursting passion into plaints thus pour'd" (IX.97–8). The relation of intercourse and discourse hinted at in Milton's earlier conflations of conversation and propagation is here exploited with (and for the purpose of) a vengeance. The words that are the substance of Satan's soliloquy are the outpouring of an inward passion that can only be delivered in solitude.[7]

Satan's position in the cosmos of *Paradise Lost* is unique. As an archangel who has rejected the telos of the Godhead, he now retains much of his former awareness but lacks rational control of his passions. He is condemned to an exquisite appreciation of his own self-enslavement. Having rejected the order of divine providence, he constantly projects alternate constitutions of his own desires; these he sees through almost as soon as he creates them. His language is shaped by his commitment to a subjectivity unrestrained by engagement with the material creation he has rejected.[8] In his soliloquy Satan runs through a series of impressions of Eden, quickly rejecting each one and replacing it with another. Thus he exults in the beauty of the garden, "O Earth, how like to Heav'n, if not preferr'd" (IX.99), only to wear himself down to the despair and degradation objectified in the shape and behavior of the snake (IX.163–77). The grammar of Satan's language and thought is epitomized as a series of suppositional statements structured "if . . . but." This "fallen conditional" construction is the grammar of a temporality in which the future is simply the negation of the past, the medium of a compulsive undoing.

After his initial exultation at seeing God's work in the garden, Satan remembers his mission and, entrapped in the story he is committed to author, soon drifts into "what might have been":

If I could joy in aught, sweet interchange
Of Hill and Valley, Rivers, Woods and Plains,

Now Land, now Sea, and Shores with Forest crown'd,
Rocks, Dens, and Caves; but I in none of these
Find place or refuge; and the more I see
Pleasures about me, so much more I feel
Torment within me, as from the hateful siege
Of contraries, all good to me becomes
Bane, and in Heav'n much worse would be my state. (IX.115–23)

Unable to resist the "but" that cancels hope, Satan often sees the truth behind his rationalizations.[9]

The syntax of Satan's language is the concrete expression of his fallen subjectivity, and its patterns can be related to the conceptual and epistemological constraints of the fallen state. When Satan denied the supremacy of God, he denied the intersubjective ground of creation. The deity is overthrown not in heaven but in the fallen sensibility, which replaces it with a fantasy of personal omnipotence. The fantasies of the fallen mind are inherently unstable, persisting only until reason or the evidence of the senses undermines them. Without recourse to intersubjective "fact," which Satan must negate to preserve the illusion of omnipotence, he is doomed to oscillate forever between the "ifs" and "buts" of a profligate fancy. The pattern is poignantly established by Satan's first words in the poem – "If thou beest he; But O how fall'n!" (I.84) – words that were read then as contextual but now appear representative.[10] Moreover, the restless dissatisfaction that results in the multiplication of fanciful hypotheses in Satan's soliloquy may now be recognized as the empty image of the propagation that is the promised fruit of the "collateral love" of Adam and Eve.

At this point the text refers at once to this intratextual juxtaposition and to a homologous structure in the text of actions. When judging or choosing, the fallen subject, attempting to author himself or herself in actions, imagines a hypothetical outcome to the considered action. The fallen mind thus shuttles endlessly between an anticipated future and a determinate set of alternative actions. The activity of anticipation and retrospection that is the necessary concomitant of judgment and choice ends only with death and the subject's release from its situated temporality. Satan's entrapment in an always hypothetical present is grounded in this experience of restlessness. His peculiar role as the archetype and progenitor of fallen subjectivity precludes his recourse to either of the strategies available to fallen men. His refusal to engage the material world (understood as God's creation) forecloses the release into historical engagement that is available to man, and his claim to immortality and immutability forecloses the final determination of meaning that makes death the "gate of life."

In a way this situating of the fallen subject restates the Aristotelian definition of tragic *poesis* as the *mimesis* of a human action, with the qualification that the action itself is necessarily a mimesis of an action completed in the imagination.[11] We may reconsider, in this light, Millicent Bell's conviction that Adam and Eve do not really fall in the dramatic climax of *Paradise Lost*. Bell feels that Milton does not present a "prime cause" to motivate the fall and that therefore, "instead of asking what caused the Fall, Milton was preoccupied . . . in employing the somewhat intractable legend to dramatize the state of fallen Man – Man as he knew him."[12] Bell refers to Adam and Eve's act of disobedience rather than to Satan's fallen condition, but the textual problems are similar. In both cases Milton extrapolates the unknown prehistory of a historically experienced present. By making the reader's present contiguous with Satan's past, Milton interprets the experienced restlessness of the fallen mind as the concrete, historical expression of its own prehistoric repetition. At this point, it may be useful to recall the temporal reversal of metaphoric ontology in speculative theology. According to this reversal, the sensible vehicle of a metaphor like that of the family in the Godhead is taken to be the temporal inscription of an intelligible original. Earthly fathers are understood as having been named *after* the heavenly father. A similar trope of temporal reversal motivates Milton's prehistory of the fall. From the experience of fallen man, Milton deduces that Satan fell because he misunderstood his relationship to God, because he believed that the absolute could be approached by accumulating increments of power, and because he confused appearance and essence. Once he rebelled, these errors were concretely expressed in his fallen state. In other words, sensible conditions after the fall are the material inscription of the intellectual errors made before it. Cause is deduced from and represented by effect.

What should be understood with respect to the so-called antecedents of the fall is that they serve dramatically to emphasize the
presence of the contingent. As J. B. Savage has shown, Adam and
Eve "maintain their freedom by ensuring the conditions on which
it depends, by resisting the possibilities that are inimical to it."[13]
The errors or near errors that they blunder into, while remaining
on the better side of sin, give point to the seriousness of the divine
charge; they indicate how the seeming inaction of remaining obedient can, of itself, refine their natures until they are "improv'd by
tract of time" (V.498). The construal of time becomes tricky with
respect to this prelapsarian period because the notions of development and progression implicit in the promise of improvement
and necessary to comprehending obedience as a significant practice
already presuppose the fall's introduction of difference into the homogeneous duration of prelapsarian time: "The Fall must have the
effect of revising our notion of the events preceding it, of causing
us to see them in relation to itself, of making us aware for the first
time of the essential historicity of things."[14] We understand the prelapsarian moments of Adam and Eve as leading up to something,
and we are correct to do so. Adam and Eve, however, experience
this time differently, as a round of pleasant and varied repetitions
to be marked by an action of propagation that will be the material
measure of their duration. The textual aporia that opens around the
portrayal of the fall and its motivation defines the disarticulation
of pre- and postlapsarian experiences of time and makes manifest
the complicated dialectic of resemblance and difference that defines
the "characters" of Adam and Eve. When Milton naturalizes the
textual aporia as tragic inevitability, he represents this dialectic as
the generic device of dramatic irony; the reader experiences the historicity of the fall while Adam and Eve remain ignorant of it until
it is too late.

Milton's motivation of the fall is thus purchased by a strategic
temporal reversal in his text – the effects of sin are recognized as
its causes. What had been conceptual abstraction before the fall,
however, is concretely expressed after. "Evil into the mind of God
or Man / May come and go, so unapprov'd, and leave / No spot
or blame behind" (V.117–19), Adam consoles Eve after her dream.
The fall before the fall anticipated in Eve's dream remains fancy's

"wild work" (V.112), the misjoined reminiscences of the previous evening's talk and the "addition strange" of satanic inspiration (V.116), until what has been imagined and rejected in Book V is performed in the concrete material presence of the fruit in Book IX. Similarly, Sin emerges from Satan's head when rebellion is intellectually conceived and planned, and Death is born when the thought of Sin is concretely embraced, propagated, as it were, in action (II.746–67).

The relationship between explicit theme and the implicit characterization we find in *Paradise Lost* is, I think, that suggested by Susanne Langer in her remarks on the achievement of "organic form" in the drama:

> It is true that tragedy usually – perhaps even always – presents a moral struggle, and that comedy very commonly castigates foibles and vices. But neither a great moral issue, nor folly inviting embarrassment and laughter, in itself furnishes an artistic principle; neither ethics nor common sense produces any image of organic form. Drama, however, always exhibits such form, it does so by creating the semblance of history, and composing its elements into a rythmic single structure. The moral context is thematic material, which, like everything that enters into a work of art, has to serve to make the primary illusion and articulate the pattern of "felt life" the artist intends.[15]

We can accept Langer's notion of a "virtual" mimesis that creates a "semblance of a history" while going beyond the romantic aesthetic of organic form to recognize the function of metaphor as the rhetorical armature on which the "single rhythmic structure" is built.

Although Langer is writing of staged drama, her argument applies to *Paradise Lost* IX as well. By choosing the dramatic structure he used in this book, Milton set in motion the dialectic of mythos and ethos that Aristotle recognized as the mainspring of a tragic form whose power it is to disclose character through the depiction of moral choice in circumstances that are first experienced by the characters as contingent, but retrospectively appear to have been the workings of an inevitable fate.[16]

The conclusion of Satan's soliloquy draws together many of the motives that adhere to him:

> O foul descent! that I who erst contended
> With Gods to sit the highest, am now constrain'd
> Into a Beast, and mixt with bestial slime,
> This essence to incarnate and imbrute,
> That to the highth of Deity aspir'd. (IX.163–7)

Satan's relationship to the snake is clearly realized. His incarnation suffers from the inevitable comparison to that of the Son. Although Satan considers his entry into the snake a "foul descent," we may remember that he has *risen* quite laboriously from hell to execute his mission. His entry into man's world will pull Earth down to commerce with hell rather than raise Satan to Earth, and it will provide the context of the other and antithetical incarnation that exalts man to Godhead. Satan's image of revenge that "bitter ere long back on itself recoils" (IX.172) anticipates this future reversal, links the coiled shape of the snake to the motion of Satan's "if . . . but" logic, and recalls the narrator's characterization of the soliloquy as an inverted orgasm: "But first from inward grief / His bursting passion into plaints thus pour'd."

Knowing that he will ultimately suffer the more himself, Satan compulsively attempts to transfer his self-hatred onto the unoffending Adam, "on him who next / Provokes my envy" (IX.174–5). The fact that Adam is, for Satan, merely a target of opportunity contributes to the tragic effect of the presentation. As the fatal confrontation of man and devil draws near, the events that mesh to bring them together promote an atmosphere of inevitability that works with the reader's prior knowledge of the story to involve him emotionally in the approaching climax.

Yet at the same time there is a strong element of the accidental and contingent in the fall – the motivelessness of Satan's envy, the time of day, Eve's hunger. The effect is simultaneously to invest each act with meaning while maintaining that, except for the eating of the fruit, the events of Adam and Eve's day are routine. Perhaps this combination of inevitability and contingency can best be appreciated if we consider that Satan had limitless time to effect the fall. Adam and Eve, though tempted on the particular day depicted in Book IX, were subject to continual temptation. Obedience is an act of will; as a pledge of faith, they would have had to hold to it eternally. As the war in heaven shows, even had they ascended the scale of nature to become as angels, they would still have remained subject to temptation. Thus the tragedy of the fall, as presented, is a mixture of the inevitable and the coincidental that, like the syntax of Satan's soliloquy, finds its ultimate credibility in a density of its mimesis that accords with our experience of life.

## III

After Satan has entered the snake, the scene shifts to the newly awakened Adam and Eve and the second "act" of the drama begins. In the separation scene, the first parents emerge as clearly recognizable human beings who bear a severe responsibility. While the text continues to assert their prelapsarian difference from the fallen reader – for example, by having them base the arguments of their domestic dispute on theological precepts – the increasingly perceptible subordination of timeless precept to immediate emotional needs tends to efface that difference, resituating Adam and Eve for the fall by placing them in the dramatically determinate temporal space that will become the norm after the fall. In the separation scene, Raphael's dogmatic assertion of the supremacy of reason over passion (VIII.561–94) is submitted to the complexities of time as Adam and Eve attempt to apply it as a concrete practice in a fully dramatized context.

Within the decorum of classical tragedy established for Book IX, this practice takes the form of an agon between Adam and Eve, each of whom struggles to control the ensuing action by establishing an interpretation of God's provision of work in the form of gardening and of Raphael's warning to "swerve not too secure" (V.238).

Eve, by asserting the value of efficiency over the "looks" and "smiles" she shares with Adam (IX.220–5), challenges the impor-

tance of the "collateral love," on which he bases his sense of self.[17]
As the separation issue becomes a test of their relationship, Adam
and Eve become more interested in their effect upon one another
than in the substance of the argument. (Eve's "I expected not to
hear" [IX.281] makes explicit the shift in her concern from the issue
of separation to the implications of Adam's reluctance to part from
her.) The voice of desire does not make itself heard beneath that
of reason because Adam and Eve are already fallen or because they
are created imperfect, but because the dispute takes place on the
level of the emotions – the argument is about how they feel. Such
attention to feeling is not authorized as such in their discourse and
is therefore displaced into a hermeneutical dispute that is, in effect,
a metaphoric exploration of their "collateral love" and of their attempts to reconcile its clear theory to the complexity of its practice.

This underlying exploration becomes apparent when Adam asks
Eve why she does not share his feelings:

> I from the influence of thy looks receive
> Access in every Virtue, in thy sight
> More wise, more watchful, stronger, if need were
> Of outward strength; while shame, thou looking on,
> Shame to be overcome or over-reacht
> Would utmost vigor raise, and rais'd unite.
> Why shouldst thou not like sense within thee feel
> When I am present, and thy trial choose
> With me, best witness of thy Virtue tri'd. (IX.309–17)

Adam at once betrays a preoccupation with Eve's feelings, as though
the issue of separation had alerted him to an interiority he had not
previously ascribed to her, and a dramatically inflected sense of the
self *staged* for the beloved other. Adam's suggestion that he and Eve
are the best witnesses of each others' virtue is related to his previously disclosed tendency to view her as "absolute" in herself
(VIII.547–55). The concrete effect of this tendency in this context
is that Eve "screens" Adam's memory of the divine witness, an
ominous anticipation – in the mind of a reader in the position of
"having already followed" the story – of the moment when Adam
will make Eve absolute by electing to fall with her.[18] Still, given

the dialectic of "collateral love" and the argument of propagation accepted by God in Book VIII, Adam's concerns appear reasonable and appropriate.

Their inquiry into the practice of "collateral love" overwhelms the "right reason" of Adam and Eve, but the ascension of passion over reason occurs by degrees in the course of the dispute, with desperately important issues at stake. An analogy may be made between Adam's lapse in the separation and the descent of the good angels into militarism during the war in heaven. In both cases there is no sin against God, but there is error in judgment brought about by difficult contexts of decision. Milton gives the argument between Adam and Eve the emotional tension and movement of an incipient domestic quarrel. Along with the ideational context, he provides the tonal movements of exasperation, competitiveness, manipulativeness, and emotional hurt that underlie this sort of confrontation. Adam is more concerned with his relationship to Eve than with their obligation to God.[19] But the error he makes, and Eve's provocation, fall short of a prematurely fallen state.

Adam and Eve allow passion to overcome reason, but until they *act* against God's commandment, they are mistaken, not sinful. The intellectual equipment God gives them to discern right from wrong is sufficient. When Adam falls it will be knowingly. But sufficiency is not a guarantee, and the error of separation allows the fall to occur, though it does not necessitate it. When Raphael chides Adam for his astronomical speculations, he first makes clear that the exercise of intellect is not, in itself, wrongful: "To ask or search I blame thee not" (VIII.66). The angel warns Adam against speculation for its own sake (to increase self-love), but Adam's concern with his relationship to Eve obeys Raphael's injunction to "be lowly wise: / Think only what concerns thee and thy being" (VIII.173–4). As creatures whose discursive intellects seek empirical confirmation, Adam and Eve learn by experience. They are created not immutable, but capable of development within the context of their temporal situation. The freedom necessary for this process is the same freedom that permits the error of separation. In dramatic terms, the fatality of this error is not in the quarrel but in the reader's apprehension.[20]

The separation arises out of the strategic confluence of a number of factors, and its status as an episode *in* the fall can only be assigned *after* the fall. From Adam and Eve's position within (rather than having already followed) the story, the argument over separation occurs contingently, as an occasion for the self-authorship of judgment and choice. The consequent events of the temptation and fall will retrospectively constitute the choice they make as a wrongful one. But "wrong" carries the meaning of mistaken until fallenness aligns their subjective position with the reader's and assigns the separation a negative moral connotation.

In *Paradise Lost* experience is one mode of revelation. Raphael warns Adam not to judge by outsides but to seek the essential nature of things. The "essence" or "truth" of things turns out to be functionally determined, on the one side by their relation to first principles, the universal and atemporal design of the universe, and on the other their temporally revealed position in the chain of second causes, beginning with creation and ending with apocalypse. In other words, the universe and its history form a signifying system, the signified of which is God's eternal word. But that system only signifies when complete; that is, when the *totum simul* that defines the unsituated subjective position of God is available to man. The meaning of events during the "Race of Time" may be rightly read only in the light of the *virtual* completion of time given by Scripture (as corrected by the indwelling Spirit in the reader). History is the passage from a virtual to an empirical meaning. It is the collective experience through which human beings achieve conformity with the divine by living the truth of revelation. The discourse of Adam and Eve in the separation scene illustrates this dynamic epistemology in microcosm. Their words are a displaced representation of the issues at hand. They argue about God's command as a way of testing their love. The argument only seems doctrinal. By moving too quickly to place their own doings in an atemporal context, they neglect the immediate historical situation in which their doctrine is to be practiced. The separation scene is a mirror image of the war in heaven. In the war the angels are absorbed by an immediate dramatic context; in the separation scene Adam and Eve lose track of an intimate and immediate context by transferring it too facilely to a cosmic context. They attempt to force "conformity divine" without respecting the mediation of time that Adam had so eloquently argued when he defined his difference from God in terms of the need for propagation, that is, the inherently temporal extension of humankind.

Eve is constituted as a more sensuous creature than Adam. It is she who observes details that are referred to Adam for interpretation. In the separation scene, Adam argues for the importance of this collaboration (IX.309–17), but the expected male and female roles are reversed insofar as Adam argues from the mundane experience of their "looks and smiles," while Eve brings to bear an interpretation of free will in its relation to "collateral love." This reversal of masculine and feminine roles links the scene to the long tradition of the emasculation of Hercules adapted by Tasso and Spenser and argues against any revisionist reading of the scene as a healthy development of Eve's independent character.[21] At the same time, it revises the tradition by rendering sexual character a function of the dramatic action and subverting the idealist tradition it imitates. The distribution of authority and the style of rhetoric within the domestic circuit of edenic love is not the function of fixed natures, but of specific temporal situations.

Eve's "feminine" sensuousness is a necessary adjunct to Adam's abstract reasoning, as his memory of passionate engagment with her is an anchor against her inadequate imitation of "male" discourse. In Book X, it will be Eve's memory of the Son's gentle aspect and promise at the judgment that helps Adam to the crucial recollection of the *protevangelium* and a restored conviction of God's mercy (966–1011), and, in book XII, it will be Eve's oneiric intuition of the correct and necessary actions called for by their revealed destiny that provides a program with which to enter life on the "subjected Plain" (610–23).[22] Milton's use of the commonplaces of Renaissance misogyny is never simple, nor is his Eve ever simpleminded. I shall argue in the next chapter that she is in fact the essential pivot on which his depiction of the restoration turns. Perhaps we are to assume that the fall itself fixes the masculine and feminine inversion of the separation in the emasculatory and misogynistic models of the mythos of Circe or the portrait of Hercules with the distaff? In the same way that the fall is depicted as presupposing its own effects, the relations of Adam and Eve in the separation scene, which are semantically open when read prospectively, appear in retrospect as an iteration of the struggle of wills it is their misfortune to begin.

## IV

When Satan returns to the stage, he adapts his rhetoric to the corruption of Eve's attention to sensory detail by supplementing his "male" argument with a wealth of "feminine" description. The fruit is "of fairest colors mixt, / Ruddy and Gold" (IX.577–8); the serpent is first attracted by "a savory odor blown, / Grateful to appetite" (IX.579–80); hunger and thirst are "powerful persuaders" that "quickn'd at the scent / Of that alluring fruit" (IX.587–8). Thus the serpent appears to engage Eve's reason with promises of the fruit's magic powers, but first he engages her senses, her appetite, her curiosity to see this beautiful and savory food and learn how a snake came to speak. The superficial appeal to reasoned argument serves only to dramatize the conflict of reason and sense that is created in the scene.[23] Satan makes Raphael's fear concrete by creating a tension between two faculties that should work together.

Satan's argument begins with the proposition that what works for a serpent would work for a woman (IX.691–2), and Eve errs in assuming that she is speaking with a serpent when, in fact, the words only appear to issue from the snake. Having achieved this deception, Satan begins to speculate on God's intentions (IX.692–715). A model of response to such speculations is Abdiel's "Shalt thou give Law to God?" (V.822), but Eve is too absorbed in the curious phenomenon of the talking snake who flatters her with apparently reasoned discourse to go beyond her habitual empiricism.[24] She forgets that the appearance of a thing may not reveal its essence, and, further, fails to distinguish nature, which is subject to her inductive logic (under the dominion of human judgment and choice), from the divine command, which is not. Satan uses the conversation he overheard in Book IV (411–39), paraphrasing Adam's "whate'er Death is" (IV.425) as "whatever thing Death be" (IX.695), to make his discourse familiar to Eve and render the situation of their dialogue less strange.

The rapid flow of the tempter's rhetorical questions invites Eve to venture answers that Satan supplies before she can consider them

(IX.691–705). In this way, he infects her language and, consequently, her subjectivity. By putting words in her mouth, he ma-
nipulates Eve into constituting a world according to his rhetoric –
a world in which hypothetical alterations of her status distract Eve's
attention from her concrete historical situation and focus it on the
immediacy of the dialogue of temptation. Satan then asserts his
central thesis that since the snake has eaten, Eve may eat, introducing
into this proposition a favorite satanic illusion – that Godhead may
be conceived as the aggregate of increments of power: "That ye
should be as Gods, since I as Man, / Internal Man, is but proportion
meet, / I of brute human, yee of human Gods" (IX.710–12).[25] Satan
introduces Eve to his peculiar way of constituting "reality" at a
bewildering pace. She begins the discourse on familiar ground and
ends it in the strange regions of the damned intellect.

According to Kathleen Swaim, "Eve's nature is sensual, vain,
and submissive but also imitative," and it is true that in her meditation on Satan's argument, Eve repeats his specious syllogisms
(IX.745–79).[26] Satan exploits this imitativeness to fashion her sensual, vain, and submissive responses. Satan exploits Eve's sensuousness to get her attention with his description of the fruit, but
this sensuousness is divinely ordained. Satan expropriates Eve's
submissiveness and imitativeness by paraphrasing her conversation
with Adam, and he corrupts her attentiveness to sensory detail by
distracting reason, its supplement. In sum, Eve's nature is subverted
by Satan. As the Father attests, she is deceived but not "self-
deprav'd." Her fall is presented as Aristotle would recommend. It
grows out of an intellectual (not a moral) error that is rooted in her
character or nature. It specifically excludes prior sin or depravity.
Moreover, the attributes of Eve's nature that will be condemned
in a postlapsarian world are in themselves morally neutral. It is
Satan's abuse of these attributes in a specific situation that establishes
a *practice* of sensuality, vanity, and mimicry on the elements of unfallen "feminity." After the Fall, Eve's complex and empathic attention to the demeanor of the judging Son will lead her to a saving
mimicry that anticipates Christ's divine submission.

Eve's fall is presented as at once contingent and historical. It is
contingent in that Eve happens on this day to be alone, to be hungry,

and to encounter Satan. It is historical because it is an irreversible act that revises both what has been – paradise, soon to be reduced to an irremedial nostalgia – and what is to come – a long day's dying on the "subjected Plain." It is, in fact, the first historical act, and it replaces the prelapsarian temporality of pleasant and varied repetition with the postlapsarian historicity of a linear progress toward inevitable death.

Alienated from the divine order, the newly fallen Eve seeks to affirm the empiricism that contributed to her fall by trying to form a new world order based, not on God and faith, but on the tree (which she equates with knowledge) and experience (IX.807–17). The thought processes represented in her soliloquy differ markedly from those of the prelapsarian Eve; she envisions herself as the initiate of a new gnostic order. The pattern of participation and interaction on which divine creation was based is now replaced by a political structure of power and manipulation. For the first time, Eve begins to fashion herself as an object of her own and Adam's contemplation, planning her appearance and calculating the effects she will promote (IX.816–30). Thus her alienation from providential order is immediately read as a division within the self.

Even though Eve's earlier speeches are logically ordered according to the concepts she explores, her soliloquy is structured on the level of the signifier, when, for example, she flies from "though secret she retire," in which "secret" refers to wisdom, to "and I perhaps am secret" (IX.810–11), a rationalization aimed at denying the inevitability of punishment. Before the fall, language had been one of the factors distinguishing bestial from human life. After the fall, the material element of language (audible sound) masters the intellectual material of reason and thus weakens the distinction of brute and human.[27]

In the same passage, Eve begins to use the "fallen conditional" construction that characterizes Satan's speech. The thought that she is "perhaps secret" initiates a series of fantastic suppositions about the possible selves she may craft to dissimulate her fallen state. However, while Satan's fantasies and rationalizations are stopped by his despairing awareness of the "dismal situation of the damned," Eve's speculations are restrained by a survival of "collateral love":

Confirm'd then I resolve,
*Adam* shall share with me in bliss or woe:
So dear I love him, that with him all deaths
I could endure, without him live no life. (IX.830–3)

The lyric close of the soliloquy prevents the reader from becoming completely alienated by Eve's scheming in the lines directly preceding it. Thus Milton maintains a high degree of identification, and never lets the reader get too far from his or her filial relationship to Eve.[28] Even though Eve considers how she might manipulate Adam by manipulating her appearance and resolves to encourage his fall, her inability to contemplate life without him anticipates the terms of his own decision to fall and keeps her within the orbit of their "collateral love." It is significant that although Eve echoes Satan earlier in the soliloquy, her final lines echo Adam (compare IX.831 and 269). Her imitation of Satan is a tragic departure, but after her fall she returns as best she can to her original teacher. Had love not arrested Eve's rationalizations, her subjectivity would have become identical to Satan's as she descended into the isolation of a dream of omnipotence.

The third "act" of Book IX ends with Eve seeking Adam, and the fall in progress. The fourth "act" includes Eve's confrontation with Adam, his fall, and the redefinition of their relationship after their love is experienced, for the first time, as "exorbitant desire."

## V

We know from as early as line 269 ("Or with her the worst endures") that Adam will not let Eve fall alone. The narrator's preface to Adam's response to the fall of Eve highlights Adam's predicament, "First to himself he inward silence broke" (IX.895). With Eve lost, the still innocent Adam has no one with whom to interact in the old way. He is placed in a poignant position, at once with his beloved yet alone. The words that issue from his inward silence portray Eve sympathetically, recognizing the essential role she has played in his constitution of his own sense of self:

> I with thee have fixt my Lot,
> Certain to undergo like doom; if Death
> Consort with thee, Death is to mee as Life;
> So forcible within my heart I feel
> The Bond of Nature draw me to my own,
> My own in thee, for what thou art is mine;
> Our State cannot be sever'd, we are one,
> One Flesh; to lose thee were to lose myself. (IX.952–9)

The plentiful monosyllables and heavy intralinear stops give the passage a measured pace to emphasize that Adam, unlike Eve, falls with considerable appreciation of what he is doing and why. While Eve was overwhelmed by the pace of Satan's temptation, Adam "scrupl'd not eat / Against his better knowledge, not deceiv'd, / But fondly overcome with Female charm" (IX.997–9). The emotional impact of Adam's fall is complex. The reader is expected to acknowledge Adam's nobility but to reject the action that appears to issue from it. Milton's Aristotelian conception of tragic character facilitates the reader's identification with Adam and grounds the fall in an error.

Arthur Barker correctly identifies that error as Adam's "failure to believe that Satan can no more win on earth than in heaven," that is, his failure of faith.[29] Adam's error is not a fault in the sense of a character flaw destined to manifest itself repeatedly in certain situations, but rather a mistake made in a difficult and highly specified moment. The pattern of a proper response to that moment can be found in the behavior of the Son, who, in Book III, responds to Adam's fall by interceding with the Father.[30] Adam, horrified at the thought of losing Eve, forgets the infinity of divine mercy. The reader may wonder what might have resulted had Adam prayed that Eve be forgiven rather than joined her in disobedience. The constitution of "what might have been" as an unrealized alternative to the experienced constitution of human life then becomes the nostalgia for a lost edenic past that afflicts the descendants of Adam and Eve.

Adam's failure is best understood in context with the Son's success. The reader knows that the first Adam's error will be redeemed by the second Adam's sacrifice. Christ's love will provide fallen man with the exemplar through which he may understand and correct Adam's error. The narrative of God's entry into time will thus repeat and repair Adam's entry into the historicity of "being toward death" by providing an eternal context in which the Christian can hear a transcendent gloss on the dramatic working out of the events of everyday life.

Once the fall is completed, the garden is transformed; paradise becomes "these wild woods forlorn." The interaction between Adam and Eve, which had been "collateral love," is transformed to "exorbitant desire":

> For never did thy Beauty since the day
> I saw thee first and wedded thee, adorn'd
> With all perfections, so inflame my sense
> With ardor to enjoy thee, fairer now
> Than ever, bounty of this virtuous Tree. (IX.1029–33)[31]

Adam's reference to "all perfections" emphasizes the loss of those perfections as sense conquers spirit and right reason, and the garden becomes the world. Adam's attempt to assert the continuity between his present desire and the Eve who answers it and the unfallen desire she was created to answer (VIII.449–51) unknowingly poses an antithesis between the day he first saw Eve, that is, the day she was created, and this tragic day when she is uncreated.

## VI

In the fifth and final "act" of the drama, Adam and Eve awake after having spent their carnal lust, to find that exorbitant desire can be recycled but not renewed. Before the fall, they were busy about their mission of propagation, with respect both to the tending of the garden and the increase of their race. Now they find themselves without purpose:

> Cover'd, but not at rest or ease of Mind,
> They sat them down to weep, nor only Tears

> Rain'd at thir Eyes, but high Winds worse within
> Began to rise, high Passions, Anger, Hate,
> Mistrust, Suspicion, Discord, and shook sore
> Thir inward State of Mind, calm Region once
> And full of Peace, now toss't and turbulent:
> For understanding rul'd not, and the Will
> Heard not her lore, both in subjection now
> To sensual Appetite, who from beneath
> Usurping over sovran Reason claim'd
> Superior sway. (IX.1120–31)

Their "state of mind" resembles the physical conditions of chaos, "toss't and turbulent," restlessly subject to "the hateful seige of contraries." The narrator's summary of the internal changes in the pair follows the orthodox theological interpretation of the fall: Reason now serves appetite. The allusion to Psalm 137.1 (IX.1121), the lament of the exiles from Zion, suggests the *ex-orbitance* or alienation of passion when "collateral love" becomes absolute desire, anachronistically engaging typology to embed the temporal *historia* of Adam and Eve as they await exile from Eden in the *veritas* of a yet unwritten biblical lament. As the Psalm represents a lyric moment in the narrative of Israel, suspended by the Babylonian captivity, the psalm of Adam and Eve's exile reflects the suspension of the narrative of man by the "self-enthrallment" of the founding couple.

Book IX ends with Adam and Eve trapped in this slavery, engaged in an agon that cannot be resolved until they are reconnected to the orbit of divine creation and can resume their mission of propagation:

> Thus they in mutual accusation spent
> The *fruitless* hours, but neither self-condemning,
> And of thir vain contest appear'd no end. (IX.1187–9, my emphasis)

Like the warring angels in Book VI, Adam and Eve reach an impasse requiring messianic intervention – that is, the sublation and redefinition of history by the temporal manifestation of grace.

Milton borrows the form of classic drama for Book IX because he borrows its theme – the strange mixture of accident and fate that seems to direct and shape our lives. He encloses this tragic form in the atemporal, essentially comic, Christian view of history. To do this Milton must tell us that we are relatively insignificant, yet that our acts are crucially important; that our enemy, the devil, is formidable and deadly, yet helpless, tormented, and doomed to defeat. He can do this because his art is mimetic, drawing its validity from the rhythm of "felt life." He warns us to keep separate the two contexts we live in – human history and Christian eternity – by showing us how we depend on dramatic context, on our immediate situation, when we construct the world we see.

# 7

## "TILL THE DAY / APPEAR OF RESPIRATION TO THE JUST"

The Tenth Book of *Paradise Lost* has a greater variety of persons in it than any other in the whole poem. The author, upon the winding up of his action, introduces all those who had any concern in it, and shows with great beauty the influence which it had upon each of them. It is like the last act of a well-written tragedy, in which all who had a part in it are generally drawn up before the audience, and represented under those circumstances in which the determination of the action places them.[1]

The tenth book of *Paradise Lost* is perhaps the busiest in the epic, and, as Joseph Addison aptly noted, the appearance of all the poem's major characters and all its locales, immediately following the severely restricted action of Book IX, gives the impression of a finale in which each character is displayed in the condition to which he or she has been brought by the now completed action of the drama.

But the action of *Paradise Lost* is not completed, and the resituating of its actors and locales is only provisional. Much of Book X portrays the aftermath of the tragedy presented in Book IX. The revisions of the world order consequent to man's disobedience are noted: the bridge between Earth and hell that is the concrete sign of Satan's league with man, the arrival of Sin and Death in paradise, the unfortunate changes in the earthly environment.

As the effects of the fall are realized on Earth, the restorative movement of the epic begins. Thus Book X serves both as denouement and transition. The judging of Adam and Eve by the

Son and their reconciliation begin the process of redemption and point toward the second action promised in the poem's opening lines. The business of the epic at this point – the rapid movement between scenes and characters – once again restores an emphasis on the act of narration; the situating and resituating of the narrator with respect to his story and his listeners ends the mimetic immediacy of Book IX and begins to present the readers *of* the story and the readers *in* the story (that is, Adam and Eve) with a universe mediated by signs that present themselves as such, as objects of interpretation.[2] The poem's second angelic narrative, that of Michael in Books XI and XII, differs from that of Raphael specifically in its generic shift from mimesis to narration, a shift reinscribed in Michael's narrative as a move from vision to audition.[3] In these final books the ascendency of narration over drama is the structural image of the thematic ascendency of time over eternity that follows the fall. Paradoxically, however, this plunge into narrative, which is also a plunge into history, provides for a saving reinscription of eternity within history and initiates the subjectivity of self-authorship in a fallen world.

## I

The final lines of Book IX stress the isolation of Adam and Eve, self-condemned to a state of moral exile in which they can no longer communicate along the circuits of "collateral love." The opening action of Book X shows that this isolation is a specific feature of their postlapsarian subjectivity. From a radically different point of view, that of the Godhead, the first parents are not alone; though fallen, they remain the objects of divine care:

> But whom send I to judge them? whom but thee
> Vicegerent Son, to thee I have transferr'd
> All Judgment, whether in Heav'n, or Earth, or Hell.
> Easy it may be seen that I intend
> Mercy colleague with Justice, sending thee
> Man's Friend, his Mediator, his design'd
> Both Ransom and Redeemer voluntary,
> And destin'd Man himself to judge Man fall'n. (X.55–62)

This passage puts into action what has already been shown in the prolepsis of Book III, while the action it initiates is itself a prolepsis of the last judgment. The narrative motif of a scene that repeats an earlier scene while anticipating a later one is continued in lines 103–8, the first in a long series of calls issued to man from the Son of God.[4] As the Son calls Adam to judgment, he recalls him from spiritual exile (Cf. III.183–90). The judgment itself, which includes both the expulsion from paradise and the *protevangelium,* reflects the double movement of the narrative, which presents the fall and the redemption simultaneously.[5] The Son clothes Adam and Eve "as Father of his Family" (X.216). Doing *his* father's bidding, the Son becomes Adam's father, as Adam is *our* father. The extension of filial love begins the work of reunifying the creation, and so the first judgment of sin becomes the occasion of sin's repair.

The signs of fallenness are mitigated as they are imposed. But, once the Son withdraws, the narrative turns to the activities of Sin and Death. The promise of ultimate redemption guarantees an ultimate remission of sin, but its fulfillment is deferred over precisely the span of human history. At Hellgate, Sin feels the effects of the fall stirring within her and proposes to Death that they "found a path / Over this Main from Hell to that new World / Where Satan now prevails" (X.256–8). The "now" in this proposition defines the present of fallen man and embraces the duration of the world from the fall of Adam to the apocalypse. The repetition of Satan's journey that establishes the road also establishes that what had been presented as a singular and difficult crossing of Chaos may now be viewed as *iterative* narration.

While building the bridge from Hell to Earth, Sin and Death encounter the returning Satan, whose charge to his progeny invites the reader to sketch in the details of fallen life after the first and before the final judgment:

> You two this way, among those numerous Orbs
> All yours, right down to Paradise descend;
> There dwell and Reign in bliss, thence on the Earth
> Dominion exercise and in the Air,
> Chiefly on Man, sole Lord of all declar'd,
> Him first make sure your thrall, and lastly kill.

My Substitutes I send ye, and Create
Plenipotent on Earth, of matchless might
Issuing from mee: on your joint vigor now
My hold of this new Kingdom all depends,
Through Sin to Death expos'd by my exploit.
If your joint power prevail, th' affairs of Hell
No detriment need fear, go and be strong. (X.397–409)

The effects of the fall are now more clearly seen. Although man is assured of the opportunity of redemption, he is "exposed" to Sin and Death until the end of time, when they will have power "over the fourth part of the earth; to kill with sword and with hunger, and with death, and with the beasts of the earth" (Rev. 6:8).

The temporality of pleasant and varied repetition and the promise of increase enjoyed by Adam and Eve before the fall is transformed – by the singular historical act of disobedience – to the object of nostalgia, as a new temporality, defined by the expectation of death, replaces it. Life, previously governed by a pattern of dependable repetitions, now becomes episodic, contingent on a daily remission of sword, hunger, beasts.[6] The future of fallen man, however, is portrayed with Milton's characteristic double vision. What is necessarily previewed by its protagonists as a radically contingent, historical drama is rationalized and rendered meaningful by a providential perspective. Thus the Father explains that the all too substantial temporal presence of Sin and Death will, in the long run, prove merely instrumental:

I call'd and drew them thither
My Hell-hounds, to lick up the draff and filth
Which man's polluting Sin with taint hath shed
On what was pure, till cramm'd and gorg'd, nigh burst
With suckt and glutted offal, at one sling
Of thy victorious Arm, well-pleasing Son,
Both *Sin,* and *Death,* and yawning *Grave* at last
Through *Chaos* hurl'd, obstruct the mouth of Hell
For ever, and seal up his ravenous Jaws.
Then Heav'n and Earth renew'd shall be made pure

To sanctity that shall receive no stain:
Till then the Curse pronounc't on both precedes. (X.629–40)

After the Father decrees the changes that manifest the curse (X.649–749), the focus of the poetry, which has been cosmic in scope, narrows, as Adam's long soliloquy presents the internal human reaction to the transformation of the universe after the fall.[7] His reactions to his sin and its consequences help the reader understand the dramatic position of newly fallen man, and Adam's interaction with Eve shows the way out of despair through a renewal of "collateral love." Adam's first reaction is to the obvious changes in paradise and the sense of loss they enforce upon him, "O miserable of happy! is this the end / Of this new glorious World" (X.720–1). The feeling of loss is joined to that of guilt, for Adam in losing paradise believes himself to have lost the opportunity of procreating God's image (X.720–41). This guilt leads him to question his responsibility as a created being:

> O fleeting joys
> Of Paradise, dear bought with lasting woes!
> Did I request thee, Maker, from my Clay
> To mould me Man, did I solicit thee
> From darkness to promote me, or here place
> In this delicious Garden? as my Will
> Concurr'd not to my being, it were but right
> And equal to reduce me to my dust,
> Desirous to resign, and render back
> All I receiv'd, unable to perform
> Thy terms too hard, by which I was to hold
> The good I sought not. (X.741–52)

What had seemed "this one, this easy charge" (IV.421) becomes "thy terms too hard."[8] Adam briefly argues that his crime was circumstantially inevitable, as Satan had argued in Book IV (58–61). But Adam rejects this argument both as a breach of contract (X.754–9) and on the basis of an analogy to his anticipated fatherhood: Adam's sons, whose curses he fears, will be born, as Adam was,

without prior consent. Will they then be released from the requirements of filial obedience (X.759–64)?

With these arguments, Adam anticipates the great movement of
the closing books of the epic. He repudiates his argument against
God under the covenant of laws by recognizing that his creation
constituted a contract that he is obliged to honor, and under the
convenant of love by understanding his obligations to God under
the tutelage of the filial analogy. The first Adam thus anticipates
(and prefigures) the mission of the second; he learns to obey God
not only according to his pledge, but also, as a son obeys his father,
out of love.[9] Adam's extrapolation of his filial relation to God from
his *proposed* filial relations to his own progeny demonstrates the
efficacy of "collateral love" (even in expectation) in maintaining a
dialectical relationship to providence and the anticipation of a deferred meaning that marks human understanding in a fallen world.
The essence of the case is contained in Adam's first argument, with
its appeal to explicit law and reason, but the second argument
translates this fixed law into the expectation of temporal experience.
Moral action is already governed by the ability to imagine a future
and assimilate that future to the known patterns of divine governance. Here, in fact, the pattern itself is derived from its expected
application.

Adam's reflection on his relation to his future progeny intensifies
his sense of guilt by leading him to consider the hereditary force
of the curse he has incurred (X.815–34). Reason leads him "through
[the] Mazes" (X.830) of his attempts to displace his guilt onto God,
to a conviction of his own guilt but no further. Reason has done
what reason can. Successful repentance requires "a sense of divine
mercy" (*CP*.VI.467), but, at this point, Adam's fear of his inability
to bear divine justice fills his heart and mind.[10] Momentarily forgetting God's infinite mercy, Adam falls into the trap of despair:

> Thus what thou desir'st,
> And what thou fear'st, alike destroys all hope
> Of refuge and concludes thee miserable
> Beyond all past example and future,
> To *Satan* only like both crime and doom.
> O Conscience, into what Abyss of fears

And horrors hast thou driv'n me; out of which
I find no way, from deep to deeper plung'd! (X.837–44)

Because he lacks an adequate conviction of God's mercy, Adam turns from "that bad Woman" (X.837), Eve, to Satan for the *other* in whom he finds his image reflected. Just so, in the heat of battle, loyal and rebel angels become mirror images. Adam, newly reformed within fallen time, identifies with and fears his exorbitant desires. His situation, like that of the warring angels, elicits and requires a messianic abridgment of linear time.

Kester Svendsen, among others, has argued that the recognition of God's mercy necessary for Adam's repentance to overcome despair presupposes his reconciliation with Eve.[11] Adam's reconciliation with Eve allows him to recall the *protevangelium* (X.1030–55) and begin to *interpret* the newly fallen world in terms of divine mercy. The interaction leading to this insight replays in reverse the separation scene of Book IX. Eve repairs the breach she had opened when her desire to work apart caused Adam to question the durability of their "collateral love." Once their trusting relationship is reestablished, Adam's despair is overwhelmed by his efforts to rescue Eve from hers. His recognition of divine mercy grows directly out of the dramatic situation of a husband who seeks to console his wife by minimizing a serious family plight, and ends by finding consolation himself. Eve's presence as another sufferer like Adam and Adam's recognition of her suffering disrupt the solipsism of sin and point the way to regeneration.

Eve, by accepting the suffering incurred in the fall, transforms the "passion" of exorbitant desires to an anticipation of the passion of suffering and so becomes, *avant la lettre,* the first Christian. First Adam is reborn in his witness of Eve's passion as second Adam will be born (and humanity reborn) from the womb of second Eve. Adam's identification with and fear of his exorbitant desires followed his (mis)recognition of his image in Satan. When he once again sees his image in Eve, he sees that the image, reflected in her, remains the image of God reflected in him. The self-enclosure of mirrored desires is broken and the spiral of "collateral love" restored. The image escapes the infinite regress of the mirror of identification and returns to the generative pattern of resemblance; love and the image flow from God through Adam to Eve and back, but also – differed and deferred – into the promise of future generations and infinite expansion. The multiplication of God's image through time as a chain of genetic resemblances is the material inscription of the temporality in which self-authorship takes place.[12]

This restoration is not easy. Eve's first approach to Adam is brutally repelled. She endures his abuse, in which he reduces her to "a crooked rib," that is, to an erstwhile and flawed part of himself (X.884–5), and renews her supplication:

> Forsake me not thus, *Adam,* witness Heav'n
> What love sincere, and reverence in my heart
> I bear thee, and unweeting have offended,
> Unhappily deceiv'd; thy suppliant
> I beg, and clasp thy knees; bereave me not,
> Whereon I live, thy gentle looks, thy aid,
> Thy counsel in this uttermost distress,
> My only strength and stay: forlorn of thee,
> Whither shall I betake me, where subsist? (X.914–22)

In Book IX, Eve complained that the efficiency of her gardening was impaired by the looks, smiles, and casual discourse (221–2) she shared with Adam, whom she now acknowledges as her "only strength and stay," thus repairing the breach in the mutuality of their love that had preceded the fall. Her humble posture toward Adam suggests the appropriate behavior of Adam toward God and invites him to imitate Eve's example.

Eve's most significant lines make explicit her desire to restore the prelapsarian hierarchy and anticipate Christ. Paraphrasing the Son's language in Book III, Eve appears to intuitively imitate a speech she has not heard:

> On me exercise not
> Thy hatred for this misery befall'n,
> On me already lost, mee than thyself
> More miserable; both have sinn'd, but thou
> Against God only, I against God and thee,
> And to the place of judgment will return,

> There with my cries importune Heaven, that all
> The sentence from thy head remov'd may light
> On me, sole cause to thee of all this woe,
> Mee mee only just object of his ire. (X.927–36)[13]

Eve's words remind Adam of his hierarchical obligations and, by combining an acknowledgment of responsibility for sin with a conviction of heaven's mercy, they help him move through despair to contrition.

Eve's submissive reminder restores Adam's sense of responsibility for her, and his desire to fulfill that charge is translated into behavior that once again manifests the image of God:

> She ended weeping, and her lowly plight,
> Immovable till peace obtain'd from fault
> Acknowledg'd and deplor'd, in *Adam* wrought
> Commiseration; soon his heart relented
> Towards her, his life so late and sole delight,
> Now at his feet submissive in distress,
> Creature so fair his reconcilement seeking,
> His counsel whom she had displeas'd, his aid;
> As one disarm'd, his anger all he lost,
> And thus with peaceful words uprais'd her soon. (X.937–46)

Eve's behavior suggests to Adam how God might be addressed and restores the circuit of "collateral love" from which prayer issues. Adam's felt compassion for Eve supplies the experiential pattern that allows him to seek compassion from God.

Beginning to fulfill his function as the more rational of the pair, Adam tells Eve that neither of them could sustain the wrath of God that will, in any case, be visited upon them both as well as upon their descendants. Their task is not to place the blame but to share the burden (X.958–65). Eve suggests continence or suicide as ways of evading the curse on their progeny and themselves. Her concern for the unborn generations and her desire to surrender a being that has become a burden recapitulate Adam's own thoughts, but his efforts to help her relieve him of self-pity: "*Adam* with such counsel nothing sway'd, / To better hopes his more attentive mind / La-

boring had rais'd" (X.1010–12). The search for "better hopes" with
which to counsel Eve leads finally to the *protevangelium:*

> I have in view, calling to mind with heed
> Part of our Sentence, that thy Seed shall bruise
> The Serpent's head; piteous amends, unless
> Be meant, whom I conjecture, our grand Foe
> *Satan,* who in the Serpent hath contriv'd
> Against us this deceit: to crush his head
> Would be revenge indeed. (X.1030–6)

Thus Adam initiates the pattern of self-authorship that is to prevail
in the fallen world. Faced with a difficult choice of action in a temporal context – to live and reproduce or not – Adam interprets the
word of God, in this case the *protevangelium,* so as to choose the
course of action consonant with the future providence has designed
and obscurely revealed. Through his judgment on the meaning of
the promised revenge and the choice that issues from that judgment,
Adam participates, of his own free will, in the creation of a divinely
ordained human history. His interpretation of the promise and the
action to which it leads write an episode in his narrative movement
toward the "nobler end" of "conformity divine."

The recollection of the promise leads Adam to remember the
mild demeanor of the Son when he delivered it (X.1046–59). Thus
the promise, the recollection of the Son's gracious presence, and
the need to console Eve, combine to create the moment at which
Adam achieves the "sense of divine mercy" necessary to complete
his repentance. Reunited in "collateral love," Adam and Eve seek
to repair their break with God:

> What better can we do, than to the place
> Repairing where he judg'd us, prostrate fall
> Before him reverent, and there confess
> Humbly our faults, and pardon beg, with tears
> Watering the ground, and with our sighs the Air
> Frequenting, sent from hearts contrite, in sign
> Of sorrow unfeign'd, and humiliation meek.
> Undoubtedly he will relent and turn

From his displeasure; in whose look serene,
When angry most he seem'd and most severe,
What else but favor, grace, and mercy shone? (X. 1086–96)

The *protevangelium* differs from the prohibition of the fruit as fallen differs from prelapsarian revelation. Whereas the command was a simple and direct assertion of divine will, the *protevangelium* requires an interpretation that includes an appeal to knowledge of God's merciful ways and the projection of alternative futures contingent on Adam and Eve's present moral choice. The first parents are now epistemologically in the historical world, progressing toward a revealed end by locating moral choice in the articulation of the episodic and configurational components of a narrative. As "authors to themselves," they are about to encounter and initiate "the story of all things."

## II

The double motion of Book X may be summarily characterized as the erection of two antithetical bridges: that built by Sin and Death, joining hell to paradise, and that built by the reconciliation and repentance of Adam and Eve, rejoining man to heaven. The remainder of *Paradise Lost* previews the process of regeneration for Adam and Eve, while continuing to insist on the pain of earthly punishment. The narrative, which had soared over the Aonian Mount, makes its way through "the race of Time" to the end of history, to leave the poem's human characters, and the reader, in the fallen world, with their race yet to be run. The two perspectives of the poem, temporal and eternal, are shown in their proper relationship to each other; history is compressed into a moral fable framed on both sides and presided over by the providence of God.

The shift in style that accompanies the compression of history within this providential frame has often irritated critics. For example, Louis Martz expresses the opinion that at some point in the composition of *Paradise Lost* XI and XII, Milton "lost touch with the central conception of his poem," giving the conclusion a theologically successful but poetically disastrous design in which "the effects of sin are presented at length with varied and relentless horror, while the effects of 'supernal grace' are for the most part given the form of brief and abstract statement."[14] The style of Books XI and XII differs from that of the first ten books of the poem and Martz's comments are indicative of the difference. The question he raises is clear: Has Milton subordinated poetry to theology and consequently produced an abstract and discursive conclusion in which the poetry flags as the conception absorbs the poetic form?

I will argue against this conclusion that the style of the final books is dictated by the conceptual and poetic design of *Paradise Lost* as a whole. The comparatively flat and rapid narrative of the last books answers to a thematic implication of Adam and Eve's entry into the fallen world and its historical temporality. Prelapsarian Adam and Eve enjoyed an unmediated access to revealed truth; they could ask God (as they do about Eve's dream in their morning prayer in Book V) and expect an answer. The preview of world history accorded them by Michael in the poem's closing books introduces a new hermeneutic situation in which revelation is primarily mediated not by the living Word, but by its written Scripture (as illuminated by the Holy Spirit). The style of Milton's poetry in these books, therefore, looks forward to the chaste style of *Paradise Regained,* a style in which truth is identified with the perception of pattern and rhetoric answers to the peculiar temporality of typology. Understood in this way, the final books appear not to be as Martz calls them, an epilogue, but the conceptual climax of the poem, the founding of a context in which what is experienced as radically contingent is – through the mediation of faith and the knowledge of biblical history – understood as both providential and significant. The vision and narration Michael provides are, in effect, a reading lesson, through which Adam is introduced to the prose of the world.

The vision granted to Adam in Books XI and XII helps him to endure the grim picture of life his empirical reason shows him, not by rejecting it but by tempering it with revealed knowledge of an eternal providence that envelopes and subsumes history. The revelation is intended to console Adam, but it requires faith in the wisdom and charity of God. In fact, the Father tells Michael to grant Adam the vision only "if patiently thy bidding they obey" (XI.112).[15] They need faith to earn the consolation as they need faith to believe it. A proper understanding of divine providence does not remit their punishment; it teaches them to endure it "sorrowing, yet in peace" (XI.117). Adam's vision is not accustomed to sorrow. His initial response to fallen nature is despair. Michael teaches him to confront the pain caused by his sin and offers him the hope of a glorious redemption at the end of time. Adam may be regenerated, but he is no longer innocent. He must learn to bear guilt and suffering, to see a fallen world with fallen eyes and to hope for a necessarily deferred justice.

What it means to be fallen is made clear. Adam, who had entertained angels and argued with God, can no longer tolerate heavenly visitors. Thus Michael comes "not in his shape Celestial, but as a Man / Clad to meet Man" (XI.239–40), and the narrator points out that the arrival of Michael and his entourage would have been "a glorious Apparition, had not doubt / And carnal fear that day dimm'd *Adam's* eye" (XI.211–12). Resituated as fallen, Adam's subjectivity transgresses its bounds and projects itself into the world of objects. His vision of Michael is infected with "doubt and carnal fear," much as Satan's first vision of hell was "mixt with obdurate pride and stedfast hate" (I.58). The eye constructs a vision by combining what appears before it with what transpires behind it, the interior winds of passion that rage in the formerly homogeneous and unitary locus of the self. Unmediated knowledge of the divine is disallowed by the confusion of subject and object.

The now necessary role of mediator, ultimately fulfilled by the Son, is first assumed by Michael's typification of the incarnation. Michael takes Adam to a hilltop so that he may view the earthly kingdoms, but before granting Adam a vision of the future, it is necessary to purge his eyes:

> But to nobler sights
> *Michael* from *Adam's* eyes the Film remov'd
> Which that false Fruit that promis'd clearer sight
> Had bred; then purg'd with Euphrasy and Rue
> The visual Nerve, for he had much to see;
> And from the Well of Life three drops instill'd.
> So deep the power of these Ingredients pierc'd,
> Ev'n to the inmost seat of mental sight,
> That *Adam* now enforc't to close his eyes,

Sunk down and all his Spirits became intranst:
But him the gentle Angel by the hand
Soon rais'd, and his attention thus recall'd. (XI.411–22)

The enumeration of medical herbs in this passage anticipates the
role of Christ as spiritual healer; the allusion to the well of life invokes the ritual of baptism. Adam is "enforc't to close his eyes";
spiritual sight after the fall involves a turn away from temporal or
carnal vision. This turn away from carnal sight, however, is not a
refusal of the world, but a strategic turn from the sensible world
to an interpretive context. The eternal gloss that corrects the sight
is itself nothing other than an event to be realized in the material
history of the future. The vision that Adam is to see, and the narration that follows, reiterate this point through their presentation
of history as a succession of episodes in which a single just man
turns away from human society to "walk with God," moves beyond
the immediate context of an event to see it in relation to the pre-
ordained future. We have seen this pattern already in play in the
repentance of Adam and Eve, achieved by a turn from their immediate situation to the promise of the *protevangelium*.

The narrator comments on the hill upon which Michael and Adam
stand:

It was a Hill
Of Paradise the highest, from whose top
The Hemisphere of Earth in clearest Ken
Stretcht out to the amplest reach of prospect lay.
Not higher that Hill nor wider looking round,
Whereon for different cause the Tempter set
Our second *Adam* in the Wilderness,
To show him all Earth's Kingdoms and thir Glory. (XI.377–84)

The hilltop visions of Adam and Christ afford the opportunity to
compare two very different mediators of vision, Michael and Satan,
and the subjectivity each seeks to situate. Satan uses the hilltop as
he had used the Tree of Life in Book IV, for "prospect" in the
visual and synchronic sense: "And so large / The Prospect was,
that here and there was room / For barren desert fountainless and

dry" (*Paradise Regained* III.263–5). Michael will use the "amplest reach of prospect" in the temporal sense, by showing not the series of alternative presents that Satan offers Christ, with the temptation to conquer earth in its spatial dimensions, but rather a chronological sketch of the human future, with the offer of a deferred conquest of time. Satan accompanies his visions with "a new train of words" (*PR*.III.266), and Michael discloses the expression of the Word as the providential destiny of material creation.

The belated recognition of the unreliability of fallen vision in Book XI puts in question the entire preceding action of the poem. The reader is reminded that he or she has witnessed Milton's verbal vision with clouded eyes. From the perspective afforded the reader after the cleansing of Adam's eyes, the proportions of the poem – its dedication of so much space to "man's first disobedience" in comparison to what is given to "one greater man" – may be seen as ironic. The fallen man's preoccupation with "tragic" time, human passion, and the actions of individual human subjects makes high drama of the eating of an apple.[16] From an exclusively human perspective, the loss of paradise is a paramount and continuing tragedy. But the exclusively human perspective is implicated in that loss; it is an empirical myopia that must be corrected by the lens of revelation. The empirical epistemology that perforce equates experience and essence leaves man vulnerable to the illusive imagery of evil, the alternative and simultaneous presents that Satan presents. In Books XI and XII, Milton's deflated and deflating poetry sacrifices the gnosis of the lyric present and the singularity of tragic inevitability to the proto-prosaic of iterative narrative and the epistemological dialectic of "configurative cognition."[17] The events revealed to Adam are revealed as singular events that are also signifying or typical, as patterned *episodes* whose narrative shape reveals the configuration of moral action in the light of a foreknown and providential destiny.

Even before the fall, Adam had to exercise caution when "reading" the Book of Nature. In Book VIII, Raphael reminds him that appearance may not be equated with essence, "that Great / Or Bright infers not Excellence" (90–1). In Book III, when Satan, disguised as a cherub, successfully deceives Uriel (681–9), we are warned that willful deception can mislead even the intuitive knowledge of an angel. After the fall, empirical observation is even more problematic. Adam's postlapsarian reading of nature in Book X is accurate, yet it leads him to the morally unacceptable position of despair. The observation of sin unmediated by faith in mercy is insupportable. Now Michael turns Adam's vision away from the "Earthly Kingdoms," the prey of Sin and Death, and directs it inward; the heart is regenerate, not the world. If one may perceive conflicting sights from the same hilltop, one must seek truth not in the object, but in the subject's adjustment to it. Michael's reading lesson teaches Adam to refine his perception from within and to author himself within the dialectic of inner truth and material circumstances that providence provides.

Thus Michael's instruction works to detach Adam from the physical landscape without obliterating that landscape – to combine the spatial and temporal senses of "prospect." The cosmic theater of action gives way to the battle in the heart of man. When Adam asks Michael for an account of the final battle of the savior and the serpent, Michael warns him to "Dream not of thir fight, / As of a Duel, or the local wounds / Of head or heel" (XII.386–8). The savior's victory, says Michael, will be achieved "not by destroying *Satan,* but his works / In thee and in they Seed" (XII.394–5).[18] We are asked again to correlate the temporal world with something we cannot see. Michael's comment on the destruction of Eden by the flood is to the point:

> Then shall this Mount
> Of Paradise by might of Waves be mov'd
> Out of his place, push'd by the horned flood,
> With all his verdure spoil'd, and Trees adrift
> Down the great River to the op'ning Gulf,
> And there take root an Island salt and bare,
> The haunt of Seals and Orcs, and Sea-mews clang.
> To teach thee that God attributes to place
> No sanctity, if none be thither brought
> By Men who there frequent, or therein dwell. (XI.829–38)

The internalization of the action is central to the development of the new covenant and its accompanying poetics, celebrated in the final books of *Paradise Lost*. When Michael promises Adam the rewards of what amounts to a good Christian life, we get the mirror image of Satan's "which way I fly is Hell; my self am Hell" (IV.75).

In the last two books of the poem, subtle juxtapositions, cross-references, and internal allusions replace local poetic effects. The reader is forced back into the text and its specific intertextuality with the Bible, as he or she joins Adam in learning to locate the moral significance of each episode in its relations to consequent episodes. Milton has Michael bring Adam and the reader to an understanding of earthly life that leads to moral action. If one is to correct one's perspective and live successfully on Earth, one does not need to perform feats of physical strength; one needs

> only add
> Deeds to thy knowledge answerable, add Faith,
> Add Vertue, Patience, Temperance, add Love,
> By name to come call'd Charity, the soul
> Of all the rest: then wilt thou not be loath
> To leave this Paradise, but shalt possess
> A Paradise within thee, happier far. (XII.581–7)

Under Michael's tutelage, Adam learns to question the panoply of "tinsel trappings [and] gorgeous Knights" (IX.36) and to appreciate the "better fortitude / Of Patience and Heroic Martyrdom" (IX.31–2). That "better fortitude" is written in the medium of historical time by "deeds" that "answer" knowledge. Milton's insistence on works, typical of radical Protestant thought in the second half of the seventeenth century and sharply opposing the Calvinist emphasis on salvation *sola fide,* represents the triumph of narrative time over doctrine. Works are the necessary manifestation of the *practice* of Godliness and the temporal mediation of the inner voice and the outer world.

Free will then is not free action, but free choice constrained by an a priori and divinely determined "right" answer. It is man's *subjection* to the universal law of a divine creation he recognizes as divinely *ordinatissima*. Milton's narrative of judgments and choices thus represents the complex practice necessary to implement Augustine's doctrine of free choice:

For only he is free in service who gladly does the will of his Lord. And consequently he who is the servant of sin is free only for sinning. . . . This is the true liberty, because of joy for the upright act; and no less is it pious servitude, because of obedience to the commandment.[19]

Submission to the logic of providential design frees men from an involuntary subjection to the far less orderly ordering of other men, an ordering that substitutes force for reason and politics for love. The Nimrod episode "reveals" this political subjection to be a temporal translation of the "dismal Situation" of the damned, a (self)enslavement to "exorbitant desire." When Adam condemns Nimrod (XII.64–78), Michael comments on liberty:

> Justly thou abhorr'st
> That Son, who on the quiet state of men
> Such trouble brought, affecting to subdue
> Rational Liberty; yet know withal,
> Since thy original lapse, true Liberty
> Is lost, which always with right Reason dwells
> Twinn'd, and from her hath no dividual being:
> Reason in man obscur'd, or not obey'd,
> Immediately inordinate desires
> And upstart Passions catch the Government
> From Reason, and to servitude reduce
> Man till then free. Therefore since hee permits
> Within himself unworthy Powers to reign
> Over free Reason, God in Judgment just
> Subjects him from without to violent Lords;
> Who oft as undeservedly enthral
> His outward freedom: Tyranny must be,
> Though to the Tyrant thereby no excuse. (XII.79–96)

Tyranny, the subjection of men by men, occurs only when the intersubjectivity of reason is already disrupted by unreasonable desire, desire in exorbitance of reason. Tyranny appears on Earth as the visible inscription in the material of history of the always prior subjection of reason to this excess of desire.[20] Michael's explanation uses the biblical intertext, the story of Nimrod, to join Raphael's narrative of Satan's rebellion in heaven and Adam's disobedience in Eden to a "revealed" narrative paradigm that organizes the complex issue of subjection (and its intrinsic relation to subjectivity) as a question of judgment and choice between two alternative patterns: subjection to the will of the Father as reason discerns it in the order of things, or subjection to the irrational excess of a desire generated in the self and beyond the orbit of "collateral love."[21] Significantly, Milton posits the absence of God's *informing* creativity not as nothingness but as Chaos, the surrender of energy to the mechanistic (and therefore unsubjected or uninformed) forces of chance. The intrapsychic correlate of Chaos is alienation or exile.

We may now return to the digression on hypocrisy in Book III (681–9) to understand more clearly the transition from the cosmic scale of Books I through VIII to the psychological focus of the poem's conclusion. Hypocrisy presupposes a subjection of the self to the self. The hypocrite submits the signifier of the self to a discourse marked by the disjunction of signification and reference. The face that Satan, disguised as an inquisitive but pious cherub (III.636–9), presents to Uriel is not a motivated synecdoche signing the inner "self," but a metonymy, a substitution of Satan's *speculation* of what Uriel desires to see.[22] The hypocrite parodies the creator by attempting to substitute his fantasies for divine ontology, and thus to circumvent God's system of signifying with things. In response to his exorbitant desire, he adds a surplus of significance to divine creation, an appearance to which no thing corresponds, and so transfers his own exorbitance to the process of signification itself, substituting for the divine logic of correspondences, the fallen logic of the supplement and differing and deferring *this* time, the time of our history, from *that* when "God shall be All in All" (III.341).[23] In Milton's terms, once reason is subjected to appetite, hypocrisy is inevitable. Hypocrisy is the place of the sign, the insertion of the empty signifier into the space where what is desired is not. Thus Satan deceives his followers in Book I and Eve lies to Adam in Book IX (856–85).

A corollary of the surrender of freedom by disobedience is idolatry, which occurs when the hypocrite, projecting his or her appetites onto the external world, begins to believe in the substantial reality of his or her fantasies. Eve displays such idolatry when she worships the Tree of Knowledge (IX.795ff). When Satan says hell resides within him, he realizes the extent to which, for him, the external world is merely a reflection of his internal psychic economy. Similarly, in Books XI and XII, the events of human history are presented as both historical events and as reflections of the internal states of those who cause them. The seed Milton plants with his comment on hypocrisy in Book III later appears as part of the pattern of human history. The just men of any age have no recourse from the chaos of mechanical causes and exorbitant desires, save faith in divine providence and revealed truth; they reject false appearances to "walk with God." To do so they must discern in their own situations the typical pattern that structures their unique experience, and judge and choose within the doubled context of the particular historical sequence and the providential rhetoric it typifies.

Other aspects of the early action of *Paradise Lost* may be revised from the retrospective viewpoint established by the poem's concluding books. As fallen readers, we may experience considerable difficulty when, in Book III, we see the Almighty without a mediator. We are uncomfortable with his absolute power because, from the fallen perspective, we have difficulty in seeing him as other than a projection of our own internal tyranny. The Nimrod episode helps us to understand this process of projection. Nimrod equates Godhead with dominion and fails to understand his place in creation as distinct from God's. Like Satan, he revolts against "paternal rule" as one

> of proud ambitious heart, who not content
> With fair equality, fraternal state,
> Will arrogate Dominion undeserv'd
> Over his brethren, and quite dispossess
> Concord and law of Nature from the Earth. (XII.25–8)

Like Satan, Nimrod is "emulous" only of strength and cannot recognize the absolute difference between God's creative merit and his own coercive force. "Not content" with "fraternal state," he attempts to depose the Father by revolting against "paternal rule." His tyranny is a corrupt (or parodic) translation of the intrinsic monarchy of heaven. God's rule is by merit, Nimrod's by might. The incarnation is the necessary correction, for it rewrites Nimrod's farcical attempt to rise to heaven as the Son's successful descent to Earth.[24] Man ruptures his connection to heaven when he tries to assume the role of God, "in despite of Heav'n, / Or from Heav'n claiming second Sovranty" (XII. 34–5). An alternative mode of imitation is offered when God condescends to be man. The monarchical emulation of divine power is countered by the submissive emulation of divine love, the imitation of Christ. The opposition of Nimrod and Christ dramatizes the reversal of the ontology of metaphor that was discussed in connection with the invocation to light.[25] The denomination of earthly behavior (and the dominion it implies) follows the revelation *in time* of a heavenly and eternal pattern.

The pattern that the incarnation will introduce on earth is one that Adam and his progeny will be able to follow. Michael explains that after the resurrection the work of the savior will be continued by his disciples:

> Men who in his Life
> Still follow'd him; to them shall leave in charge
> To teach all nations what of him they learn'd
> And his Salvation, them who shall believe
> Baptizing in the profluent stream, the sign
> Of washing them from guilt of sin to Life
> Pure, and in mind prepar'd, if so befall,
> For death, like that which the redeemer di'd. (XII.438–45)

The teaching of the apostles most often takes the form of the narrative history of the life of Christ. In the Synoptic Gospels, believers may find the pattern of pure life and recognize that the readiness "for death, like that which the redeemer di'd" is all. A moral life imitates the story of Christ and looks forward to a death that is at once a humiliation and an exaltation.[26] Thus Adam is offered not a doctrine, but a way of life – a narrative induction into the peculiar temporality of "being toward" a death that is conceived not as the end of being, but as the end of situated being, the end of being-there. We shall discuss in the next chapter how the exchange of life for death, epitomized and effected by Christ's passion, changes the end toward which every life story tends into a new beginning and thus underlies the rhetorical design of Milton's narration.

## III

Michael's instruction helps Adam turn away from the mechanical and restrictive aspects of earthly life to aspire to the eternal life made possible by faith. Part of this instruction is a careful explanation of death that shows Adam its various corporal forms, but reduces bodily death to a moment in a dialectical movement through the "Gate of Life" (XII.571). Death is first represented in this dialectic as the "bottomless perdition" into which the fallen angels are thrown "there to dwell / In Adamantine Chains and Penal fire" (I.47–8), then as a bodily transformation, and finally as a transition to eternal life.

Fallen Adam initially conceives of death as a literal return to the dust from whence he came and, consequently, as a relief from strife and toil (XI.547–53).[27] A similar idea of ultimate escape into non-being is expressed in Book II by Moloch, "More destroy'd than thus / We should be quite abolisht and expire" (92–3), and by Belial, "To perish rather, swallow'd up and lost / In the wide womb of uncreated night, / Devoid of sense and motion" (149–51). As a corrective, Michael repeatedly emphasizes the importance of understanding material appearance in terms of spiritual implication.

The first vision of death shown to Adam, the murder of Abel, calls on Adam to infer spiritual states from sensible signs. Cain's appearance as a "sweaty Reaper," his offering of "the green Ear, and the yellow Sheaf," imply his impiety, just as Abel's contrasting devotion is signified by his "meek" demeanor and his sacrifice of the "firstlings of his Flock / Choicest and best" (XI.434–8). God's preference is signed by "propitious Fire from Heav'n," distinguishing the plenitude of Abel's offering from the emptiness of Cain's (XI.441–3). Cain's murder of his brother is the visible acting out of his inner rage (XI.444), and, as Abel dies, he "groan[s] out his Soul with gushing blood effus'd" (XI.447); material and immaterial vitality are joined, yet distinct.

Michael adds to the vision a verbal gloss that locates the event as the initial link in a chain of subsequent events:

> But the bloody Fact
> Will be aveng'd, and th' other's Faith approv'd
> Lose no reward, though here thou see him die,
> Rolling in dust and gore. (XI.457–60)

Adam, however, remains riveted by the physical scene and his response ignores the promise of justice:

> Alas, both for the deed and for the cause!
> But have I now seen Death? Is this the way
> I must return to native dust? O sight
> Of terror, foul and ugly to behold,
> Horrid to think, how horrible to feel! (XI.461–5)

The intralineal punctuation (especially the two question marks) of Adam's response conveys the staccato rhythm of violent death. It is as though Cain's act has been translated directly into the structure of Adam's speech. The final line, with its caesura between two alliterative units, schematizes the state of Adam's perception. Significantly his mimetic language abstracts from the specific content of Abel's death a sound pattern that comes to signify the structure of death and can be extrapolated to other situations. But Adam is still overwhelmed by physical feeling. The pain of the body predominates over the conceptual abstraction of death from a situated physical experience to a pattern of speech and thought.

Michael further elaborates the distinction between a death and death itself:

> Death thou hast seen
> In his first shape on man; but many shapes
> Of Death, and many are the ways that lead
> To his grim Cave, all dismal; yet to sense
> More terrible at th' entrance than within. (XI.466–70)

Adam is made to confront the physical nature of death and then asked to go beyond it to an understanding of the instrumentality of death. Death is the instrument of justice. For the elect, death is not an end but a transition after which all pain ceases. Michael recommends Christian fortitude and submission to the will of God: "Nor love thy Life, nor hate; but what thou liv'st / Live well, how long or short permit to Heav'n" (XI.552–3). Thus Adam is shown the rigorous enforcement of the fall, death, and taught a response that offers an alternative to despair. Like the destruction of Eden and the expulsion itself, the visions of death adjust Adam's sight to something beyond "the Earthly Kingdoms and thir glory."

Although the death of the body is "terrible at th' entrance," it represents Adam's passage from the woes of fallen nature, not into oblivion but into "second Life." The Father describes death as one of the instruments of regeneration:

> I at first with two fair gifts
> Created him endowed, with Happiness
> And Immortality: that fondly lost,
> This other serv'd but to eternize woe;
> Till I provided Death; so Death becomes
> His final remedy, and after Life
> Tri'd in sharp tribulation, and refin'd
> By Faith and faithful works, to second Life,
> Wak't in the renovation of the just,
> Resigns him up with Heav'n and Earth renew'd. (XI.57–66)

When Adam and Eve are granted grace and death, their "final remedy," their resurrection has already begun. The process of creation and re-creation continues to move toward the day when

> Hell, her numbers full,
> Thenceforth shall be for ever shut. Meanwhile
> The World shall burn, and from her ashes spring
> New Heav'n and Earth, wherein the just shall dwell
> And after all thir tribulations long
> See golden days, fruitful of golden deeds,
> With Joy and Love triumphing, and fair Truth.

Then thou thy regal Sceptre shalt lay by,
For regal Sceptre then no more shall need,
God shall be All in All. (III.332–41)

The structure of prefiguration and subsequent fulfillment that Milton employs in *Paradise Lost* recapitulates the process of historical revelation it is meant to portray. To speak of the subordination of poetry to theology in the epic is to miss Milton's mediation of the two discourses by the specific temporality of narrative. The last two books of the poem reinterpret the first ten, as the New Testament reinterprets the Old. They make explicit what was previously implied and teach us that revelation partakes of a structure of double implication that also characterizes narrative.[28] The prehistory of man, supplied in the first ten books of *Paradise Lost,* is, like the Mosaic laws,

> but giv'n
> With purpose to resign them in full time
> Up to a better Cov'nant, disciplin'd
> From shadowy Types to Truth, from Flesh to Spirit,
> From imposition of strict Laws, to free
> Acceptance of large Grace, from servile fear
> To filial, works of Law to works of Faith. (XII.300–6)

The poetic license of the first ten books is justified by the material reality of the biblical history it is to gloss. In Milton's revised and corrected empiricism, history is interpreted by the same figures it validates, as the episodes of any narrative are glossed and validated in the retrospection of the reader who has grasped the configuration of the whole.[29]

In these last, historical books, Milton shows the effects of sin more graphically than those of grace because, until the last judgment and its synchronization of figure and truth – that is, its effacement of difference in the image and deferral in time – the figure of Sin will continue to take the historical shape of so many temporally situated sins. The figure of grace, however, asserts its potency only through the paired mediations of faith and works. Thus, it becomes manifest only in retrospect, as the pattern underlying such events

175

as Adam's reconciliation with Eve, his memory of the Son's demeanor at the judgment, and his insight into the meaning of the *protevangelium*.

Until the "full time" of truth, the effects of sin must be endured. As in the war in heaven, the promise of justice will be fulfilled only by a messianic abridgement of time that retrospectively abrogates the logic of narrative and effects a lyric closure – the identity of type and truth, flesh and spirit, subject and act, when "God shall be All in All":

> Truth shall retire
> Bestuck with sland'rous darts, and works of Faith
> Rarely be found: so shall the World go on,
> To good malignant, to bad men benign,
> Under her own weight groaning, till the day
> Appear of respiration to the just,
> And vengeance to the wicked, at return
> Of him so lately promis'd to thy aid,
> The Woman's seed, obscurely then foretold,
> Now amplier known thy Saviour and thy Lord. (XII.535–44)

The final action of the second coming can exist in the narrative text only as an anticipation, for narrative cannot narrate its own demise.

# 8

# THE REVELATION OF HISTORY

T HE LENS THROUGH WHICH I HAVE VIEWED
*PARADISE LOST* is shaped by three assumptions about
the function and process of narrative. The first is that the
subjects of a narrative are defined by what may be predicated of
them. If I ask someone to define his subjectivity – that is, to explain
who he is – he will inevitably tell me a story. This story will necessarily be structured by a series of predications: I was born in the
city of . . . , I attended school at . . . , and so on.[1] My sense of
this person (and his of himself) will be determined by the attributes
and actions of which he can be conceived to be the subject.[2] If he
attempts to be exhaustive, his story will eventually include an account of my question and an attempt to narrate his narration of its
answer. Walter Benjamin appreciates this parabolic conundrum in
an essay entitled "The Storyteller," where he remarks that

> not only a man's knowledge or wisdom, but above all his real
> life – and this is the stuff that stories are made of – first assumes
> transmissible form at the moment of his death. Just as a se-
> quence of images is set in motion inside a man as his life comes
> to an end – unfolding the views of himself under which he
> has encountered himself without being aware of it – suddenly
> in his expression and look the unforgettable emerges and im-
> parts to everything that concerned him that authority which
> even the poorest wretch in dying possesses for the living
> around him.[3]

177

Since we cannot narrate our own deaths, this final authority, conferred by completion, is always deferred to a place just beyond the boundaries of our experience. We understand the things we do by imagining their consequences, and since each action interlocks with subsequent actions, it is only death that confers a final significance on the episodes of our experience. The end of our imagined story forms for us a personal eschatology with reference to which our view of ourselves is structured and on the basis of which moral choices are made. Without this story form, which connects present experience to a remembered past and an anticipated future, experience remains a set of contingent events, devoid of significance. Thus my second assumption is that narrative is always constituted in an act of reflection – contingent experience becomes meaningful when it is understood as an episode in a completed story.

The transfer of experience into narrative leads to a third assumption: The articulation of experience in narrative is ordered not only by reference to a story structure always broader than the events it includes, but also by the limited predicative operations grammar and rhetoric make available.[4]

Like the individual life history I proposed to elicit, *Paradise Lost* is constrained by its exhaustive ambition to thematize its own narration by including it within an eschatological framework. "For now we see through a glass, darkly; but then face to face: now I know in part; but then shall I know even as also I am known" (1 Cor. 13:12). The Pauline dictum invokes two orders of vision and sets them into a temporal sequence. Knowledge then, in the kingdom, will be complete, essential, intuitive. The temporal demarcation between the two orders is not absolute. Revealed truth, imparted to man by a benevolent creator, allows him to interpret his mortal vision through the gloss of an eternal vision.

When Milton intends to relate "things invisible to mortal sight," he faces a specific and language-bound problem. He conflates two visions – one temporal, empirical, mimetic; the other eternal, revelatory. These visions are double, but each is projected into the single linear discourse of a poetic narrative. Two stories – one of "man's first disobedience" and the other of "one greater Man" – are entwined so that each provides the hermeneutic necessary for

the interpretation of the other in a dialectic of personal and apocalyptic eschatologies. The rhetoric that accomplishes this suturing
of two stories performs the conflation of reading and writing implied
by the notion of "self-authorship." The rhetorical pivots at which
Milton's narrative turns from a temporally situated vision to an
eternal and universal one locate the privileged moments at which
the Miltonic subject authors itself by freely enacting the judgments
and choices it makes in accord with its providential role. It is at
these moments that a modern experience of historical significance
is at once revealed and sublated into a renewed affirmation of providence. The revelation of history is also the revelation of a particular
kind of narrative cognition, the narrative of the self authored as a
subject, moving through time, capable of change, yet recognizably
self-identical.

The poetic problem Milton faces is duplicated within *Paradise
Lost* when Raphael narrates the hexameron: "What words or tongue
of Seraph can suffice, / Or heart of man suffice to comprehend?"
(VII. 113–14) such a narrative. The problem is explicitly verbal:
"Immediate are the Acts of God, more swift / Than time or motion,
but to human ears / Cannot without process of speech be told"
(VII. 176–8). A reading of the metaphorical structure of *Paradise Lost,*
which views narrative as a cognitive instrument that reduces contingency to causation by imposing a significant pattern, ex post
facto, on a series of events, will show that "the process of speech"
represented by the poem illustrates and enables the conceptualization
of the two orders of vision implied by Saint Paul as separate epistemological orders, one of being, the other of becoming, mediated
by a specific text, Holy Scripture. By employing this master text,
the Christian construes the apparently contingent events of his or
her personal narrative as providential, as both physical-historical
and spiritual-eternal moments in the dialectical practice that William
Ames designates "living to God."[5] This dialectic, represented in
Milton's poem by a narrative structure that promotes the reading
of one set of events through the perspective of two contrastive endings, rewrites the Thomistic distinction of appearance and essence
as a confrontation of heaven and history. The dialectical antithesis
of eternal essence and historical appearance is mediated and resolved

within the poem by the sacrifice of Christ, which confers eternal salvation through a historical death, and by the universal history supplied by Scripture.

To accomplish this mediation, the narrative structure of *Paradise Lost* purports to disclose an ontological progression from analogy to identity that is projected rhetorically in the poem by a dialectical progression from metaphor to synecdoche. By inviting the reader to transcend the gloomy ending of his personal narrative by assimilating it to that of Christ, *Paradise Lost* conflates a prelapsarian and monistic view of human life with a postlapsarian and dualistic one. Both visions are mediated by a pivotal equivocation on the word "death" as it pertains to Christ and to man. To conclude our study of *Paradise Lost,* we may elaborate the specific rhetoric underlying this narrative structure and elucidate its ground in the epistemological assumptions of the speculative theological tradition.

The exchange of the individual Christian's mortality for the immortality of Christ begins with the use of Scripture as a gloss on his present experience. The anticipated congruence between the individual's future and the future of the world revealed by Scripture induces a series of temporal reversals that finally place death as not the end of life but its prelude.

When, in *Paradise Lost* XI and XII, Michael supplies a synopsis of biblical history, Adam is given what Milton's readers already have, a view of history whole. Milton divides Michael's revelation into two parts. The account from Abel to Noah is visually presented, the remainder is narrated. Thus the latter part of Adam's preparation for life on the "subjected Plain" is given in the form of much of Scripture itself, that is, as a series of thematically linked, exemplary narratives. The shift follows the initiation of a new covenant, signaled by God's rainbow, and a proleptic reference to the end of time:

> Day and Night,
> Seed-time and Harvest, Heat and hoary Frost
> Shall hold thir course, till fire purge all things new,
> Both Heav'n and Earth, wherein the just shall dwell. (XI.898–901)

The prolepsis is further strengthened by the typological reference to Noah as "one just Man" (XI.890) and the coordination of the destruction by water and the coming destruction by fire. The "invisibility" of the revelation after the flood foreshadows the more necessary invisibility of events after the fire. Adam must learn to understand what he sees and hears without sight of "objects divine / [that] Must needs impair and weary human sense" (XII.9–10).[6] As the nature of a man's life is only understood at his death, so that of history is available only through history's end. This final perspective is made available by Scripture and verified by the Holy Spirit, just as Michael makes it available to Adam.[7] Milton accepts the reality and the importance of the visible world but insists on the active participation of reason – "searching, trying, examining" – and grace in using God's gifts to overcome the limitations of sense and see into the meaning of things.[8]

For Milton, the necessary supplement to the appearance of things is their participation in the fulfillment of divine providence. The world is known historically, as already unfolded to the all-seeing eye of heaven. Unlike the two worlds of Plato's *Republic,* Milton's temporal and eternal realms are not absolutely separate. They are two orders of knowledge pertaining to a single set of phenomena. The world of pure being is the world as it will be for regenerate man and as it already is for God, "beholding from his prospect high, / Wherein past, present, future he beholds" (III.77–8).[9] From the standpoint of Milton's God, history is already a category of being by virtue of its participation in the completed design of creation. Man, however, experiences his world as one of becoming, of continual definition and redefinition, subject to contingency and fortune. The Christian's recourse is to place his experience not in the context of personal ends, but in the eternal sphere of providence. In this way the creature aspires to become within history what, in God's mind, he already is.[10] History is thus the medium in which man writes his na 1e in the ink of his choices and the text that he reads in search of "conformity divine." Ultimately, through the example of Christ, who exchanges immortality for death, the faithful man learns to exchange death for immortality by positing eternal being as his personal end. This is the message Adam reads in Michael's historical revelation.[11]

Adam juxtaposes two sets of readings, one derived from sensory experience, the other from revelation. The latter "measures" and therefore interprets "this transient World, the Race of time, / Till time stand fixt" (XII. 554–5). The confused flow of events about to begin with Adam's descent to the "subjected Plain" may be understood because Michael has "predicted" the events to which it tends and the eternal principles that underlie them: "that suffering for Truth's sake / Is fortitude to highest victory, / And to the faithful Death the Gate of Life" (XII. 569–71). The word "death" serves as a pivot between the two readings. It refers to physical extinction in the reading derived from sensory experience and to resurrection and rebirth to eternity at the end of the reading derived from revelation. Acceptance of this rhetorical extension of "death" as a literal representation of the dual nature of Christ preserves the mediation of heaven and history represented by the use of one word with two different meanings while asserting that its basis is not linguistic but historical. For the believing Christian the meaning of "death" is revised and extended not by the rhetorical device of metaphor but by the historical death and resurrection of Christ. This historical revision of death as the gate of life is merely re-presented by Milton's rhetorical device. Adam reads this meaning in Michael's prophecy just prior to the expulsion from Eden, yet his perspective is the end rather than the beginning of time.

According to this scheme all the contingent events encountered in the world are understood before they occur. By his effort to make his end a return to the Logos, Adam "lives to God"; his life becomes the becoming of being. Faith precedes knowledge and makes it possible by supplying the context in which knowledge is received. The narrative move here initiates a practice under which the discourse of mundane experience is evaluated by projecting it into the history of the world as it is already known through revelation. The individual understands the events of his life as contingent from his temporal perspective, but providential, and therefore significant, from the perspective of the last days. He deduces, as best he can, the significance that the future will disclose by assimilating his life story to the master narrative of biblical revelation. By doing so, he looks forward to the recitation of his life before the judgment seat.

Each man passing through death is asked the question with which I began my consideration of narrative, that is, is asked to give an account of his life. Milton writes in the *Christian Doctrine:* "Matt. xii, 36, 37: *every idle word that men speak, they will be called to account for it on the day of judgment: for according to your words you will be justified, and according to your words you will be condemned.* – that is, if our words are honest but our deeds do not answer to them" (*CP*.VI.622–3).[12] This transitional narrative, spoken with the authority of completeness that only death confers, determines whether one will be admitted through the "Gate of Life" or condemned to the "second" or eternal death.

We may at this point begin to consider more microscopically the rhetoric through which Milton represents the process whereby historical experience is integrated with a scripturally derived sense of providence. Milton's task in *Paradise Lost* is to portray appearances as they are perceived by man's senses, to demonstrate the inherent limitations of this empiricism, and to explore the intimate relationship between human perceptions and the intelligible but suprasensible workings of providence that stabilize the ultimate meaning of what we perceive. The particular "process of speech" appropriate to this enterprise is metaphor. Because it presents two implicitly related terms, metaphor demands of the reader a twofold interpretation that parallels the double interpretation of experience in the contexts of lived history and eternal providence. This is especially true of metaphors in which only one term is stated. The "things invisible to mortal sight" in *Paradise Lost* are the tenors of metaphors whose vehicles are drawn from representative human experience. This rhetorical innovation, which achieves a redescription of the world as given to the senses in terms of the world as given in revelation, is properly dialectical. The implicit world of the metaphor's tenor negates yet preserves its vehicle. The redescription is privileged by the Christian revelation that proclaims that the transformed vision will ultimately subsume the negated empirical vision in whose terms the world must be described.[13] Human history is then understood as the progressive motion of the empirically perceived world toward "conformity divine." The adequation of vehicle and tenor is the rhetorical image of what is understood to be the ontologically real work of providence as executed by individual human subjects. Providence expresses itself through time as the progressive rationalization of the external world to conform it to a divine design that God's grace has made present in the regenerate heart.[14]

To judge, choose, and act correctly, the reader is asked to reflect on his or her temporal experience in the context of an eternal world: The apocalyptic eschatology of revelation supplements and revises the personal narrative within which experience is encountered. The process is, in fact, reminiscent of that found in the New Testament parables in which judgments typical of everyday life are portrayed as inadequate to or inappropriate in the kingdom of grace. The substitution of one eschatology for another gives rise to a dual narrative by asking the reader to interpret one set of events twice. The change in prospective endings allows the spiritual term of the metaphor to redescribe the negated yet preserved empirical term. The tension between the two terms defines the dual nature of the Christian: fallen, yet regenerate, mortal, yet immortal. With the metaphorically induced ambiguity of the word "death" extended to invoke two complete and distinct orders of meaning, Christians find themselves, like Adam, standing at the end of their own lives, producing the history by which they will be judged. Milton's representation of this practice, based on a rhetorical maneuver, in turn, demonstrates the tropological process by which speculative theology develops.

Milton uses continuing metaphors in varied contexts to imitate, in the reader's experience, the inadequacies of empirical judgment. The vehicles of these metaphors form the discursive surface of the text, and the tenors provide the literary illusion of grace. The corrected vision of earthly events that is, in effect, the referent of Milton's poem emerges as the synthesis of a single story told from two points of view.[15]

Milton's use of the theological metaphor that names the first and second members of the Godhead, Father and Son, was determined by his religion, but the theological metaphors arose out of human perceptions and were answerable to human needs. They were living metaphors – ad hoc cognitive instruments that innovated a new articulation of experience.[16] By reinserting the terms of speculative theology in a narrative structure, Milton restores to their nominal language the authority of metaphor; he discloses the significance of a paradigmatic substitution by reinserting it in a predicative frame.

Paul Ricoeur argues that the metaphoric use of "Father" and "Son" to denominate aspects of the Trinity is distinct from that of speculative theology, because the metaphor necessarily retains and transports its "proper" or sensual meaning into a spiritual tenor, and therefore falls short of a true sublation of the physical into the intellectual. Although speculative theology removes the concept of the persons in the Trinity from its rhetorical ontology, poetic metaphor constantly reasserts that ontology by reading the attributes of its corporeal vehicle into its spiritual tenor. The reading of *Paradise Lost* I have proposed indicates the way in which metaphor permits a mimesis of the conceptual operation of speculative theology – a mimesis that discloses the founding of the concept itself.[17]

The paternity of God, the Father, assimilates the creative action of the deity to the procreative action experienced in the world. "Father" is the vehicle for a metaphor, the tenor of which is the perfect creator who accepts responsibility for his creatures as a father does for his family.[18] The metaphor describes a relationship rather than a state of affairs, and its vehicle interlocks with the vehicles of associated metaphors to form a two-tiered narrative. If God is our father, we are his children. If the second person in the Trinity is the Father's Son, he is our brother. The relationships of the metaphoric vehicles imply the less tangible relationships of their tenors. The brotherhood of man in Christ is implicit in the theological metaphor, yet, in the poem, the metaphor creates a structure that transfers the interpretation of earthly events into an eternal context. This dialectic is governed by the backward, revisionary glance that exchanges, for the empirical eschatology of death and nothingness, the revelatory eschatology of eternal life.

This mode of metaphoric implication and the sublation of the sensible into the suprasensible narrative is briefly suggested by the threading of two narrative sequences at the opening of Book III:

> Hail, holy Light, offspring of Heav'n first-born,
> Or of th' Eternal Coeternal beam
> May I express thee unblam'd? since God is Light,
> And never but in unapproached Light
> Dwelt from Eternity, dwelt then in thee,
> Bright effluence of bright essence increate. (III. 1–6)

Here the dialectic of the sensible and the spiritual is mediated by the observable relation of the sun to radiant light. The continuum of identity and difference in the relations *lux–lumen,* father–son, fountain–stream (III.7–8) manifests itself in predicative contexts in which both terms of the relation operate simultaneously. Historically, these metaphors are unidirectional: The vehicles are grounded in the sensible from which the tenors extrapolate a suprasensible world. However, once these metaphors are established, they begin to be read in the other direction. The family is understood as something that ought to be like the Godhead; the earthly father is expected to imitate the heavenly. Milton's poem reverses the historical development of the trope in this way. The sensible vehicle of the metaphor – that is, the earthly family – is presented as a historical manifestation of the eternal family of the Holy Trinity.[19] In this way the visible world is at once taken as real and meaningful in itself and as a moment in universal history.

Raphael's ambivalent description of his accommodated discourse suggests the interpenetration of the two spheres implied by the poem's metaphorical structure and the ontological privilege extended to the suprasensible sphere:

> How last unfold
> The secrets of another World, perhaps
> Not lawful to reveal? yet for thy good
> This is dispens't, and what surmounts the reach
> Of human sense, I shall delineate so,
> By lik'ning spiritual to corporal forms,
> As may express them best, though what if Earth
> Be but the shadow of Heav'n, and things therein
> Each to other like, more than on Earth is thought? (V.568–76)

The metaphoric identification of spiritual and corporeal forms is here given ontological force. Accommodated discourse, then, is possibly more than discourse "as if." Spiritual terms may be not simply analogous to corporeal terms but their more brilliant originals as well. The text is then a representation of the motion of history toward its apocalyptic terminus, and the rhetorical motion from metaphor to synecdoche is the shadow of providence.[20]

Actions taken in the visible world have consequences in both realms. Although the earthly consequences occur in an immediate dramatic context, the realization of their participation in a providential design is deferred until the individual crosses the boundary of mortality to appreciate life in the presence of God and in the absence of his former mundane context. The materialist interpretation of the visible world is presented as terminating in the death of the subject and the utter negation of his narrative. The spiritual interpretation is presented as terminating in an apocalyptic transcendence of death: the negation of negation that is a crossing of the categorical bar from beings to being. This promised transcendence will emerge from the confrontation of death with life in the incarnate Son of God.

The Son's account of this confrontation in his colloquy with the Father in Book III (243–65) reveals again the ambivalence between "being" understood as an all-inclusive unity and "being" understood as implicit in attribution or predication: "Thou hast giv'n me to possess / Life in myself for ever, by thee I live" (III.243–4). The same ambivalence continues in the disparity between "While by thee rais'd I ruin all my Foes" (III.258) and "the multitude of my redeem'd" (III.260) until "reconcilment" is achieved by a return to the Godhead: "Wrath shall be no more / Thenceforth, but in thy presence Joy entire" (III.264–5). The rhetorical restructuring of experience affords a redescription in language that offers the transcendence of grammar as the transcendence of death. The text appeals directly to the reader's experience, abstracts that experience from its situational context, and integrates it into an inclusive view of history, the *eschata* of which are supplied by revelation.

Examination of two of the poem's principal metaphors will exemplify the way in which this rhetorical movement from metaphor to synecdoche – from the assertion of comparability to that of identity within a larger structure – acts as an armature on which the narrative is built. The identification of knowledge and food, especially as concentrated in the forbidden fruit, and the identification of man and God in the incarnate Christ function as decisive and antithetical moments in this dialectical movement.

Early in Book VII, Adam, having heard Raphael's narration of the war in heaven, asks the cause and method of creation. The angel explains that though he cannot express, nor Adam understand, a full account of "Almighty works," "Yet what thou canst attain, which best may serve / To glorify the Maker, and infer / Thee also happier, shall not be withheld" (VII.115–17). The legitimacy of Adam's request for knowledge is judged according to its purpose. Useful knowledge informs Adam of his personal happiness, increasing his appreciation of God's goodness. Knowledge is useful only when the signs that bear it become transparent so that the divinity they signify may be grasped. Adam must move through the sensible sign to an experience of divine love, which is, ultimately, like holy light, an emanation of God himself, the medium in which the synecdochic members of his body merge.[21] Thus Raphael stipulates the "heart" of man as the faculty that comprehends creation.[22] Insofar as God is identified with love, the signified is understood to be possessed whenever the apprehension of the sign evokes the emotion.

Near the end of his visit to Eden, Raphael warns Adam to keep distinct the sensual and spiritual attractions of Eve:

> In loving thou dost well, in passion not,
> Wherein true Love consists not; Love refines
> The thoughts, and heart enlarges, hath his seat
> In Reason, and is judicious, is the scale
> By which to heav'nly Love thou may'st ascend,
> Not sunk in carnal pleasure, for which cause
> Among the Beasts no mate for thee was found. (VIII.588–94)

If Adam properly understands "Almighty works," his knowledge of creation will be refined to love for his creator, for it is the heart that "digests" knowledge. The intellectual nourishment Adam may justly seek is capable of this transubstantiation: "What wee, not to explore the secrets ask / Of his Eternal Empire, but the more / To magnify his works, the more we know" (VII.95–7). The Love–love relation, making the empirical affection continuous with a putatively divine origin, finally represents God in man and announces the narrative's location of the literal. As Augustine writes in the *Christian Doctrine,* the tyranny of lust being thus overthrown, charity reigns through its supremely just laws of love to God for His own sake, and love to one's self and one's neighbor for God's sake. Accordingly, in regard to figurative expressions, a rule such as the following will be observed, to carefully turn over in our minds and meditate upon what we read till an interpretation be found that tends to establish the reign of love. Now, when taken literally it at once gives a meaning of this kind, the expression is not to be considered figurative.[23]

Raphael clarifies the sense of transubstantial knowledge when he compares knowledge to food, cautioning against intellectual indigestion (VII.126–30). Digestion transforms food into the finer substance of the body that eats it (V.414–16). Potentially the refinement of food and eater can continue; Adam, becoming more and more ethereal, will "transubstantiate" lighter and lighter food until "from these corporal nutriments" he may at last "turn all to Spirit" (V.496–7). To achieve this destiny, Adam must exert "temperance over appetite" and refrain from eating the fruit of indigestible knowledge. If Adam eats food inappropriate to his state, he will be unable to refine its substance to his own. The figure of the forbidden fruit is, then, a metaphor assimilating the physical to the intellectual process of "digestion." Once again, two chains of significance are joined by a single, troped word. The fruit signifies both food and knowledge. But, as with the analogy of God and man in Christ, the placement of the fruit in a narrative to be accepted as historical fact asserts that this particular fruit was knowledge and food. Its historical existence as such provides an ontological ground to the rhetorical manipulation of reference achieved by the metaphor. To eat this fruit is to disobey God and thus experience evil. In Milton's poem, the act of eating it results in both physical and intellectual indigestion.

The prohibited fruit provides an antithetical term in Milton's Christian dialectic. The apprehension of Christ's Passion requires the sublation of the corporeal in the spiritual, the transmutation of sensory knowledge to spiritual affection. The attempt to obtain spiritual (misunderstood as magical) powers by eating the fruit incorrectly reverses the dialectic. Transcendent knowledge is thought to subsist in its (arbitrary) signifier. This misunderstanding calls for a physical/physiological digestion that reduces the equivocal signifier in the wrong direction, concentrating its dual qualities in the corporeal/temporal vehicle. Thus the signifier of obedience ("the nobler end" of "conformity divine") is assimilated, ironically, through disobedience, the knowledge of evil attained by doing evil.

The misreading of the metaphor is understood by Aquinas as the failure to distinguish between a name and the origin of what the name signifies:

> When we say he [God] is good or wise we do not simply mean that he causes wisdom or goodness, but that he possesses these perfections transcendently. We conclude, therefore, that from the point of view of what the word means it is used primarily of God and derivatively of creatures, for what the word means—the perfection it signifies—flows from God to the creature. But from the point of view of our use of the word we apply it first to creatures because we know them first.[24]

Milton's narrative represents this signified–signifier relationship as a relationship between interlocking chains of significations. This representation is the mimesis that ultimately negates, yet preserves, the experience of mundane contingency by portraying it as a specifically mortal access to the eternal world of providence. Thus the apparent contingency of naming is reduced by its inclusion in a completed history that already exists in its completeness but remains inaccessible to mortal vision. Mundane experience, understood in the light of faith and revelation, is, or will turn out to be, providentially significant. When living well, that is, in Ames's phrase, "living to God," man uses faith, reason, and understanding to interpret the sensible world, as he experiences it, and to move toward its intelligible form. In this way, worldly experience participates in the mediation of man and God. But more is at stake than purely intellectual understanding or Neoplatonic self-perfection. The actions through which historical individuals "live to God" are the performance of works that transform the world of experience in the direction of "conformity divine."

In *Paradise Lost,* the apocalyptic revision of history, which integrates earthly and universal history, generates a poetic language in which God as *ens* becomes also *est;* the "is" of attribution is lent an ontological force by its implicit derivation from the fountain of all being.[25] The poem images this extension of being as light, the Holy Spirit, or, most inclusively, love. Its positive achievement is the promised incarnation of the Son, and its antithesis is Satan, whose frenzied actions are revised and negated (though not without mundane consequences) when viewed in the perspective of a totalizing providential history.

The eating of the apple is, in *Paradise Lost,* a hermeneutic failure and a founding of error, the opening of the space in which error wanders. Milton portrays interpretation itself as a refining process through which one is dialectically raised from the sensually perceived sign through an intellectual mediation to an experience of spiritual significance. For Milton, the material signifier is meaningful not in itself but as an element in a story, for access to truth is conferred not by the object or a sign, but by the act of understanding its function in a completed message.

It is not difficult to see in Milton's depiction of the forbidden fruit and Eve's fall the shadow of the Roman Catholic notion of transubstantiation, which (in Milton's view) also invests a material signifier with power that is exclusively God's, viewing the sign as a thing separable from the value God imparts to it.[26] Eve's misreading of the signifier, like the Roman notion of the Lord's Supper (as Milton understood it), confuses the sacrament, the seal of a covenant to be fulfilled by the practice of obedience, with a "consecrated element" capable of imparting an effect through its own virtue (IX.745–79). Her sin is not simply eating the fruit, but also disobeying God's command.[27] Satan's temptation urges Eve to her misunderstanding of the fruit's mode of signification by substituting for God's command a corrupted and corrupting "gospel preached," a false verbal gloss on the arbitrary visual signifier.[28] In this way he stands as the prototype of the wolves who "shall succeed for teachers" after the ministry of the Apostles and who will leave the truth "only in those written Records pure, / Though not but by the Spirit understood" (XII.507–14). Experienced in sin and sophisticated in his knowledge of sacramental hermeneutics, Satan derives ironic humor from the trivial nature of the fruit itself when he reports to the devils: "Him by fraud I have seduc'd / From his Creator, and the more to increase / Your wonder, with an Apple" (X.485–7).

The significance of the apple now emerges as retrospectively defined by the consequences of its fraudulent provisional meaning. Satan's discourse invests the forbidden fruit with a talismanic power that Eve's sin makes true. The homology of action and discourse implicit in the metaphor of self-authorship is enacted by the interdependence of Eve's self-definition as fallen and the emergence of the fruit's meaning from the intersection of a narrative discourse – Eve's imagined transcendence through disobedience and the power of the fruit – and a historical act based on the sacrifice of an eternal truth to what is, in effect, a narrative desire. Self-authorship is purchased at the price of precisely the sort of talismanic signifier Eve believes the fruit to be. The freedom of the self to judge and choose and thereby to define itself is at one with the play of the sign, emptied of itself and submitted to the temporal processes of discourse.[29]

When, after her fall, Eve mistakes the effects of disobedience for the power of the fruit, her idolatrous invocation of the tree institutionalizes her misreading of the fruit, creating a daily ceremony of misunderstanding:

> O Sovran, virtuous, precious of all Trees
> In Paradise, of operation blest
> To Sapience, hitherto obscur'd, infam'd,
> And thy fair Fruit let hang, as to no end
> Created; but henceforth my early care. (IX.795–9)

Eve's unintended pun on "sapience" signifies the reduction of knowledge to taste that attends her identification of physical and divine power. Thus the circle closes on the identification of knowledge and food. Eve has interpreted the fruit in terms of an immediate end – her presumed ascension to Godhead. By doing so, she opens a breach between the chain of signifiers terminating in God and the one terminating in corporeal death, sacrificing the former to the latter. Her progeny therefore must pass through mortality to find again eternal life.

The route to a reestablished communion passes through the life of Christ, which teaches man the way to sublate the literal term of the metaphor. In the incarnate Christ, the mortal man is preserved, yet transcended by the God. Adam, to digest the lighter, spiritual food of obedience, must renounce the physical ingestion of the forbidden fruit, just as Christ renounces the satanic banquet (and the earthly throne) in *Paradise Regained.*[30]

The two terms of the filial metaphor in *Paradise Lost* achieve synthesis in the incarnation of the Son, the historical moment when the tenor and the vehicle of the metaphor merge; and the narrative promises us that the equation of the metaphoric terms will be literal. When the Son incarnate descends into the sphere of appearances and enters the world of fallen man, the metaphor appears to collapse into a single term incorporating the attributes of its former vehicle and tenor, just as the metaphoric identification of knowledge and food collapsed in the forbidden fruit. What distinguishes the incarnation of the Son from his earlier descents into the world – to effect its creation in Book VII and to judge Adam and Eve in Book X – is his passage through death, the mortal man's "Gate of Life." Christ's death on the cross effects the reversal of the eschatological dialectic; by assuming the personal eschatology of an individual man, he shows man how to assume the apocalyptic eschatology of heaven. The Gospel accounts of Christ's acts, acts based on his assessment of "history in its prophetic aspect," complete the record in the light of which each Christian may conduct his or her own meditation "of things past and to come" and thus discover the way through sensible, corporeal death to spiritual, eternal life.[31] At the moment when Christ is both God and man, the spheres of history and eternity coincide; the direct connection of man and God that the fall had ruptured is restored.[32] The narration at this point requires that Christ's actions be at once compatible and incompatible with one or the other of the two lexical categories he occupies. A developed narrative would require a series of characterizing predications, which would pull apart the equivocal sign and disclose its internal discontinuity. Milton "solves" this problem in *Paradise Lost* by placing the incarnation beyond the limits of the narrative (except as a promise whose fulfillment is both anticipated and remembered). In *Paradise Regained,* he defines Christ's special status by having him rigorously renounce action – thus, like God, Christ becomes an unmoved mover, while to some degree he shares man's puzzlements.

Christ's restriction to circumscribed moments of participation within the narrative then signals the reassertion of the problem that the narrative is generated to solve; the divine cannot be assimilated to the temporal structure of human life through the temporalizing device of narration. The Son acts within his mythic realm and Jesus acts on earth, but the figure is exhausted in the Passion, which is not narrated but described. The absence of the divine signifier from mundane discourse becomes the mark of his transcendental reality. The constitutional gap in the narrative becomes the locus of the eternal. Thus Ignatius of Antioch takes as a mark of salvation the ability to hear the silence of the Word:

> It is better to be silent and be real, than to talk and to be unreal. Teaching is good, if the teacher does what he says. There is then one teacher "who spoke and it came to pass," and what he has done even in silence is worthy of the Father. He who has the word [*logos*] of Jesus for a true possession can also hear his silence, that he may be perfect, *that he may act through his speech,* and be understood through his silence. Nothing is hid from the Lord, but even our secret things are near him. Let us therefore do all things as though he were dwelling in us, that we may be his temples, and that he may be our God in us. [Emphasis mine.][33]

God's descent to earth is to enable man's ascent to heaven. This restoration is, however, deferred until the end of time, when "God shall be All in All." This deferral matches the deferral of the Passion to a place suggested by, but beyond the limits of, the narrative. The Father tells the Son that in the golden age "thou thy regal Scepter shalt lay by, / For regal Scepter then no more shall need" (III.339–40). The symbols of authority will not be needed when God is "All in All" because things will be known essentially; the signifier will regain its identity with the signified. Metaphor will become synecdoche, and the signified will always be God. This consummation is implicit in the series of literary synecdoches that bind Adam, mankind, and "one greater Man," in the poem's opening lines. The destruction of the filial metaphor by the equation of its terms in the incarnation prefigures the obsolescence of all metaphor (indeed of language) when, "wak't in the renovation of the just" (XI.65), we see without benefit of such accommodations: "Then shall I know even as also I am known." Until then, the play of metaphor will displace the prelapsarian "poetry of nouns" in favor of a language of relationships and predications. The restoration will redeem the noun by making all relationships identities, all nouns functions of a divine substance, which, in itself, exhausts the lexicon of potential predicates.[34]

Historical experience is a necessary moment in the dialectic of revision and redefinition that leads man to this reunification with God. I have attempted to show the precise way in which Milton's narrative articulates its mimesis of this dialectical process. Possessed of the Gospel, Milton's readers are enjoined to follow a path through the wilderness that has already been prepared for them, a path through history to eternity, through death to life. Milton's text, standing metonymically for the universal history given in the Bible, thus becomes "the gospel preached, which instructs us in the signification of the visible sign," the word that makes history a sacrament.

*Paradise Lost* presents two constitutions of man's temporal being. One, prelapsarian and monistic, posits a continual refinement in perception in which knowledge increases faith and faith increases knowledge until man "improv'd by tract of time" (V.498) ascends to the kingdom.[35] The other, postlapsarian and dualistic, implies a cognitive hierarchy in which the sphere of essence stands above that of protean appearance, remaining impenetrable to man's vision "til one greater Man" rejoin the ruptured spheres, render the analogues identities, and prepare the way for the restoration of a monistic universe in which God is "All in All." Adam's impertinent eating of the apple is the event in the story that revises the story, substituting the perspective of the two eschatologies for the ascent to the kingdom, the disobedience that "brought Death into the World, and all our woe" (I.3). The Passion, which brings death into God's world, is an event beyond the boundaries of the narrative that will "restore us, and regain the blissful Seat" (I.5). The Passion itself prefigures the Second Coming and the apocalypse; it revises but cannot complete the narrative. Thus Christ is present in *Paradise Lost* primarily as a promise, as the telos of the dialectic.

The apocalypse remains outside the narrative because it allows no transition, no contingencies, no movement. When predication ceases, narrative fades into description, and we find the subject has been removed to another time and another place. This distance in time and space cannot be reduced by narrative because the destruction of narrative is the price of its reduction, and because it is narrative itself that produces the "self-authored" subject of Milton's epic, the subject who chooses a path through history and language to produce out of its own free choices the distinct acts and words that will define what it was only in that moment when it is no longer. Thus Milton's story of all things necessarily ends where we begin:

> In either hand the hast'ning Angel caught
> Our ling'ring Parents, and to th' Eastern Gate
> Led them direct, and down the Cliff as fast
> To the subjected Plain; then disappear'd.
> They looking back, all th' Eastern side beheld
> Of Paradise, so late thir happy seat,
> Wav'd over by that flaming Brand, the Gate
> With dreadful Faces throng'd and fiery Arms:
> Some natural tears they dropp'd, but wip'd them soon;
> The World was all before them, where to choose
> Thir place of rest, and Providence thir guide:
> They hand in hand with wand'ring steps and slow,
> Through *Eden* took thir solitary way. (XII.637–49)

*Paradise Lost,* in its ending, reveals itself as not the history of all things but its preface. The containment of its figurative processes is not narrative but thematic, in so far as the poem narrates the impossibility of its own narration in any terms other than those that reproduce mankind in its mediated relationship to eternity, looking backward in search of its future.

# NOTES

CHAPTER I

1. *Paradise Lost* III.116–25. All citations of Milton's poetry are from *John Milton: Complete Poems and Major Prose,* ed. Merritt Y. Hughes (Indianapolis, 1957). Citations of Milton's prose are from *Complete Prose Works of John Milton,* ed. Don M. Wolfe et al., 8 vols., (New Haven, 1953–80), hereafter abbreviated *CP.*

2. *OED,* s.v. "author," entries 4, 1, 2a, and 3a, respectively. Seventeenth-century dictionaries generally notice the derivation from *augere;* see, for example, the entries for Augment and Author in John Minsheu's *The Guide Into Tongues* (London, 1617). A glance at the entry for Author in the index to the *Columbia Edition* of Milton's works (ed. F. A. Patterson, [New York, 1931–38]) indicates that he used the word to refer to himself as a writer of texts (see for examples the endnote to "The Passion" and the headnote to "Lycidas"), as well as in the other ways mentioned in my text. As my argument develops, it should become clear that the gathering of meanings under the word "author" remained, for Milton, an active process of metaphoric extension, in which each meaning illuminates the others.

3. I would like to thank Ernest B. Gilman for bringing to my attention the relevance of the derivation of "author" from the Latin *augere* to the theme of accumulation and addition in my study of seventeenth-century subjectivity and self-presentation, and Richard Harrier for useful bibliographical and conceptual help in my efforts to understand the usage of "author" in the Renaissance and seventeenth century.

4. For discussions of the two perspectives on narrative "events," see Jurij Lotman, *The Structure of the Artistic Text,* trans. Ronald Vroon, Michigan Slavic Contributions #7 (Ann Arbor, 1977), pp. 28–31; Jonathan Culler, "Fabula and Sjuzhet in the Analysis of Narrative:

Some American Considerations," *Poetics Today* 1 (Spring 1980): 27–37; and my "The Narrative of the Subject and the Rhetoric of the Self," *Papers on Language and Literature* 18 (1982): 398–415.

5. Cf. Andrew Milner's discussion of individualism and the interior voice in the "world vision of revolutionary independency" in *John Milton and the English Revolution: A Study in the Sociology of Literature* (London, 1981), pp. 50–9.

6. The notion of writing with the logos by reading what is written in the heart is adapted from the idealist tradition of epideictic poetry in which one becomes what one loves through contemplation. See Joel Fineman, *"Shakespeare's Perjured Eye": The Invention of Poetic Subjectivity in the Sonnets* (Berkeley, 1986), pp. 1–48.

7. On the development of historical consciousness in the seventeenth century, see Hershel Baker, *The Race of Time* (Toronto, 1947). A concise statement of the combination of Christian and historical understanding I will be discussing appears in C. A. Patrides, *The Grand Design of God: The Literary Form of the Christian View of History* (London, 1972), p. 7: "[The New Testament extension of] historical typology [and its enthusiastic reception] had the threefold purpose of confirming that historical events are non-recurring and irreversible, that they imply a design according to which the created order advances onward, and that they are meaningful only in so far as they are seen to relate to the advent of the Messiah."

8. Two seminal works are William G. Madsen's *From Shadowy Types to Truth: Studies in Milton's Symbolism* (New Haven, 1968) and Barbara Lewalski's *Protestant Poetics and Seventeenth-Century Religious Lyric* (Princeton, 1979). A notably sophisticated view of the consciousness of time implied by typological hermeneutics is found in Edward Tayler, *Milton's Poetry: Its Development in Time* (Pittsburgh, 1979).

9. Aristotle, the *Poetics,* 1450a, quoted from Aristotle, *On Poetry and Style,* trans. G. M. A. Grube, The Library of the Liberal Arts (Indianapolis, 1958), p. 13.

10. Ibid., p. 14. For a relevant discussion of Aristotle's *Poetics* and the relationship of plot to action, see Paul Ricoeur, *Time and Narrative,* vol. 1, trans. Kathleen McLaughlin and David Pellauer (Chicago, 1984), pp. 31–51.

11. On improvement by "tract of time," see Mary Ann Radzinowicz, "Man as a 'Probationer of Immortality': *Paradise Lost* XI and XII," in *Approaches to Paradise Lost: The York Centenary Lectures,* ed. C. A. Patrides (Toronto, 1968), pp. 34–9; Barbara Kiefer Lewalski, "In-

nocence and Experience in Milton's Eden," in *New Essays on Paradise Lost,* ed. Thomas Kranidas (Berekely, 1969), pp. 86–117; and Diane Kelsey McColley, *Milton's Eve* (Urbana, Ill., 1983), pp. 193–5. Contra, see Mary Nyquist, "Reading the Fall: Discourse and Drama in *Paradise Lost,*" *English Literary Renaissance* 14 (1984): 199–229.

12. Tzvetan Todorov observes that the subject of a narrative moves between the poles of change and continuity: "Narrative is constituted in the tension of two formal categories, difference and resemblance; the exclusive presence of one of these brings us into a type of discourse which is not narrative. . . . The simple relation of successive facts does not constitute a narrative: these facts must be organized, which is to say, ultimately, that they must have elements in common. But if all the elements are in common, there is no longer a narrative, for there is no longer anything to recount. Now, transformation represents precisely a synthesis of differences and resemblance; it links two facts without their being able to be identified." *The Poetics of Prose,* trans. Richard Howard (Ithaca, N.Y., 1977), p. 233. To conceive of oneself as both self-identical and changing, as moving though time yet remaining in touch with a point of origin, is to find the common ground between text and actions necessary to be author to oneself.

13. Several recent books examine the formation and presentation of images of the self in the Renaissance. See Stephen Greenblatt, *Renaissance Self-Fashioning: From More to Shakespeare* (Chicago, 1980); Judith Anderson, *Biographical Truth: The Representation of Historical Persons in Tudor–Stuart Writing* (New Haven, 1984); and Richard Helgerson, *Self-Crowned Laureates: Spenser, Jonson, Milton, and the Literary System* (Berkeley, 1983). See also, Anne Ferry's discussion of the language used to refer to self and individuality in Renaissance sonnet sequences in *The "Inward" Language: Sonnets of Wyatt, Sidney, Shakespeare, Donne* (Chicago, 1983).

14. As *Paradise Lost* is correctly identified in the commendatory poem of S. B. published with the second edition: "Qui legis Amissam Paradisum, grandia magni / Carmina *Miltoni,* quid nisi cuncta legis? / Res cunctas, & cunctarum primordia rerum, / Et fata, & fines continet iste liber." This formulation gives the narrative corollary of Lewalski's observation that the essential concern of Protestant meditation is "to trace the interrelation between the biblical text and the Christian's own experience, so that the one is seen to be the reflection or manifestation of the other. . . . The Christian's experience is to comment upon the biblical text, and the text upon his experience" (*Protestant*

*Poetics,* pp. 154–5). Milton's rewriting of Genesis enacts this dialogic commentary in narrative form by demonstrating the relationship of the beginning, middle, and end of time and situating present experience as a perpetual middle. On the Augustinian ground of such a concept of time, see Paul Ricoeur, *Time and Narrative,* vol. 1, pp. 5–30.

15. I take the two phrases in quotation marks from Louis O. Mink, "History and Fiction as Modes of Comprehension," *New Literary History* 1 (1970): 541.

16. Paul Ricoeur, "Explanation and Understanding: Some Remarkable Connections among the Theory of the Text, Theory of Actions, and Theory of History," in *The Philosophy of Paul Ricoeur: An Anthology of his Work,* ed. Charles E. Reagan and David Stuart (Boston, 1978), p. 160. See also, "The Model of the Text: Meaningful Action considered as a Text," *Social Research* 38 (1971), repr. in *Interpretive Social Science: A Reader,* ed. Paul Rabinow and William M. Sullivan (Berkeley, 1979), pp. 73–101.

17. Ricoeur, "Explanation and Understanding," pp. 160–1.

18. Ibid., p. 161.

19. Ibid., p. 157. The reformation and counterreformation are marked by an increased interest in motivation as the signs of grace become internalized. The visible actions of taking the sacraments are devalued by the reformed theologians in favor of a diligent examination of the internal state of the individual.

20. Or, to use terms closer to Milton's time, its final cause. Ricoeur develops his model of the narrative text to explore the experience of time in terms of the temporal categories of Heideggerian phenomenology: *"The primary direction of care is toward the future.* Through care, we are always 'ahead of' ourselves." "Narrative Time," *Critical Inquiry* 7 (1980): 181 (Ricoeur's emphasis). (Much, but not all, of the material in this essay appears in reworked form and a broadened context in *Time and Narrative,* vol. 1, pp. 52–94.)

21. Various Christian views of history are surveyed in Patrides, *The Grand Design of God.* For an extended discussion of Milton's dialectical use of biblical eschatology, see Chapter 8 in this book.

22. See Ricoeur, "Narrative Time," pp. 182–3; and Martin Heidegger, *Being and Time,* II.5.74, trans. John Macquarrie and Edward Robinson (New York, 1962), p. 436. See also Ricoeur's comparison of Heidegger's phenomenology of time to Augustine's, *Time and Narrative,* vol. 1, pp. 82–7.

23.   The dialectical connection between the resurrection of each believer and the postapocalyptic renovation of heaven and earth supplies a clue to Milton's mortalism.

24.   Louis O. Mink, "History and Fiction," p. 546 (Mink's emphasis). Cf. Alasdair MacIntyre, *After Virtue: A Study in Moral Theory* (Notre Dame, Ind., 1981), pp. 197–209. MacIntyre's argument for a narrative constitution of a unified self is in some respects similar to the one developed here and elaborated at the beginning of Chapter 8. But although MacIntyre sees the homology between the structure of actions and of narrative, he argues, against Mink, that actions are always already taken within and from a narrative constitution of the self. This view is unsatisfactory on two grounds: 1) It loses sight of the dialectical interplay of provisional narrativization leading to actions in various contingent circumstances and the continual retrospective revision necessary to make these provisional narratives episodes in the larger narrative in which individual character emerges; that is, precisely the relationship of providence and revelation to moral action in Milton's presentation of "self-authorship"; and 2) By failing to recognize the temporal space between immediate action and retrospective narrativization – the difference, in Mink's terms, between following and having already followed a story – MacIntyre underestimates the priority of narrative rhetoric in the shaping of character in action; again, it is Milton's presentation of providence and his deferral of semantic plenitude to the end of time that provides, as it were, the grammar of historical actions in which unity of self appears to be achieved. There are other possible enclosing narratives or, let us say, rationalizations for deferring meaning beyond death, including the inherited social and historical traditions favored by MacIntyre, but I shall argue (in Chapter 8) that the effect of the enclosing or world historical narrative on the individual life history is necessarily mediated by some formal aspects of narrativization per se.

25.   Cf. Ricoeur, "Narrative Time," p. 180: "Finally, the recollection of the story governed as a whole by its way of ending constitutes an alternative to the representation of time as moving from the past forward into the future, according to the well-known metaphor of the arrow of time. It is as though recollection inverted the so-called natural order of time. By reading the end in the beginning and the beginning in the end, we learn also to read time itself backward, as the recapitulating of the initial conditions of a course of action in its terminal consequences. In this way, a plot establishes human action not only

within time . . . but within memory. Memory, accordingly, *repeats* the course of events according to an order that is the counterpart of time as 'stretching along' between a beginning and an end."

26. Mink, "History and Fiction," p. 551 (Mink's emphasis). See also Ricoeur, "Narrative Time," pp. 179–80.

27. Lewalski, *Protestant Poetics,* p. 131.

28. See Milton's well-known assertion in the *Christian Doctrine* that "each passage of scripture has only a single sense, though in the Old Testament this sense is often a combination of the historical and the typological" (*CP.*VI.581).

29. On Milton's Arminianism, see Maurice Kelley's introduction to the *Christian Doctrine, CP.*VI.74–86; and Dennis Danielson, *Milton's Good God: A Study in Literary Theodicy* (Cambridge, 1982), esp. pp. 82–91.

30. John Donne, *The Epithalamions, Anniversaries and Epicedes,* ed. with an introduction and commentary by W. Milgate (Oxford, 1978). For Bacon, see, for example, the assertion in the *Novum Organum* that technological progress will restore man's prelapsarian dominion over creation. *The Works of Francis Bacon,* collected and edited by James Spedding, Robert Leslie Ellis, and Douglas Denon Heath, 13 vols. (Boston, 1863), vol. 8, p. 350. See also Milton's "Baconian" Prolusion VII, *CP.*I.296, 301–2. Anthony Low makes a similar argument and provides additional references in *The Georgic Revolution in Seventeenth-Century English Literature* (Princeton, 1985), pp. 117–54.

31. See, for examples, Christopher Hill, *The World Turned Upside Down: Radical Ideas in the English Revolution* (New York, 1972), passim, but esp. pp. 40–5, and "The Agrarian Legislation of the Revolution" in *Puritanism and Revolution: Studies in Interpretation of the English Revolution of the Seventeenth Century* (New York, 1964), pp. 153–96; and Lawrence Stone, *The Causes of the English Revolution, 1529–1642* (New York, 1972), pp. 66–7. For a discussion of the evolution in economic concepts and terminology that accompanies these changes, see Joyce Oldham Appleby, *Economic Thought and Ideology in Seventeenth-Century England* (Princeton, 1978). For a thorough and stimulating discussion of the form of *Paradise Lost* in terms of the ideology of emergent capitalism, see Christopher Kendrick, *Milton: A Study in Ideology and Form* (New York and London, 1986). Kendrick's book, which became available only after the present study was in press, often reaches conclusions similar to my own, although its method is quite different.

32. See Mary Ann Radzinowicz's discussion of this passage in *Toward*

*Samson Agonistes: The Growth of Milton's Mind* (Princeton, 1978), p. 84, and her general discussion of revelation in history, pp. 69–86.

33. William Whitaker, *Holy Scripture, Against the Papists, especially Bellarmine and Stapleton* [Cambridge, 1588], trans. and ed. William Fitzgerald (Cambridge, 1849), pp. 407–8. Georgia Christopher discusses the Reformation tendency to read the Hebrew Scriptures as a continuous, historical narrative and to resist dismembering them into a series of moral illustrations or prefigurations, arguing that Luther came to see "the Old Testament less as a thesaurus of types than as a history deserving close attention in itself. The issue of faith, he held, was the same for the patriarchs as for his contemporaries: man was confronted by God's oracle. Luther's relative deemphasis of typological symbolism in favor of a 'realistic' reading seems to be part of a cultural trend also evident in the interpretation of epic." (*Milton and the Science of the Saints* [Princeton, 1982], p. 4). Where Christopher sees a "deemphasis" of typology, I see a profound revision of types to effect their historical contextualization; however, we both note the same tendency toward a more novelistic or, as she puts it, "realistic" mode of reading.

34. An earlier but analogous case of social pressure resulting in doctrinal innovation is the redefinition of the prohibition of usury in mercantile Italy. *The Merchant of Venice* records the ambiguities of the Christian view of usury in this transitional period.

35. See the discussion of *The Tenure of Kings and Magistrates* in Radzinowicz, *Toward Samson Agonistes,* pp. 76–8.

36. See Balachandra Rajan's comments on the Osiris passage in *Areopagitica* in *The Form of the Unfinished: English Poetics from Spenser to Pound* (Princeton, 1985): "The principle of an evolving consciousness, arising from the consolidations of its own past and putting into a progressively built relationship the eternally present and the historically attained, is brought dramatically into the field of inquiry" (p. 96); and on the historical pressures favoring the Miltonic conception of "the search for truth": "The multiplicity of sects . . . had to be legitimized as a creative ferment out of which was to emerge that reading consensus which is once again held before us as a horizon. The Puritan problem was to construct an intermediate model of the attainment of truth which retreated from absolutism without altogether renouncing it and without capitulating to the relativities of history" (p. 100).

37. *The Faerie Queene,* as a dynastic romance, may be considered as somewhat apart from this national project to produce an English epic,

but Milton's references to Spenser suggest that Milton saw him as within that tradition.

38. See for example the poem to Book II.

39. On the endlessness of Spenser's narrative, see Jonathan Goldberg, *Endlesse Worke: Spenser and the Structures of Discourse* (Baltimore, 1981); and my "Augustine, Spenser, Milton and the Christian Ego," *New Orleans Review* 11 (1984): 9–17.

40. The tension between an increasingly inescapable sense of historical causation and allegory's tendency to reduce temporal progress to spatial pattern may be read in the letter to Raleigh, which prefaced the 1590 edition of *The Faerie Queene*: "For the Methode of a Poet historical is not such, as of an Historiographer. For an Historiographer discourseth of affayres orderly as they were donne, accounting as well the times as the actions, but a Poet thrusteth into the middest, euen where it most concerneth him, and there recoursing to the thinges forepaste, and diuining of things to come, maketh a pleasing Analysis of all. The beginning therefore of my history, if it were to be told by an Historiographer should be the twelfth booke, which is the last . . . " (Edmund Spenser, *The Faerie Queene,* ed. Thomas P. Roche, Jr., with the assistance of C. Patrick O'Donnell, Jr. [New Haven, 1981], pp. 16–17). The nonexistent twelfth book is to recount the assigning of the quests and thus to locate the meaning of the already narrated events in a deferred account of their temporal origin. Milton's approach to the epic requirement of a beginning in medias res is markedly different. Imploring his muse to "say first what *cause /* Mov'd our Grand Parents . . . to fall off / From thir Creator" (I.28–31), he locates the failure of Satan's rebellion as the proximate link in the chain of interlocking causes and effects that form the episodes of his narrative.

41. See for examples Low, *The Georgic Revolution* and William A. Sessions, "Spenser's Georgics," *English Literary Renaissance* 10 (1980): 202–38.

42. Sessions, p. 216.

43. Cf. Roland Barthes's characterization of the epic as a "narrative broken at the functional level but unitary at the actantial level" in "Introduction to the Structural Analysis of Narratives," in *Image Music Text,* trans. Stephen Heath (New York, 1977), p. 104.

44. In his discussion of the mixed genre of *Paradise Lost,* Rajan notes the criticism of Milton for confusing tragic and epic genres that begins with Dryden (pp. 105–10). For an analysis of the rhetoric through which Milton integrates epic and tragic, see "Augustine, Spenser, Milton and the Christian Ego," 15–17. An extended comparison of

the rhetorical procedures of Spenser and Milton will appear in my forthcoming study, *The Story of All Things: The Rhetoric of the Self in Renaissance Poetic Narrative.*

45. Erich Auerbach, "Figura," in *Scenes from the Drama of European Literature* (New York, 1959), p. 47; reissued, with a forward by Paolo Valesio (Minneapolis, 1984).

46. See Section II of this chapter.

## CHAPTER 2

1. For a fuller discussion of the logical implications of tropes in narrative, see my "The Subject of Narrative and the Rhetoric of the Self," *Papers on Language and Literature* 18 (1982): 398–415. Because the nomenclature of rhetorical tropes is a vexed and confusing issue, I want to emphasize that the distinction I offer between metonymic and synecdochic readings of the opening lines of *Paradise Lost* is concerned only with the logical alternatives of difference and resemblance. I specify as varieties of metonymy or irony those tropes that imply the mutual exclusivity or difference of the troped and "literal" terms. Metonymy *(transnominatio)* calls one thing by the name of another. It can only be read as trope when that to which the name is applied is kept separate from the thing "properly" named. Irony is always read against a "literal" reading that it precisely is not. It negates the adequacy of representation to represented. I specify as metaphor or synecdoche tropes that imply the similarity, or even the predicative interchangeability, of the troped and "literal" terms. Synecdoche asserts that what may be predicated of the part may also and automatically be predicated of the whole; it thereby creates a homogenous class of which any integral member contains, in essence, the power of action of the whole. Metaphor asserts that what may be predicated of one term may also and automatically be predicated of the other. The organization of tropes into two logically distinct groups probably begins with the Ramists' attempts to clarify relations between tropes "according to method." It may be seen, for example, in Abraham Fraunce's *The Arcadian Rhetorike:* "There be two kindes of tropes. The first conteineth *Metonymia,* the change of name: and *Ironia,* scoffing or iesting speach: the second comprehendeth a *Metaphore* and *Synecdoche,*" (ed. from the Edition of 1588 by Ethel Seaton, published for the Luttrell Society [Oxford, 1950], p. 4, abbreviations expanded). Fraunce does not specify the reasons for his groupings. For a modern discussion, see Kenneth Burke, "The Four Master Tropes," in *A Grammar of Motives* (Berkeley, 1969), pp. 503–17.

Read as a metonymy, the substitution of "Man's" for "Adam's" disjoins Adam from Man by emphasizing that his disobedience is the cause or origin of Man's disobedience. He is prior to, and the efficient cause of, fallen (disobedient) man. The subsequent appearance of "one greater man," repairs the disjuncture and turns the metonymy of effect for cause into a synecdoche of the member. See Fraunce: "The *Metonymia* of the cause is double, of the efficient, or materiall cause: of the efficient, as when the Autor & inuenter is put for the things by him inuented & found" (p. 4); "The *Metonymia* of the thing caused is when we attribute that to the efficient which is made by the efficient" (p. 7); and: "*Synecdoche* of the part is, when by the part wee meane the whole, and it is either of the member or of the speciall. Of the member, when by one integrall member the whole is signified" (p. 21). Cf. Georgia Christopher's discussion of the use of alternative metaphoric and metonymic readings in Puritan discourse in *Milton and the Science of the Saints* (Princeton, 1982), pp. 125–6.

2. On Milton's transformations of time into space, see Christopher Collins, "Milton's Early Cosmos and the Fall of Mulciber," in *Urbane Milton: The Latin Poetry, Milton Studies* XIX, ed. James A. Freeman and Anthony Low (Pittsburgh, 1984): 37–52.

3. My phenomenology of the satanic subject is shadowed by a psychoanalytic etiology that cannot be developed or accommodated in the main body of my text but will be suggested in the notes. In psychoanalytic terms, one might say of Satan's loss of contact with the material world that, after a narcissistic withdrawal of libido from the father, he regresses to a stage characterized by primary process.

4. Here I would join Jacques Lacan's argument that "the form in which language is expressed itself defines subjectivity. . . . In other words, it refers itself to the discourse of the other [that is, the unconscious]" in *Ecrits: A Selection*, trans. Alan Sheridan (New York, 1977), p. 85. In Lacan's "topography of the unconscious," desire slips along a series of metonymic signs of its repressed object "indicating that it is the connexion between signifier and signifier that permits the elision in which the signifier installs the lack-of-being in the object relation" (*Ecrits: A Selection*, p. 164).

5. See Jack Foley, " 'Sin Not Time': Satan's First Speech in *Paradise Lost*," *ELH* 37 (1970): 38.

6. Cf. Lacan, "I identify myself in language, but only by losing myself in it like an object. What is realized in my history is not the past definite of what was, since it is no more, or even the present perfect of what has been in what I am, but the future anterior of what I shall

have been for what I am in the process of becoming" (*Ecrits: A Se-lection*, p. 86).

7. Cf. Paul Ricoeur's discussion of Augustine's definition of the experience of time as a *distentio animi* (*Confessions* XI) in *Time and Narrative*, vol. 1, trans. Kathleen McLaughlin and David Pellauer (Chicago, 1984), pp. 5–30.

8. See Chapter 6, Section ii in this book.

9. The OED records no uses of "subject," in the modern philosophical sense, "for the mind or ego considered as the subject of all knowledge" before the eighteenth century, but cites transitional uses from 1682 and 1697. The change in the use of the word "subject" is only one indicator of a general shift toward understanding the self or mind as an interior space in which exterior objects are known, a conception that is already clear in the Cartesian "cogito." Anne Ferry provides a detailed account of the development of an English vocabulary with which to express the notion of the self as an interior space in *The "Inward" Language: Sonnets of Wyatt, Sidney, Shakespeare, Donne* (Chicago, 1983).

10. I am indebted to my student, Tom Waite, for his suggestion that there is a curious resemblance between Beelzebub and Milton's contemporary, Descartes. I do not presume that this relationship was intended, but one might consider that Milton's epic supplies a social dialectic that is the horizon of Cartesian self-certainty.

11. A view taken by A. J. A. Waldock, *Paradise Lost and its Critics* (New York, 1947), p. 83.

12. Lacan's theory of the "mirror stage" grounds the ego and aggression in the dialectic of appropriation and alienation that accompanies the discovery of the self as image and the perceived need to protect the image from appropriation by another: "This moment in which the mirror-stage comes to an end inaugurates, by the identification with the *imago* of the counterpart and the drama of primordial jealousy . . . , the dialectic that will henceforth link the *I* to socially elaborated situations" (*Ecrits: A Selection*, p. 5). The "primordial jealousy" of Satan for the Father could well serve as the mythological narrative of which Lacan's genesis of the ego is the theoretical counterpart. Insofar as Lacan's mirror stage partially displaces Freud's more social "myth" (the term is Freud's own) of the emergence of the ego after the rebellion of the brothers against the father of the primal horde, one suspects it is. (See *Group Psychology and the Analysis of the Ego* in *The Standard Edition of the Complete Works of Sigmund Freud*, ed. and trans. James Strachey and Anna Freud [London, 1957], XVIII, pp.

135–6. Hereafter cited as *SE*.) Milton's narrative thus leads to a digression on Lacan's resituating of the ego – away from Freud's social anthropology and toward the Christian story of precreation.

13. For a discussion of the logical implications of irony, see my "The Narrative of the Subject and the Rhetoric of the Self," 410, and "Hayden White and Literary Criticism: The Tropology of Discourse," *Papers on Language and Literature* 17 (1981): 430–3.

14. But Cf. Andrew Milner's discussion of Lukács in *John Milton and the English Revolution: A Study in the Sociology of Literature* (London, 1981), pp. 14–17, 23–37. Milner's objections to Lukács pertain more to his prescriptiveness and his notion of class consciousness than to his distinction between realism and modernism. Leopold Damrosch, Jr., discusses Milton's narrative in relation to Lukács's earlier (Hegelian) *Theory of the Novel* in *God's Plot and Man's Stories: Studies in the Fictional Imagination from Milton to Fielding* (Chicago, 1985), pp. 13–15, 78. Damrosch argues that "*Paradise Lost* stands poised between myth and novel because of its double focus: Adam and Eve are novelistic while the narrator is prophetic. Or more accurately, Adam and Eve *become* novelistic, and it is precisely that transition – from prelapsarian unity to postlapsarian dividedness – that embodies Milton's explanation of the origin of evil" (120). His argument converges with mine at some points, especially with respect to the consciousness of Satan.

15. Lukács, *Realism in Our Time: Literature and the Class Struggle,* trans. John and Necke Mander (New York, 1971), p. 22.

16. Ibid.

17. Cf. Damrosch, p. 94; Frank Kermode, *Romantic Image* (New York, 1957), pp. 138–62; and Herman Rapaport, *Milton and the Postmodern* (Lincoln, Neb., 1983), pp. 168–207.

18. The deprecation of warlike heroism by its unsavory origins has been noted by many Miltonists, notably John M. Steadman in *Milton and The Renaissance Hero* (Oxford, 1967).

19. For a discussion of "conversation" and the "collateral love" that is the antithesis of Satan's "exorbitant desires," see Chapter 5, Section iii in this book.

20. Cf. R. A. Shoaf's discussion of narcissism, "proof," and confusion in *Milton, Poet of Duality: A Study of Semiosis in the Poetry and Prose* (New Haven, 1985), pp. 129–31, 144–53.

21. On this and other proleptic similes, see James Whaler, "The Miltonic Simile," *PMLA* 46 (1931): 1034–74, and "Animal Simile in *Paradise Lost,*" *PMLA* 47 (1932): 534–53.

22. On Milton's strategic use of "seems," see Julia M. Walker, " 'For each seem'd either': Free Will and Predestination in *Paradise Lost*," *Milton Quarterly* 20 (March 1986): 13–16.

23. On the Homeric and Vergilian origins and implications of the bee simile, see Davis P. Harding, *The Club of Hercules: Studies in the Classical Background of Paradise Lost* (Urbana, Ill., 1962), pp. 103–8; and James A. Freeman, *Milton and the Martial Muse: Paradise Lost and European Traditions of War* (Princeton, 1980), pp. 186–99.

24. See Augustine, *De Civitate Dei*, 2, ii; and Milton, *CP*.VI.478.

25. William Empson, *Milton's God*, rev. ed. (London, 1965), p. 57n.

26. Cf. Arnold Stein's remarks on Milton's use of sources in contexts that are supposed to predate them in *The Art of Presence: The Poet and Paradise Lost* (Berkeley, 1977), pp. 32, 87–9.

27. On Milton's use of Hesiod's version of the cephalic birth of Athena, see Philip Gallagher, " 'Real or Allegoric': The Ontology of Sin and Death in *Paradise Lost*," *English Literary Renaissance* 6 (1976): 317–35, esp. 332–4.

28. The significance of Sin as the origin of wordplay and the loss of the presence of the thing that occurs with substitution for it of the sign is noted in Rapaport, p. 26, in Maureen Quilligan's *Milton's Spenser: The Politics of Reading* (Ithaca, N.Y., 1983), pp. 85 n. 5, 92; and in Shoaf, pp. 23–4 and passim.

29. Quilligan, *Milton's Spenser*, pp. 85–6.

30. Ibid., p. 86.

31. On uncreation and narcissism, see Joseph Summers, *The Muses' Method: An Introduction to Paradise Lost* (Cambridge, Mass., 1970), pp. 88–9; and Michael Lieb, *The Dialectics of Creation: Patterns of Birth and Regeneration in Paradise Lost* (Amherst, Mass., 1970), pp. 142–60.

32. Summers, *The Muses' Method*, pp. 46, 48.

### CHAPTER 3

1. On the problem of portraying God in heaven, see Leland Ryken, *The Apocalyptic Vision in Paradise Lost* (Ithaca, N.Y., 1970), p. 132.

2. Critics have often noted the absence of a sustained and direct treatment of the crucifixion from Milton's work. For a review of the relevant literature and a discussion of the relationship of the absence of the Passion in Milton's poetry to problems of narration, see my " 'In Pensive trance and anguish and ecstatick fit': Milton on the Passion," in *A Fine Tuning: Sharpening Perceptions of Seventeenth-Century Theological Poetry*, ed. Mary T. Maleski (Columbia, Mo., in press).

3. Noting that although the Father and Son are clearly differentiated in Book III, they are never differentiated outside the boundaries of heaven, C. A. Patrides concludes that "the distinction was introduced by Milton for dramatic purposes, although in the end it is the one God with whom he is concerned." "The Godhead in *Paradise Lost: Dogma or Drama?" JEGP* 64 (1965): 32; repr. in W. B. Hunter, C. A. Patrides, J. H. Adamson, *Bright Essence: Studies in Milton's Theology* (Salt Lake City, 1971).

4. References for this view include: John Peter, *A Critique of Paradise Lost* (New York and London, 1960), p. 18; J. B. Broadbent, *Some Graver Subject: An Essay on Paradise Lost* (New York, 1967), pp. 144–57; William Empson, *Milton's God*, rev. ed. (London, 1965), passim; and A. J. A. Waldock, *Paradise Lost and its Critics* (Cambridge, 1947), pp. 97–118. Even Milton's staunchest defenders have expressed difficulty with his presentation of the Father. See, for examples, Douglas Bush, *Paradise Lost in our Time* (Ithaca, N.Y., 1945), p. 43; C. S. Lewis, *A Preface to Paradise Lost* (New York, 1962), pp. 130–1; C. A. Patrides, *Milton and the Christian Tradition* (Oxford, 1966), pp. 156–8. Milton's God is defended in Irene Samuel, "The Dialogue in Heaven: A Reconsideration of *Paradise Lost,* III.1–417," *PMLA* 72 (1957): 601–11; and Anthony Low, "Milton's God: Authority in *Paradise Lost,*" *Milton Studies* IV, ed. James D. Simmonds (Pittsburgh, 1972), pp. 19–38.

5. Frank Kermode, "Adam Unparadised," in *The Living Milton* (London, 1960), p. 91.

6. Stanley Fish, *Surprised by Sin: The Reader in Paradise Lost* (New York, 1967), p. 83.

7. See Milton's discussion of the Father in *The Christian Doctrine, CP.*VI.133–52, especially his insistence on accepting as literal, rather than anthropomorphic, the revelations of God's form in Scripture (136) and on the impossibility of defining the Father's essence: "Since it has no causes, we cannot define the 'divine nature'. . . . But though God, by his very nature, transcends everything, including definition, some description of him may be gathered from his names and attributes" (137–8).

8. The best discussion of the Platonic and Neoplatonic traditions relevant to Milton's presentation of the Trinity is William B. Hunter, Jr., "Milton's Arianism Reconsidered," *Harvard Theological Review* 52 (1959): 8–35; repr. in *Bright Essence*, pp. 29–51.

9. See, for examples, Albert Cirillo, " 'Hail Holy Light' and Divine Time in *Paradise Lost," JEGP* 68 (1969): 45–56; Merritt Y. Hughes,

"Milton and the Symbol of Light," in *Ten Perspectives on Milton* (New Haven and London, 1965), pp. 98–104; William B. Hunter, Jr., "The Meaning of Holy Light in *Paradise Lost*," *MLN* 74 (1959): 580–92, rev. and repr. in expanded form in *Bright Essence* as "Milton's Muse"; and Maurice Kelly, *This Great Argument: A Study of Milton's De Doctrina Chistiana as a Gloss upon Paradise Lost* (Gloucester, Mass., 1962), p. 94.

10. The Fourth Gospel provides the necessary scriptural warrant. Arguments for identifying the Son as the addressee of all the invocations appear in Hunter, "The Meaning of Holy Light in *Paradise Lost*." Cf. Kerrigan's argument in *The Sacred Complex: On the Psychogenesis of Paradise Lost* (Cambridge, Mass., 1983), pp. 149–53. Kerrigan identifies the three common critical positions on the invocation to holy light – that the light invoked is the light of Genesis 1:3, that it is the Son, and that it is the Holy Spirit – and raises significant objections to each, concluding that holy light symbolizes "what becomes of orthodoxy's Holy Spirit after Milton has disassembled the triune Godhead and erected in its place his own dyad of uncreated Father and created Son" (150). The rhetorical ground is that of my larger argument – that the foundation of Milton's speculative theology remains poetic metaphor and that the Son and Father are dialectically linked by this trope and its inherent bias toward the orthodox view that the Holy Spirit *proceeds* from the love of Father and Son. Kerrigan's analysis of Milton's revision of the Holy Spirit supplies a psychogenetic ontology for Milton's method of incorporating this rhetorical effect into the narrative line of his poem.

11. See Jacques Derrida, "White Mythology," *New Literary History* 6 (1974): 68: "When we search for metaphor, what could we find *other* than this return to the same? For are we not searching for resemblance? And when we try to determine the *dominant* metaphor of a group which interests us because of its capacity to gather things together, thus what else should we expect but the metaphor of domination augmented by that power of dissimulation which allows it to escape domination in its turn, what else but God or the Sun?"

12. C. A. Patrides, "Milton and the Arian Controversy," *Proceedings of the American Philosophical Society* 120 (1976): 245–52.

13. St. Athanasius, *Against the Arians,* II, 33 in *Nicene and Post-Nicene Fathers,* trans. Cardinal Newman, 2d Series (Oxford, 1892), p. 4. Patrides's discussion of this passage appears in "Milton and the Arian Controversy," p. 208.

14. The contentious debate on the nature of Milton's antitrinitarianism

seems to me to neglect the philological bases of his arguments. Milton's understanding of the Godhead is quite literally a matter of words. See my " 'In Pensive trance and anguish and ecstatick fit': Milton on the Passion."

15. See Paul Ricoeur, *The Rule of Metaphor,* trans. Robert Czerny with Kathleen McLaughlin and John Costello, S.J. (Toronto, 1977), p. 292; and the discussion of speculation in Chapter 8 of this book.

16. See Ryken, *The Apocalyptic Vision,* p. 39.

17. St. Thomas Aquinas, *Summa theologiae* (Ia, qu. 13, art. 6), ed. and trans. Herbert McCabe, O.P. (Latin Text and English Translation) (New York, 1963), 3:71.

18. Empson, *Milton's God,* p. 119.

19. Anthony Low, *The Blaze of Noon* (New York, 1974), p. 24.

20. On the relationship of sequence to consequence in narrative, see Roland Barthes, "Introduction to the Structural Analysis of Narratives," in *Image Music Text,* trans. Stephen Heath (New York, 1977), pp. 97–104.

21. See Samuel, "The Dialogue in Heaven," p.603.

22. See Chapter 1, Section i.

23. Cf. Milton's moving use of the same metaphor in his last sonnet – "Love, sweetness, goodness in her person shin'd" – and his missing of the "human face divine" in the invocation to light (III.44) and the sonnet on his blindness (XXII).

24. Cf. *Paradise Lost* VII.163–73.

25. See note 17 above.

26. Empson, *Milton's God,* p. 120.

27. Ibid.

28. Cf. Hegel's dialectic of the unhappy consciousness, *Phenomenology of the Spirit,* trans. A. V. Miller, with analysis of the text and foreword by J. N. Findlay (Oxford, 1979): "Thus there exist for consciousness three different ways in which individuality is linked with the Unchangeable. Firstly, it again appears to itself as opposed to the Unchangeable, and is thrown back to the beginning of the struggle which is throughout the element in which the whole relationship subsists. Secondly, consciousness learns that individuality belongs to the Unchangeable itself, so that it assumes the form of individuality into which the entire mode of existence passes. Thirdly, it finds its own self as this particular individual in the Unchangeable. The first Unchangeable it knows only as the alien Being who passes judgement on the particular individual; since, secondly, the Unchangeable is a

form of individuality like itself, consciousness becomes, thirdly, Spirit, and experiences the joy of finding itself therein, and becomes aware of the reconciliation of its individuality with the universal" (p. 128).

29. See Kerrigan, *The Sacred Complex,* p. 151.

30. J. B. Leishman, *The Monarch of Wit: Analytical and Comparative Study of the the Poetry of John Donne* (London, 1951), p. 121.

31. The process Milton depicts anticipates Freud's theory of the resolution of the Oedipal complex through the introjection of the Father as ego-ideal and the displacement of the heroic from the temporally situated world of actions to the atemporal world of fantasy. See *Group Psychology and the Analysis of the Ego, SE,* XVIII, pp. 135–6 and my discussion of the relevant passages in "The Subject of Narrative and the Rhetoric of the Self," 411–12. Lacan's rewriting of Oedipal resolution as the acquisition of the name of the Father and the gaining of access to the signifier of the self in the discourse of signs is even closer to Milton's language. The scepter allows the Son to act in the name of the Father. The apocalyptic identification of Father and Sons suggests the infinitely deferred fulfillment of Oedipal desire (displaced into an appropriate object after a latency period envisaged by Milton as human history). The "subjection" of the angels to the Son, which precipitates Satan's rebellion, may be understood as the primal repression through which the Son surrenders the object of desire so as to gain access to its signs.

32. We may here recall the homophony of *nom* and *non* exploited by Lacan when he refers to Oedipal resolution as acquisition of the *nom du pere.*

33. See Frank L. Huntley, "A Justification of Milton's 'Paradise of Fools' (*Paradise Lost* III. 437–99)," *ELH* 21 (1954): 109.

CHAPTER 4

1. Cf. Hegel's description of work as the negation of the object and its appropriation for self-consciousness in the dialectic of Lordship and Bondage, *Phenomenology of the Spirit,* trans. A. V. Miller (Oxford, 1979), pp. 117–19. The importance of propagation is discussed in Section IV of this chapter.

2. The tasks of procreation and gardening are assigned by the biblical commands to "be fruitful and multiply" so as to "replenish and subdue" the earth (Gen. 1:27) and to "dress and keep" the garden (Gen. 2:15). For the exegetical tradition with respect to Gen. 2:15 and the divine requirement that man work, see Diane Kelsey McColley, *Mil-*

ton's Eve (Urbana, Ill., 1983), pp. 121–3; and Anthony Low, *The Georgic Revolution in Seventeenth-Century English Literature* (Princeton, 1985), pp. 155–220.

3. J. B. Broadbent notes that "the characters of *Paradise Lost* do not soliloquize until they have fallen" in *Some Graver Subject: An Essay on Paradise Lost* (New York, 1967), p. 80.

4. John Peter apparently fails to notice this realization of Satan's when he accuses Milton of unfairly causing Satan to abandon "his habitual disregard of facts" by acquiescing to the sign of the scales at the conclusion of Book IV (1.1013–15). Then, as in his address to the Sun, Satan directly confronts absolute truth, and finds that defiance in the light is more difficult than in the "darkness visible" of hell. Satan is consistent: In direct confrontation with God's works he is evasive, not defiant. See Peter, *A Critique of Paradise Lost* (New York, 1960), p. 55. Similarly, Waldock's claim that the Satan who appears in Book IV is a "new Satan" unrelated to the character of that name in Books I and II fails to recognize the underlying process of rationalization that begins with Satan's exposure to creation. See A. J. A. Waldock, *Paradise Lost and its Critics* (New York and Cambridge, 1947), p. 82.

5. Cf. Book I.105–24.

6. See *CP*.VI.305–11 for Milton's argument that God created the universe out of his own substance.

7. See Chapter 1, Section ii of this book, and Tzvetan Todorov, *The Poetics of Prose,* trans. Richard Howard (Ithaca, N.Y., 1977), p. 233.

8. On the sacramental or memorial function of the Trees of Life and Knowledge, see William Ames, *The Marrow of Sacred Divinity, Drawne Out of The holy Scripture, and the Interpreters thereof, and brought into Method* (London, 1642), p. 48; John Calvin, *Institutes of the Christian Religion* (Philadelphia, 1936), bk. 4, chap. 14, par. 12, and Philo Judaeus, *Works in Ten Volumes,* trans. F. H. Colson and G. H. Whitaker, Loeb Classical Library (London, 1929), I, p. 123.

9. Water was a frequent emblem of divine circulation. See, for examples, Henry Vaughan's "The Morning-watch" and Andrew Marvell's "On a Drop of Dew."

10. For historical surveys of Eden and the Golden Age in literature, see A. Bartlett Giamatti, *The Earthly Paradise and the Renaissance Epic* (Princeton, 1966); and Harry Levin, *The Myth of the Golden Age in the Renaissance* (Bloomington, Ind., 1969). From a psychoanalytic perspective, the myth of the Golden Age might be considered a displaced fantasy of the unmediated self before the formation of the ego, which is necessarily purchased at the price of a constitutive alienation:

the symbolic castration of the latency period and the introjection of
the father as an image to which the self must aspire. The Golden Age
would then be the social projection of the pre-Oedipal unity with the
nourishing mother, a possibility that bears on the maternal conception
of Eve developed in this chapter.

11. The classic work on the experience of reading *Paradise Lost* remains
Stanley Fish's *Surprised by Sin: The Reader in Paradise Lost* (New York,
1967). See also, Robert Crosman, *Reading Paradise Lost* (Bloomington,
Ind., 1980).

12. See Fish, *Surprised by Sin,* pp. 142–57; and Christopher Ricks, *Milton's
Grand Style* (Oxford, 1963), pp. 109–17.

13. Cf. Dennis H. Burden, *The Logical Epic: A Study of the Argument of
Paradise Lost* (London, 1967), pp. 49–50.

14. William G. Riggs's remarks on prelapsarian curiosity are relevant:
"The pursuit of knowledge in Eden involves fundamentally a matter
of intention: the proper end of curiosity is the glorification of God
not man. Man is asked, in the midst of the exhilaration of an expanding
consciousness, to rejoice in personal limitation, hierarchical inferiority,
and infinite debt for all he surveys. He is asked to respond to an
increasing awareness of his own powers with an increasing reverence
for powers not his own. . . . At the heart of Milton's vision of Eden
lies the painful realization that just such tensions – not their resolution
– define the character of our lives" (*The Christian Poet in Paradise Lost*
[Berkeley, 1972], p. 61).

15. See Burden, *The Logical Epic,* pp. 82–4. For an extended discussion
of the allusion to Narcissus, with a full review of the literature, see
McColley, *Milton's Eve,* pp. 74–85. Cleanth Brooks suggests that the
transfer of Eve's affections from her image in the pool to Adam "recapitulates the whole process of the child's growing up and transferring
the affections to the other sex,"Eve's Awakening," in *Essays in Honor
of Walter Clyde Curry* (Nashville, 1954), p. 285. Giamatti considers
the allusion to the tale of Narcissus (Ovid's *Metamorphoses,* III, ll.
402–510) in lines 460–91 an "overt suggestion of narcissism" intended
"not to lessen our immediate estimate of Eve so much as to provide
a repository of doubt for later exploitation," in *The Earthly Garden,*
pp. 315–23. Between them Brooks and Giamatti provide the prospective and retrospective readings of the event that are joined in Milton's text. It should be remembered, however, that Eve obeys the
exterior voice; the voice ignored by Narcissus is that of *Echo.* The
dialectic of self and other is implicit in the poles of Eve's resemblance
to *and difference from* Narcissus. It is also worth recalling in this context

the odd fact that when the Lady of Milton's *Mask* invokes the aid of *Echo,* it is Comus who appears (II.230–45).

16. William Kerrigan's explanation of the transfer of Eve's affection from her image in the pool to Adam advances the discussion of narcissism from an Ovidian to a Freudian context: "A divine voice interrupts the reverie of Eve. She must love, not an image of herself, but 'hee / Whose image thou art' (IV.471–2) – a directive that substitutes Adam for the image in the pool by identifying Eve as the living image of her beloved. Her entrancement with her form is transferred, as it were, to Adam, lifting the figure reflected in the mirror of narcissism into the higher dialectics of mutual love" (*The Sacred Complex: On the Psychogenesis of Paradise Lost* [Cambridge, Mass., 1983], p. 70). The move from Ovid to Freud performs the temporalization that is the theme of my argument, for what had been a mortal entrapment of Narcissus may now be rewritten as a stage in the ontology of the normal personality.

17. In Freud's discussion of the turn from the self to another, propagation is explicitly the point: "The individual does actually carry on a twofold existence: one to serve his own purposes and the other as a link in a chain, which he serves against his will, or at least involuntarily. The individual himself regards sexuality as one of his own ends; whereas from another point of view he is an appendage to his germplasm, at whose disposal he puts his energies in return for a bonus of pleasure. He is the mortal vehicle of a (possibly) immortal substance – like the inheritor of an entailed property, who is only the temporary holder of an estate which survives him. The separation of the sexual instincts from the ego instincts would simply reflect this two-fold function of the individual." "On Narcissism: An Introduction," *SE,* XIV, p. 78. The alignment of Freud's text and our discussion of Eve is not without discomfort. His use of the masculine pronoun separates him from our discussion of Eve, underlining one of the limitations of his discourse. Moreover, unfallen Eve does not act involuntarily; but the picture of a self turned at once toward itself and its progeny, as well as the notion of an "entailed property" are clearly present in *Paradise Lost.* It may also be noted that the male-initiated, self-serving desire Freud describes appears in Milton's Adam, moments after the fall (IX.1017–33).

18. This structure is further defined by Adam's desire for "collateral love" when he retells the story of Eve's creation in Book VIII. See Chap. 5, Section III in this book.

19. On the return of the Logos to itself in the form of collective prayer, see Augustine, *Confessions*, XIII, chap. 23; and the understanding of the angelic chorus that Adam and Eve are to "multiply a Race of Worshippers" (*Paradise Lost* VII.630).
20. On "seed," see Kathleen M. Swaim, "Flower, Fruit, and Seed: A Reading of *Paradise Lost*," in *Milton Studies* V, ed. James Simmonds (Pittsburgh, 1973), pp. 155–76.
21. Cf. McColley, *Milton's Eve*, p. 82. On creation *ex deo*, see C. A. Patrides, *Milton and the Christian Tradition* (Oxford, 1966), pp. 32–3; J. H. Adamson, "The Creation," in *Bright Essence: Studies in Milton's Theology* (Salt Lake City, 1973), pp. 81–102; and Maurice Kelley's introduction to the *Christian Doctrine, CP*.VI.87–90.
22. Cf. James Earl's argument – in his stimulating article, "Eve's Narcissism," *Milton Quarterly* 19 (March 1985) – that because "Adam is not an image of [Eve] – just as God is not an image of Adam, though Adam is an image of God, . . . Adam is not an appropriate symbol of [Eve's] self. In fact, he can only symbolize to her her own insufficiency. One day she will find the true image of herself, in her children, and she will experience then that narcissistic fulfillment which a man finds first in his mother and then finds restored to him in his wife, and which a woman also finds first in her mother and then again in her baby" (16).

CHAPTER 5

1. J. B. Broadbent, *Some Graver Subject: An Essay on Paradise Lost* (New York, 1967), p. 202.
2. See Thomas Kranidas, "Adam and Eve in the Garden: A Study of *Paradise Lost*, Book V," *Studies in English Literature* 4 (1964): 72–3.
3. For the theological background of Raphael's statement, see Walter Clyde Curry, *Milton's Ontology, Cosmogony and Physics* (Lexington, Ky., 1957), pp. 160–77; and Robert H. West, *Milton and the Angels* (Athens, Ga., 1955), pp. 164–9.
4. The propensity of evil for stubborn repetition is further dramatized by the devils' decision to continue the fight against God after they concede that God is "almighty" (I.105–24, 139–55), the quick healing of Satan after he is wounded by Michael (VI.344), and the appeal of the satanic legions to "more valid Arms" after their first failure in battle against the loyal angels (VI.430–45).
5. See Chapter 1 in this book, Section III and note 25.

6. See, for example, Richard Baxter, *The Saints Everlasting Rest* (London, 1650): "Heretikes may seem holy for a little while, but at last all false doctrines likely end in wicked lives" ("The Dedication of the Whole," n.p.). On the educational purpose of the angelic discourse, see George Williamson, "The Education of Adam," *Modern Philology* 61 (1963): 96–109. I agree with Williamson's conclusions but wish to illustrate here the poetic and thematic need for the specifically narrative-dramatic presentation of the discourse and its implications for Adam and the reader.

7. A similar argument is made by Philip Gallagher in "The Role of Raphael in *Samson Agonistes*," in *Milton Studies* XVIII, ed. James Simmonds (Pittsburgh, 1983), pp. 255–94.

8. See Thucydides: "As to the speeches that were made by different men, either as they were about to begin the war or when they were engaged therein, it has been difficult to recall with strict accuracy the words actually spoken, both for me as regards that which I myself heard, and for those who from various other sources have brought me reports. Therefore the speeches are given in the language which, as it seemed to me, the several speakers would express, on the subjects under consideration, the sentiments most befitting the occasion, though at the same time I have adhered as closely as possible to the general sense of what was actually said." (Quoted from the translation of Charles Forster Smith [Cambridge, Mass., 1919, rev. and repr. 1929], I, p. 39.) Milton's rejection of this method for his "History of Britain" is discussed by Irene Samuel in "Milton and the Ancients on the Writing of History," *Milton Studies* II, ed. James Simmonds (Pittsburgh, 1970), pp. 143–4. See also Nancy S. Struever, *The Language of History in the Renaissance: Rhetoric and Historical Consciousness in Florentine Humanism* (Princeton, 1970), p. 19: "Thucydidian learning is historical on two levels: It pertains to the phenomenal world of flux and it takes place within the development of the learner's own identity. . . . Thucydides saw the historian's task as to *imitate* dialogue, particularly where dialogue in historical fact was obscure or even lacking." Struever traces the revival of Thucydidian rhetoric by the Renaissance humanists and relates it to their experience of oratory in practical politics as representatives of their city-states. Milton's political career would have acquainted him with the style and its uses.

9. The connection of hypocrisy and temporality is also implicit in Satan's momentarily successful deception of Uriel in Book III: "For neither Man nor Angel can discern / Hypocrisy, the only evil that walks / Invisible, except to God alone" (682–4). The dissimulation unravels

when Uriel spies the succession of inward passions manifested in Satan's rapidly changing facial expressions (IV. 114–30). On the growing recognition in the Renaissance of the distinction between a private "real" self and a crafted public self, see Stephen Greenblatt, *Renaissance Self-Fashioning: From More to Shakespeare* (Chicago, 1980).

10. On Raphael's didactic use of the Abdiel episode, see Mason Tung, "The Abdiel Epsiode: A Contextual Reading," *Studies in Philology* 62 (1965): 595–609.

11. Milton follows Augustine (*Christian Doctrine*, III, 15, 23) in arguing that one should always prefer the sense of scripture consonant with God's charity. Thus charity becomes a hermeneutic guide to the meaning not only of scriptural passages but – through the typological prolepsis – lived experience. See *CP.VI.*533. On Milton's observance of "the rule of charity," see Theodore L. Huguelet, "The Rule of Charity in Milton's Divorce Tracts," in *Milton Studies* VI, ed. James Simmonds (Pittsburgh, 1974), pp. 199–214.

12. Cf. Michael Lieb, *The Dialectics of Creation: Patterns of Birth and Regeneration in Paradise Lost* (Amherst, Mass., 1970), pp. 18–19; and Arnold Stein, *Answerable Style: Essays on Paradise Lost* (Minneapolis, 1953), p. 32.

13. William Riggs argues in *The Christian Hero in Paradise Lost* (Berkeley, 1972) that the war in heaven is not mock but "mocked heroic in which the poetic manner is intentionally depreciated by its inability to answer adequately the demands of a heavenly subject" (p. 120). A similar view is expressed by Louis L. Martz in *Poet of Exile: A Study of Milton's Poetry* (New Haven, 1980), p. 210. But the effect of Raphael's heroic narrative is quite otherwise if we take note of the angelic narrator's implication in it – that is, of Raphael's own evident excitement. Furthermore, an ironic genre parody would be a peculiar choice of vehicle for Raphael's task of communicating a present danger to the generically ignorant Adam.

14. Thus Milton Miller correctly notes the "curious lack of differentiation" between good and rebel angels in the "matter of the passions aroused by battle" in "*Paradise Lost:* The Double Standard," *University of Toronto Quarterly* 20 (1951): 191. James G. Mengert argues in " 'Styling the Strife of Glory': The War in Heaven," *Milton Studies* XIV, ed. James Simmonds (Pittsburgh, 1980) that "Milton's procedure signals the end of both the heroic and the allegorical traditions. For the former is predicated on the physical itself as a value, while the latter is predicated on the ability of physical activity and things to adumbrate 'corresponding' spiritual and psychological values. What is at stake, fun-

damentally, is the analogical universe. . . . Milton is part of the tradition because he does, after all, use the battle to convey a spiritual meaning. He is the last of that tradition because his meaning is that spiritual meaning has no necessary correspondence to the vehicle used to convey it" (p. 103). In my view, what Milton does is less to demolish the analogical universe than to contextualize it, to show that actions in time have variable symbolic values that depend on a variety of factors, including occasion and intention. If he ends an allegorical tradition, it is because his contextualized and temporalized allegory turns out to be what might be called "realism." It might further be noted that Milton's shift of allegorical correspondence from the timeless to that which is worked out in varying historical contexts accords with the reformation's preference for a historicizing typological hermeneutics.

15. John Steadman, *Milton and the Renaissance Hero* (Oxford, 1967), p. 31.

16. Romans 12 is generally relevant to Milton's presentation of the war in heaven. Verses 3–6 bear especially on the condition of the angels under the Son's "great Vice-gerent Reign" (V.609). Cf. *Paradise Lost* V.831–45.

17. John Calvin, *On the Epistle of Paul the Apostle to the Romans,* trans. and ed. John Owen (Edinburgh, 1849), pp. 473–4 (my emphasis).

18. Ibid., pp. 472–3. The Pauline concept of "standing" is discussed in reference to Milton's war in heaven by Michael Lieb in *The Poetics of the Holy: A Reading of Paradise Lost* (Chapel Hill, N.C., 1981), p. 301.

19. See Matt. 17, Mark 9, Luke 9. Cf. *Paradise Lost* XII.441–5.

20. Milton, in providing a narration of the war in heaven, puts himself (or, within his fiction, Raphael) in the position of one who fills a gap in history, and he assures verisimilitude by structuring his account according to a biblical analogue. See William Nelson, *Fact or Fiction: The Dilemma of the Renaissance Storyteller* (Cambridge, Mass., 1973), p. 93 and the discussion of Raleigh on p. 43. See also James H. Sims, "The Miltonic Narrator and Scriptural Tradition: An Afterword," in *Milton and the Scriptural Tradition: The Bible into Poetry,* ed. James H. Sims and Leland Ryken (Columbia, Mo., 1984), pp. 192–205.

21. See, for examples, the Son's anticipation of the Father's reconciliation of mercy and justice (III.144–66), and the Father's reply (III.171–2). The Son's ability to anticipate his own resurrection and that of redeemed mankind from his knowledge of the Father's nature (III.245–65) recalls Abdiel's application of deductive logic to grasp the good

intention behind the Son's exaltation and its divinely ordained outcome (V.822–30).

22. Calvin, *Institutes of the Christian Religion,* Bk. I, Chap. 1, Par. 17, trans. John Allen (Philadelphia, 1936), I p. 233.

23. See Geoffrey Hartman, "Adam on the Grass with Balsamum," *ELH* 36 (1969) 168–92.

24. A considerable literature has developed around Milton's insistence on the physiological materiality of angelic digestion, the dramatic function of the meal shared in Eden, and the symbolic communion of Earth and heaven it implies. Curry provides the theological background and indicates the function of the scene in relating physical to spiritual digestion: "[Milton] observes that man is able by vital processes to sublimate the fruit of trees to sensitive and animal spirits, thence to intellectual, whence the soul receives discursive reason. And since angels differ from man in degree of perfection only and not in kind, they too are able to receive gross nutriment and convert it to their proper substance. These considerations lead to the conclusion that in time the purified spirits of men may achieve the conversion of their crass bodies into an ethereal substance like that which is formed in the bodies of angels" (*Milton's Ontology, Cosmogony and Physics,* pp. 170–1). The dramatic function of the meal is treated by Anthony Low in "Angels and Food in *Paradise Lost,*" *Milton Studies* I, ed. James Simmonds (1969), pp. 135–45; and by Thomas Kranidas in "Adam and Eve in the Garden: A Study of *Paradise Lost,* Book V," *Studies in English Literature* 4 (1964): 71–83. Neither Low nor Kranidas integrates the angelic "transubstantiation" into the metaphor of eating that Milton exploits as a vehicle for his epistemology throughout the poem. Jack Goldman argues in "Perspectives of Raphael's Meal in *Paradise Lost,* Book V," *Milton Quarterly* 11 (1977): 31–7, that the meal of Abraham and the angels in Genesis 18 is the source of the scene in *Paradise Lost.* Goldman's connection of this scene to the Hebrew sacrifice strengthens my own conclusion that the meal in *Paradise Lost* V is a prelapsarian communion.

25. See Chapter 3 in this book, Section II.

26. Calvin, *Institutes* (Bk. IV, Chap. 14, Par. 16), vol. II, p. 571.

27. For a summary of the various positions taken by Milton's contemporaries with respect to the nature of the sacrament, see Horton Davies, *The Worship of the English Puritans* (Westminster, 1948), p. 213.

28. *Savoy Declaration,* Chap. 39, Sec. 7, cited in Davies, *The Worship of the English Puritans,* p. 213.

29. Calvin, *Institutes* (Bk. V, Chap. 14, Par. 4), vol. II, p. 557.

30. Georgia Christopher discusses Calvin's view of the efficacy of sacra-
    mental tropes in *Milton and the Science of the Saints* (Princeton, 1982),
    pp. 120–33.
31. William Ames, *The Marrow of Sacred Divinity, Drawne Out of the holy
    Scriptures, and the Interpreters thereof, and brought into Method* (London,
    1642), pp. 184–5.
32. See Calvin, *Institutes* (Bk. IV, Chap. 14, Par. 12), vol. II, p. 566:
    "Therefore, as by bread and other aliments he feeds our bodies, as
    by the sun he enlightens the world, as by fire he produces warmth,
    – yet bread, the sun, and fire are nothing but instruments by which
    he dispenses his blessings to us, – so he nourishes our faith in a spiritual
    manner by the sacraments, which are instituted for the purpose of
    placing his promises before our eyes for our contemplation, and of
    serving as pledges of them."
33. See for example the definition given in the Ramist rhetoric of Abraham
    Fraunce: "A *Metonymia* of the adiunct, is, when by the adiunct we
    expresse the subiect," in *The Arcadian Rhetoric,* ed. from the edition
    of 1588 by Ethel Seaton, for the Luttrell Society (Oxford, 1950), p.
    9.
34. I should like to express my gratitude to Joan Bennett, whose comments
    on an earlier presentation of this material have contributed to what
    I hope is a more rigorous understanding of the preaching of the gospel
    in Eden.
35. See Ames, *Marrow*, p. 48: "Unto this covenant there were two Sym-
    boles, or Sacraments adjoyned. In one of which the reward due to
    Obedience was sealed by a Tree, namely of Life, and in the other the
    punishment of disobedience was sealed by a Tree, namely of knowl-
    edge of good and evil: that was a Sacrament of Life, this a Sacrament
    of Death." See also Calvin, *Institutes* (Bk. IV, Chap. 14, Par. 12),
    vol. II, p. 565: "Now, it is so true that the sacraments are confirmations
    of our faith, that sometimes, when the Lord intends to take away the
    confidence of those things which had been promised in the sacraments,
    he removes the sacraments themselves. When he deprived Adam of
    the gift of immortality, he expelled him from the garden of Eden,
    saying, 'Lest he put forth his hand, and take also of the tree of life,
    and eat, and live for ever.' What can be the meaning of this language?
    Could the fruit restore to Adam the incorruption from which he had
    now fallen? Certainly not. But it was the same as if the Lord had
    said, Lest he should cherish a vain confidence, if he retain the symbol
    of my promise, let him be deprived of that which might give him
    some hope of immortality." Cf. *Paradise Lost* XI.93–8.

36. Within this framework, we may consider the ritual reenactment of the temptation to which the devils are condemned (X.504–77) as a parody of the ritual of Holy Communion practiced in the Mass, and the transformation of the fruit to ashes as a summary comment on the fate of the Gospel in the hands of the Roman Church.

37. See Chapter 4, Section IV in this book.

38. See Chapter 3, Section III in this book.

39. See Mary Ann Radzinowicz's commentary in *Paradise Lost Books VII–VIII*, ed. David Aers and Mary Ann Radzinowicz (Cambridge, 1974), p. 51; and Joseph Summers, *The Muse's Method: An Introduction to Paradise Lost* (Cambridge, Mass., 1962), p. 147.

40. *OED*, s.v. "converse."

41. See Chapter 4, Section IV in this book.

42. Cf. After the fall, Eve wild efend her self-assertion in the separtion scene with the question: "Was I to have never parted from thy side? / As good have grown there still a lifeless Rib" (IX.1153–4). And Adam wil seek to reduce her to just such a condition: "All but a Rib / Crooked by nature, bent, as now appears, / More to the part sinister from me drawn, / Well if thrown out, as supernumerary / To my just number found" (X.884–8).

CHAPTER 6

1. Christopher Ricks discusses the significant echoes of the invocation to Book I in the opening lines of Book IX in *Milton's Grand Style* (Oxford, 1963), p. 69.

2. Martin Heidegger, *Being and Time,* trans. John Macquarrie and Edward Robinson (New York, 1962), pp. 276–311. For Heidegger, Dasein can only grasp its "possibly *Being-a-whole*" through the horizon of the "something still outstanding" that remains to be experienced. "The 'end' of Being-in-the-world is death. This end, which belongs to the potentiality-for-Being – that is to say, to existence – limits and determines in every case whether totality is possible for Dasein. . . . But as something of the character of Dasein, death *is* only in an existentiell *Being towards death [Sein zum Tode]*. The existential structure of such Being proves to be the ontologically constitutive state of Dasein's potentiality-for-Being-a-whole. Thus the whole existing Dasein allows itself to be brought into our existential fore-having" (pp. 276–7). ("Existentiell" *[existenziell]* understanding is "the understanding of oneself that leads along [the] way" to an understanding of being as such [p. 33]. It is thus a sort of middle voice between analytic

223

[ontological] and merely experiential [ontic] knowledge.) In terms of our discussion of the temporality of narrative, "existentiell *Being towards death*" is analogous to experiencing an episode in a story with conscious reference to the episode's participation in the story's foreknown outcome. For a thorough correlation of Heidegger's categories in the analytic of the temporality of Dasein and the temporality of narrative, see Paul Ricoeur, *Time and Narrative,* vol. 1, trans. Kathleen McLaughlin and David Pellauer (Chicago, 1984), pp. 54–64, and "Narrative Time," *Critical Inquiry* 7(1980): 169–90.

It may be objected that the experience of life as a temporalized progress of discovery whose horizon is death simply situates man within the universal epistemological structure of the hermeneutic circle and that the recognition of this situation is in no way peculiar to Milton. Leaving aside the to me still open question of the universalizability of the hermeneutic circle as a temporal noetic structure, it should be clear that what I am pointing to is the self-conscious *narrative* thematization of the "being toward death" in Milton's text, and that this thematization is historically specified. Milton's narrative presentation of the coming to consciousness of fallen man of and through "being toward death" participates in the historical reenvisaging of subjectivity under the metaphor of authorship that is, in turn, the theme of my argument. In other words, the hermeneutic circle may or may not be a formal feature of subjectivity per se, but its implications are felt and projected differently according to the constraints of a given historical context. To make of Milton a Heideggerean is to enlist and appropriate his name as a type foreshadowing a revelation that will become philosophical only in the twentieth century. To see something Miltonic in Heidegger is to reverse this *nachtraglichkeit* and materialize the typological as genealogical. The typological view is typically formalist, the genealogical view, historicist. By taking them together we approach, however asymptotically, a history of forms that incorporates an awareness of the forms of history.

3. The five-act tragic structure of *Paradise Lost* IX has previously been noted by William Shaw in "Book IX of *Paradise Lost:* The 'Tragedy' of Adam," (Ph.D. diss., Ohio University, 1971).

4. On the relative immediacy of "mimetic" as opposed to "pure" (reported) narrative, see Gérard Genette, *Narrative Discourse: An Essay in Method,* trans. Jane E. Lewin (Ithaca, N.Y., 1980), pp. 161–9. As the marks of the presence of the narrator (in this case by the reduction of the narrator to the role of choral commentator and the elimination of reference to the situation of the narrating) are effaced and the nar-

rative approaches the condition of drama, the disjunction between the time of telling (narration) and the story time (diegesis) is obscured, and the illusion of action subsumes the act of narrating. A parallel argument, with somewhat different emphases and conclusions is made by Mary Nyquist in "Reading the Fall: Discourse in Drama in *Paradise Lost*," *English Literary Renaissance*, 14 (1948): 199–229.

5. *OED*, s.v. "involve."

6. Cf. Jackson I. Cope's suggestion that "the choice of sexuality as the chief image of evil at crucial points in *Paradise Lost* was no personal or merely traditional accident, but perhaps the most important single stroke of unifying genius in the epic," in *The Metaphoric Structure of Paradise Lost* (Baltimore, 1962), p. 80. It may be noted, however, that Milton does not use sexuality per se as an image of evil, but rather the sexuality that executes "exorbitant desire."

7. See the discussion of Eve's fall, Chapter 5, Section II in this book. In Freudian terms, Satan manifests an inability to transfer libido from ego to object (as Eve transfers her narcissistic libido to Adam in Book IV). In his essay "On Narcissism: An Introduction," Freud writes: "The relations of self-regard to eroticism – that is, to libidinal object-cathexes – may be expressed concisely in the following way. Two cases must be distinguished, according to whether the erotic cathexes are ego-syntonic, or, on the contrary, have suffered repression. In the former case (where the use made of the libido is ego-syntonic), love is assessed like any other activity of the ego. Loving in itself, in so far as it involves longing and deprivation, lowers self-regard; whereas being loved, having one's love returned, and possessing the loved object, raises it once more. When libido is repressed, the erotic cathexis is felt as severe depletion of the ego, the satisfaction of love is impossible, and the re-enrichment of the ego can be effected only by a withdrawal of libido from its objects. The return of the object-libido to the ego and its transformation into narcissism represents *[Darstellt]*, as it were, a happy love once more; and, on the other hand, it is also true that a real happy love corresponds to the primal conditions in which object-libido and ego-libido cannot be distinguished" (*SE* XIV, pp. 99–100). The "primal conditions" in Satan's case are those in effect before his fall. When Satan reconceives of himself as "self-begot," he represses desire for a reciprocating love in which his ego would be replenished by a shared father-love devolving through the ranks of angels "more near united" by the mediation of the Son. He preserves his ego by withdrawing libido from objects and investing it only in the productions of his own mind –

his children, as it were. Since these phantasms cannot reciprocate his love, he soon withdraws to a narcissistic position, releasing aggression toward his "alter egos." On this process, see Jacques Lacan, "Agressivity in Psychoanalysis," in *Ecrits: A Selection,* trans. Alan Sheridan (New York, 1977), pp. 8–29.

8. Lee A. Jacobus places Satan's unstable subjectivity within the context of the Calvinist dependence on self-knowledge. To know oneself it is necessary to know God; Satan, by denying God, denies himself. See "Self-Knowledge in *Paradise Lost,*" *Milton Studies* III, ed. James Simmonds (Pittsburgh, 1971), p. 104–7, and Calvin, *Institutes of the Christian Religion,* Bk. I, Chap. I, Par. ii. What interests me here is Milton's realization of the doctrine in dramatic poetry, the specifically literary technique that makes the reader feel the "truth" by concretizing Calvin's abstraction.

9. On the rationalizations in *Paradise Lost,* see Northrop Frye, *The Return of Eden* (Toronto, 1965), pp. 97–8.

10. See the discussion of Satan's fallen syntax, Chapter 2 in this book.

11. On the mimetic basis of *Paradise Lost,* see Irene Samuel, "The Development of Milton's Poetics," *PMLA* 92 (1977): 231–40.

12. Millicent Bell, "The Fallacy of the Fall in *Paradise Lost,*" *PMLA* 68 (1953): 864–5. See also the exchange between Bell and Wayne Shumaker, *PMLA* 70 (1955): 1185–1203; and A. J. A. Waldock, *Paradise Lost and its Critics* (New York and Cambridge, 1947), p. 40.

13. J. B. Savage, "Freedom and Necessity in *Paradise Lost,*" *ELH* 44 (1977): 299.

14. Ibid., p. 300. See also Mary Ann Radzinowicz, "Man as a 'Probationer of Immortality': *Paradise Lost* XI and XII," in *Approaches to Paradise Lost: The York Centenary Lectures,* ed. C. A. Patrides (Toronto, 1968).

15. Susanne Langer, *Feeling and Form* (New York, 1953), p. 326.

16. See Chapter 1, Section II in this book. See also Antony Low, "*Samson Agonistes:* Theology, Poetry, Truth," *Milton Quarterly* 13 (1979): 100–1.

17. Compare Eve's rejection of looks, smiles, and casual discourse to Adam's assertion to Raphael that "neither her out-side form'd so fair, nor aught / In procreation common to all kinds / . . . / So much delights me, as those graceful acts, / Those thousand decencies that daily flow / From all her words and actions, mixt with Love" (VIII.596–602). See Arnold Stein, *Answerable Style: Essays on Paradise Lost* (Minneapolis, 1953), p. 95. Dianne McColley's contention that the separation is a positive step in Adam's and Eve's developing understanding of their relationship, "the result of a responsible and con-

sidered choice whose outcome might have been, though it was not, the greater good of the unfallen race" (*Milton's Eve* [Urbana, Ill., 1983], pp. 141) is attractive and logically argued, but ignores the emotions underlying the scene. The reader, knowing what the result of the separation will be, can hardly urge Eve on in her assertion of independence. Further, as I shall argue, the tone, diction, and pacing of the dialogue are easily referred to the experience of marital discord in a fallen world. The existence of a strong defense for Eve's behavior, such as that advanced by McColley, strengthens the effect of apprehension by keeping Eve within the reader's sympathetic grasp, but the dramatic context of the argument (and it is an argument) emphasizes the displacement of affect from fears about their love to pseudo-abstract discourse on God's doctrine. The reduction of theology to a merely instrumental use in a marital dispute is not recuperated by the impressive doctrinal contexts that McColley cites in support of her developmental conception of the separation. A formal argument may also be raised against McColley's reading, which turns the separation scene into a *debat,* even though the tragic decorum of Book IX leads one to expect an agon. Adam's exasperated, "Go" (IX.372), is a pivot at which control passes from him to Eve, the result of a struggle for power not of a compelling argument. Adam releases Eve precisely because he needs her freely rendered conversation, "thy stay, not free, absents thee more" (IX.372). Eve can be the mirror in which Adam sees and reproduces his ideal self only by being other than Adam, "manlike but different sex" (VIII.472). His decision to let her go is perhaps logically sound, as McColley argues, but it comes as the self-realization of the limits of command. Adam can compel Eve to stay only by alienating her, a self-defeating prospect. On the adversarial aspect of the separation scene, see R. A. Shoaf, *Milton, Poet of Duality: An Study of Semiosis in the Poetry and Prose* (New Haven, 1985), p. 116.

18. Of course, Adam's argument derives from Plato's *Symposium,* where it corresponds to a low rung on the ladder of contemplation, occupied by one above physical (procreative) love but not yet ascended to a vision of moral beauty apart from a morally beautiful individual.

19. See Joseph Summers, *The Muse's Method: An Introduction to Paradise Lost* (Cambridge, Mass., 1970), p. 174. On the question of force and its relation to command, see Anthony Low, "The Parting in the Garden in *Paradise Lost, PQ* 48 (1968): 30–5.

20. Cf. Nyquist's remarks on the "illusion of tragic inevitability," "Reading the Fall," pp. 223–9.

21. Cf. Torquato Tasso, *Gerusalemme Liberata,* XVI.3, and the disarmed Verdant in the arms of Acrasia, Edmund Spenser, *Faerie Queene,* II, xii.79–80.

22. On the significance of Eve's dream just before the expulsion and her "political" response to it, see Maureen Quilligan, *Milton's Spenser: The Politics of Reading* (Ithaca, N.Y., 1983), pp. 241–2. Quilligan's chapter on "The Gender of the Reader" is an extremely useful explication of the complexity of Milton's deployment of the "feminine."

23. See Kathleen M. Swaim, "The Art of the Maze in Book IX of *Paradise Lost,*" *Studies in English Literature* 12 (1972): 138.

24. As Stanley Fish has noted in *Surprised by Sin: The Reader in Paradise Lost* (New York, 1967), pp. 253–4. On Eve's empiricism, see Lee Jacobus, *Sudden Apprehensions: Aspects of Knowledge in Paradise Lost* (The Hague, 1976), pp. 144–66.

25. On Satan's attachment to an incremental conception of deity, see Chapter 2 in this book.

26. Swaim, "Art of the Maze," p. 139. Fish, noting that Eve's temptation of Adam is "a tissue of Satanic echoes," sees this repetition of arguments as evidence that Eve "takes Satan at face value" (*Surpised by Sin,* p. 253).

27. See Fish, *Surprised by Sin,* p. 95.

28. See Anthony Low, *The Blaze of Noon: A Reading of Samson Agonistes* (New York, 1974), p. 28.

29. Arthur Barker, "Structural and Doctrinal Patterns in Milton's Later Poems," in *Essays in English Literature from the Renaissance to the Victorian Age Presented to A. S. P. Woodhouse* (Toronto, 1964), p. 91.

30. See Low, *The Blaze of Noon,* pp. 23–4, 30–1.

31. See Cleanth Brooks, "Eve's Awakening," in *Essays in Honor of Walter Clyde Curry* (Nashville, 1954), p. 295.

CHAPTER 7

1. Joseph Addison, *Spectator,* no. 357, April 9, 1972, in *Addison: Criticism on Paradise Lost,* ed. Albert S. Cook (New York, 1968), p. 26.

2. On the need to interpret signs after the fall, see R. A. Shoaf, *Milton, Poet of Duality: A Study of Semiosis in the Poetry and Prose* (New Haven, 1985), pp. 30–9.

3. See Gérard Genette, *Narrative Discourse: An Essay in Method,* trans. Jane E. Lewin (Ithaca, N.Y., 1980), pp. 162–4. Genette notes that the presentation of a story can vary along a continuum from pure

mimesis – performance by actors – to pure narrative – summary report. Raphael's narratives of the war in heaven and of creation are high on the mimetic end of the scale. Michael's prophecies begin with the mimetic vision of Cain and Abel but become progressively less mimetic until the decisive break with visual representation after the narration of the flood. The marks of the narrator's presence in the text vary inversely with the degree of mimesis employed in narrating the story.

4.  On the relationship of iterative to singulative narration, see Genette, *Narrative Discourse,* pp. 113–27. Genette's argument that "in the classical narrative and even up to Balzac, iterative sections are almost always functionally subordinate to singulative scenes, for which the iterative sections provide a sort of formative frame or background" (116–17) is put in question by Milton's reversal of these priorities. In *Paradise Lost* the singulative scenes – separation, temptation, restoration – are presented as the originary frames of a projected series of iterations.

5.  On the *protevangelium,* see C. A. Patrides, *Milton and the Christian Tradition* (Oxford, 1966), pp. 123–8; and Georgia B. Christopher, *Milton and the Science of the Saints* (Princeton, 1982), pp. 13–14, 138–40.

6.  Cf. Thomas Browne's remark in the *Religio Medici* that " 'tis in the power of every hand to destroy us, and wee are beholding unto every one wee meete hee doth not kill us." Quoted from *The Prose of Sir Thomas Browne,* ed. Norman Endicott (New York, 1967), pp. 51–2.

7.  George M. Muldrow points out (in "The Beginning of Adam's Repentance," *PQ* 46 [1967]) that this speech is comparable to Satan's speech on Niphrates (IV.32–113) and that "the contrast between Satan's and Adam's speeches begins in the setting. Whereas it was the order of God's universe which occasioned Satan's introspection, it is the newly-appeared disorder which disturbs Adam" (202).

8.  Adam here raises the issue of belatedness linked to the narrative condition of the subject. To conceive of the self as such is to discover oneself as a character in another's story. See Sigmund Freud, *Beyond the Pleasure Principle, SE,* XVIII, pp. 14–17; and my discussion of these pages in "The Narrative of the Subject and the Rhetoric of the Self," *Papers in Language and Literature* 18 (1982): 414–15.

9.  See Arnold Stein, *Answerable Style: Essays on Paradise Lost* (Minneapolis, 1953), p. 118.

10. Adam proceeds through the degrees of repentance distinguished by

Milton in the *Christian Doctrine:* "Recognition of sin, contrition, confession, abandonment of evil and conversion to good" (*CP*.VI.468).

11. Kester Svendsen, "Adam's Soliloquy in Book X of *Paradise Lost,*" *College English* 10 (1949): 368. See also Jun Harada, "The Mechanism of Human Reconciliation in *Paradise Lost,*" *PQ* 50 (1973): 543–52; and Joseph Summers, *The Muse's Method: An Introduction to Paradise Lost* (Cambridge, Mass., 1962), p. 176. Georgia B. Christopher argues that it is not Eve's assumption of the guilt, but rather Adam's recollection of the *protevangelium* that opens the way to full repentance (p. 144). Although the *protevangelium* provides Adam with the necessary "sense of divine mercy," Christopher's argument ignores the fact that it is the reconciliation with Eve that allows Adam to recall and understand the Son's promise when he does.

12. On the differing and deferring of signifiers that guarantees the absence of the signified as the price of signification itself, see Jacques Derrida, "Differance," in *Speech and Phenomena and Other Essays on Husserl's Theory of Signs,* trans. David B. Allison (Evanston, Ill., 1973), pp. 129–60. My point is that God's presence in the world *through* his image(s) similarly guarantees his absence. The surplus of signification that remains after the emanation and return of light or love is at once the generations of men and the Word made flesh. The presence of God marks the eclipse of signification when the Son will put off the signs of vicegerency and "God Shall be All in All." The resolution of resemblance into identity will, at this apocalyptic moment, supply the presence of God that has been *represented* as differed and deferred through history, but, in the same and everlasting moment, time and the subject, whose medium is precisely the *differance* so effaced, must disappear.

13. Joseph Summers points out the important prosodic echoing of the Son (III.236–41) in these lines. Such tonal interrelationships used "to suggest, to reinforce, and even to create meaning . . . consciously apprehended or not" dispose the reader to credit Eve's acceptance of blame. *The Muse's Method: An Introduction to Paradise Lost* (Cambridge, Mass., 1970), p. 178.

14. Louis Martz, *The Paradise Within: Studies in Vaughan, Traherne and Milton* (New Haven, 1964), pp. 142, 150. See also C. S. Lewis, *A Preface to Paradise Lost* (1942; repr. New York, 1961), p. 129.

15. See Balachandra Rajan, *The Lofty Rhyme: A Study of Milton's Poetry* (London, 1970), p. 129.

16. As Satan expects, see X.485–93.

17.  On configurative cognition, see Chapter 1 in this book, Section II and note 12.

18.  See Rajan, *The Lofty Rhyme*, pp. 80–1. Cf. *Paradise Lost* VI.295–353. Michael fought the kind of battle Adam expects, but Satan was not destroyed; the physical victory is inconclusive.

19.  *Saint Augustine's Enchiridion,* ed. and trans. Ernest Evans (London, 1953), p. 28. I am indebted to Anthony Low for this reference.

20.  Cf. *Paradise Regained* II.450ff, IV.145ff.

21.  On free will as the freedom to choose correctly, see Northrop Frye, *The Return of Eden* (Toronto, 1965), p. 21; and Rajan, *The Lofty Rhyme,* p. 68.

22.  Milton's presentation of the fall parallels the psychoanalytic myth of the Oedipal stage, particularly in the semiotic version given by Lacan. In Lacan's theory the Oedipal complex is "resolved" when the subject enters the "Symbolic," that is the register of perception in which signs are substituted for things. The Oedipal subject accepts the law of the father (*nom du pere,* which is also the *non du pere*) by repressing its desire for the thing in favor of its acquisition of the name – much as Freud's grandson substitutes his mastery of a button and the syllables *fort / da* for the presence of his mother in *Beyond the Pleasure Principle* (see note 8 above). When this "fall" into the symbolic occurs, the subject acquires a signifier that represents him in the symbolic discourse, but is never commensurate with the repressed or barred subject sacrificed in its favor. The sliding of signifiers through metonymy allows the subject to move from one to another signifier of the repressed Oedipal desire in search of that missing part of itself. But Cf. William Kerrigan, *The Sacred Complex: On the Psychogenesis of Paradise Lost* (Cambridge, Mass., 1983), pp. 281–3, 292.

23.  In Freudian terms, the reality principle is overcome by the pleasure principle and the psyche regresses to primary process. Such a resurgence of primary process – the hallucinatory fulfillment of desire without regard to reality – is consistent with the retraction of libido from its objects in narcissism, discussed in this book in Chapter 2. On the logic of the supplement, see Jacques Derrida, "Structure, Sign and Play in the Discourse of the Human Sciences," in *Writing and Difference,* trans. Alan Bass (Chicago, 1978), pp. 278–93. See also Derrida's "The Supplement of Copula: Philosophy *before* Linguistics" in *Textual Strategies: Perspectives in Post-Structuralist Criticism,* ed. Josué V. Harari (Ithaca, N.Y., 1979), pp. 82–120.

24.  See Frye, *The Return of Eden,* p. 111.

25.  See Chapter 3, Section II in this book.

26. Cf. *Paradise Lost* III.305–19.
27. See William Kerrigan's discussion of Milton's mortalism and its implications for *Paradise Lost* in "The Heretical Milton: From Assumption to Mortalism," *English Literary Renaissance* 5 (1975): 125–66.
28. On the double implication of narrative functions, see Roland Barthes, "Introduction to the Structural Analysis of Narrative," in *Image Music Text,* trans. Stephen Heath (New York, 1977), pp. 101–4.
29. Cf. Jonathan Culler, "Fabula and Sjuzhet in the Analysis of Narrative: Some American Discussions," *Poetics Today* 1 (1980): 27–37.

CHAPTER 8

1. See A.-J. Greimas and J. Courtès, "The Cognitive Dimension of Narrative Discourse," *New Literary History* 7 (1976): 477 n. 5: "From a grammatical point of view, narrative is definable as a (more or less long) series of *states* between which are inserted transformations, that is, reflexive or transitive operations, insuring the passage from one state to another." The movement – the "between which" – is then a mark of narrative, and its achievement, whether transitive or reflexive, engages the predicative apparatus of language. It is for this reason that throughout this chapter rhetoric will be examined from a semantic rather than a semiotic perspective; for it is only on the level of discourse or message that semantic impertinence is detected, and it is the reader's reduction of this impertinence by the construction of an alternative context that is my principal theme. For an exhaustive discussion of the predicative operation of metaphor on the level of discourse, see Paul Ricoeur, *The Rule of Metaphor,* trans. Robert Czerny with Kathleen McLaughlin and John Costello, S. J. (Toronto, 1977), esp. pp. 65–100.
2. The relationship of a subject to its predicates within the structure of a story was recognized by Aristotle in his definition of tragedy as the mimesis of an action and his argument that mythos is prior to ethos (*Poetics,* 1448b, 1450a–b). The same relationship of mythos and ethos is recognized in Northrop Frye's theory of modes, where the criterion of modal classification is the power of action of the hero (*Anatomy of Criticism* [Princeton, 1957], pp. 33–5). Tzvetan Todorov argues that "the grammatical subject is always devoid of internal properties, for these derive only from a temporary junction with a predicate" (*The Poetics of Prose,* trans. Richard Howard [Ithaca, N.Y., 1977], p. 111). In another context, psychoanalysis, Jacques Lacan's definition of the subject as a signifier for another signifier has similar implications.

See, for example, his discussion of the barred subject and its signifier(s) in *The Four Fundamental Concepts of Psycho-Analysis,* ed. Jacques-Alain Miller, trans. Alan Sheridan (New York, 1978), pp. 141–2. See also my "The Subject of Narrative and the Rhetoric of the Self," *Papers on Language and Literature* 18 (1982): 398–417.

3. Walter Benjamin, *Illuminations,* ed. and with an introduction by Hannah Arendt, trans. Harry Zohn (New York, 1977), p. 94.

4. On the relationship of language to thought, see Emile Benveniste, "Categories of Thought and Language," in *Problems in General Linguistics,* trans. Mary Elizabeth Meek (Coral Gables, Fla., 1971), esp. pp. 56, 75. On the use of rhetoric to innovate new predicative categories, see Paul de Man, "Semiology and Rhetoric," in *Textual Strategies: Perspectives in Post-Structuralist Criticism,* ed. Josué V. Harari (Ithaca, N.Y., 1979), pp. 121–40. Hayden White's investigations of the rhetorical contribution to the constitution of narrative are notably specific; see, for example, *Tropics of Discourse: Essays in Cultural Criticism* (Baltimore, 1978), pp. 1–25.

5. William Ames, *The Marrow of Sacred Divinity, Drawne Out of The holy Scripture, and the Interpreters thereof, and brought into Method* (London, 1642), p. 8: "Therefore Divinity is better defined by that good life whereby we live to God, then by a blessed life whereby we live to ourselves." Edward Phillips reports that Ames (along with Wolleb) was frequently among the "ablest of divines" consulted by Milton during the composition of the *Christian Doctrine* (William Godwin, *Lives of Edward and John Phillips* [London, 1815], pp. 363–4, cited in Maurice Kelley, "Milton's Debt to Wolleb's *Compendium Theologiae Christianae,*" *PMLA* 50 [1935]: 157). The index to the Yale edition of the *Christian Doctrine* lists fifty references to the *Marrow.* Largely a redaction of Calvin's *Institutes,* the *Marrow* provides a convenient entry into Milton's theological context because its Ramist mode of organization and expression highlights the contributions of rhetoric to speculative thought. I use the term "dialectical" in the Heglian sense.

6. In reference to Michael's shift to narration, Barbara Lewalski notes that, "Whereas Adam's (and mankind's) intemperance and vainglory are a kind of moral blindness to be cured by a sharper sight, ambition in Adam and Eve was traditionally identified with the desire to know good and evil, to *see too clearly* into 'objects divine' unsuited to human sense" ("Structure and the Symbolism of Vision in Michael's Prophecy, *Paradise Lost,* Books XI–XII" *PQ* 42 [1963]: 27–8). It is worth noting here that the virtue of patience is implied. It is necessary to

wait until "objects divine" and a refined human sense are commensurate. Human sense must be raised to an appropriate spiritual level lest "objects divine" be degraded by corporeal perception, that is, perceived in a degraded way. William Madsen, in *From Shadowy Type to Truth: Studies in Milton's Symbolism* (New Haven, 1968), pp. 174–5, discusses the Puritan's distrust of visible images and preference for the word, especially the scriptural word, but he fails to consider the degree to which visual experience may be recuperated by reference to a correctly chosen (that is, scriptural) verbal gloss.

7. See, for example, *Of Reformation, CP.*I.566. See also *Paradise Lost* XII.412–22; III.45–55.

8. Irene Samuel points out the Platonic inflection of Milton's references to "Truth, absolute and independent of particular truths, giving to them not gaining from them, real existence" (*Plato and Milton* [1947; repr., Ithaca, N.Y., 1965], p. 141; see also, pp. 140–7). The quotation in the text is from *CP.*I.556.

9. See also *Christian Doctrine, CP.*VI.154: "For God's foreknowledge is simply his wisdom under another name, or that idea of all things which, to speak in human terms, he had in mind before he decreed anything."

10. Cf. Philo: "God, being God, assumed that a beautiful copy would never be produced apart from a beautiful pattern. . . . So when He willed to create this visible world He first fully formed the intelligible world" (*On the Account of the World's Creation Given by Moses [De Opificio Mundi]*, in *Works in Ten Volumes*, trans. F. H. Colson and G. H. Whitaker, Loeb Classical Library [London, 1929], I:15; see also Ames, p. 24). Madsen sees an antithesis between the Neoplatonic emphasis "on the present, the Eternal Now which bodies forth the rational structure of the universe," and the Hebrew emphasis "on history as the embodiment of God's purpose" (p. 85), in view of which "*Paradise Lost* may be described in some respects as anti-Neoplatonic not only in its symbolic method but also in its central thematic concerns" (p. 83). Madsen is correct to distinguish Milton's hermeneutics from those of the Neoplatonists, but Christian typology may be seen as a synthesis of Platonic allegory and Hebraic history rather than as the antithesis of the former. Milton's practice dialectically subsumes the allegorical meaning by reading it through an anagogic or eschatological antitype. The common use of ethical analogies between contemporary problems and biblical episodes, both in the Puritan sermon literature of the seventeenth century and in Milton's own writing, suggests that Milton's insistence on the historical and

occasionally typological sense of Scripture (*CP*.VI.581) does not exclude the analogy of scriptural episodes to the ethical conundrums faced by a Christian in the world of experience. At issue is the way in which the typological or historicized version of the relations between the sensible and intelligible (that is, between history and providence), by creating a dynamic as opposed to a strictly ontological epistemology, also creates a narratable one. For examples, see William Whitaker's discussion of hermeneutics in *Holy Scripture, Against the Papists, especially Bellarmine and Stapleton* [Cambridge, 1588], trans. and ed. William Fitzgerald (Cambridge, 1849), pp. 406–7; and Milton's use of the "one just man" motif in *Paradise Lost* (most notably in Abdiel) as both a type of Christ and an ethical injunction to a Christian mode of action.

11. See also *Paradise Regained* III.43–107.
12. See also Rev. 20:12.
13. On the relation of mythos to mimesis and the operation of metaphorical redescription, see Ricoeur, *The Rule of Metaphor*, pp. 244–6.
14. Cf. Andrew Milner's interesting discussion of the distinction between empiricism and rationalism in seventeenth-century ideology and the relationship of rationalism to "Protestant individualism" (*John Milton and the English Revolution: A Study in the Sociology of Literature* [London and New York, 1981], pp. 115–18). Milner's understanding of empiricism as a concern with the "objective" or external world and of rationalism as the privileging of an internal structure of reason fails to recognize the degree to which the categories of interior and exterior are mediated by a belief in the orderliness of a world constructed according to God's "holy mathematics." Reason is not an internal structure imposed upon the world, but rather the tool by which one discovers the proportional harmony that expresses the single design of nature and the human mind. The mediation of mind and nature by a divine design that subsumes both leads to an important hermeneutic signpost. Perception of nature is correct only when what is perceived accords with reason. In Milton's temporalized hermeneutics one goes further, working the matter of the world until it looks like that which reason indicates it really is. The assumptions behind such a notion of "good works" ought not be confused with the more thorough-going, dualistic rationalism of, say, Descartes.
15. These interlocking metaphors should not be confused with those of ahistorical allegory. Here the tenor of the metaphor comes into view only when the vehicle is translated from mundane history to divine

providence by virtue of an anagogic or eschatological perspective. Tenor and vehicle are then a rhetorical representation of the type–antitype relationship, and the difference between them is displaced from a semantic to a temporal impertinence.

16. C. A. Patrides contrasts Milton's use of the Father–Son metaphor as lexicalized language in the *Christian Doctrine* with the fully metaphorical use of the same language in *Paradise Lost* in "Milton and the Arian Controversy," *Proceedings of the American Philosophical Association* 120 (1976): 245–52.

17. See Chapter 3, Section II in this book.

18. See William Kerrigan, *The Prophetic Milton* (Charlottesville, Va., 1974), pp. 40–1.

19. Kenneth Burke notes that with the extension of personality to deity by analogy from empirical usages "a theological dialectic reverses its direction, . . . conceives of personality here and now infused by the genius of the analogical extension" (*The Rhetoric of Religion: Studies in Logology* [Boston, 1961], p. 36). It may be added that this reversal is interior to the dialectic of the metaphor that negates and preserves the figuration of a single signifier operating in and seeming to articulate two distinct registers of meaning. The "theological dialectic" is simply a version of metaphor presented as concept.

20. Madsen contends that "Milton is using 'shadow' here not in the Platonic or Neoplatonic sense, but in its familiar Christian sense of 'foreshadowing' or 'adumbration' (pp. 88–9). But there is neither need nor possibility of choosing one or the other meaning of "shadow." From Adam's temporal point of view, earth "foreshadows" heaven, earthly types conceal anagogic antitypes; but from the perspective of revealed providence, earthly forms are allegorical signs of heavenly originals and may be appropriated to create the context of ethical choice on earth. The creation of such a context is the explicit purpose of Raphael's narration of heavenly events.

21. Compare Rom. 12:4–5 and I Cor. 12:12 to Abdiel's understanding of the exaltation of the Son, *Paradise Lost* V.827–31. The notion of mediation between the individual and the universal and unchangeable, here disclosed by the reduction of metaphor to synecdoche, will later be conceptualized by Hegel as the dialectic of the unhappy consciousness (see Chapter 3 in this book, note 28).

22. See Rom. 10:10, and Chapter 5, Section II in this book.

23. Augustine, *Christian Doctrine* 3.15,23, trans. Robert J. F. Shaw in *A Select Library of the Nicene and Post-Nicene Fathers of the Christian Church*, ed. Philip Schaff (New York, 1887), first series, II:563. See also

*CP*.VI.533: "Thus anyone with any sense interprets the precepts of Christ in the sermon on the mount not in a literal way but in a way that is in keeping with the spirit of charity."

24. Aquinas, *Summa theologiae*, ed. and trans. Herbert McCabe, O. P. (Latin text, English translation) (New York, 1963), 3:71. The Latin text makes clear the senses of logical and temporal priority: "Cum enim dicitur, *Deus est bonus*, vel *sapiens*, non solum significatur quod ipse sit causa sapientiae vel bonitatis, sed quod haec in eo eminentius praexistunt. Unde secundum hoc dicendum est quod quantum perfectiones in creaturas manant; sed quantum ad impositionem nominis per prius a nobis imponuntur creaturis, quas prius cognoscimus." See also Ricoeur's important discussion of *"analogia entis"* (*The Rule of Metaphor*, pp. 272–80, esp. pp. 278–9). For a Protestant restatement of the epistemological point in question, see Ames, *Marrow*, pp. 24–5.

25. For a historical consideration of the problem, see Walter Clyde Curry, *Milton's Ontology, Cosmogony and Physics* (Lexington, Ky., 1957), pp. 24–43. On the ontological supplement implicit in the copula of attribution, see Jacques Derrida, "The Supplement of Copula: Philosophy *before* Linguistics," in Harari, ed., *Textual Strategies*, pp. 82–120.

26. See Chapter 5 in this book, Section II and note 36.

27. See John Calvin, *Institutes of the Christian Religion* (Bk. IV, Chap. 14, Par. 3), trans. John Allen (Philadelphia, 1936), II:557: "Now because we have souls enclosed in bodies, he gives us spiritual things under visible emblems; not because there are such qualities in the nature of the things presented to us in the sacraments, but because they have been designated by God to this signification" (after Chrysostom).

28. On the corruption of the Word, see Mary Nyquist, "The Father's Word/Satan's Wrath," *PMLA* 100 (1985): 187–202.

29. Cf. Herman Rapaport's discussion of Milton's "thanatopraxie," in *Milton and the Postmodern* (Lincoln, Neb., 1983), pp. 11–21.

30. "Alas how simple, to these Cates compar'd, / Was that crude Apple that diverted *Eve!*" (*Paradise Regained* II.348–9). See Barbara Lewalski, "Time and History in *Paradise Regained*," in *The Prison and the Pinnacle*, ed. Balachandra Rajan (London, 1973), p. 70; and, on Christ's relationship to his human predecessors, see p. 77.

31. Lewalski, "Time and History in *Paradise Regained*," p. 74.

32. See, for example, Calvin, *Institutes* (Bk. IV, Chap. 8, Par. 7), II:421: "But when, at length, the Wisdom of God was manifested in the flesh, it openly declared to us all that the human mind is capable of

comprehending, or ought to think, concerning the heavenly Father. Now, therefore, since Christ, the Sun of Righteousness, has shone upon us, we enjoy the full splendour of Divine truth, resembling the brightness of the noonday, whereas the light enjoyed before was a kind of twilight."

33. Ignatius of Antioch, *Epistle to the Ephesians,* trans. Kirsopp Lake, *The Apostolic Fathers,* Loeb Classical Library, 2 vols. (London, 1925), I:189. Compare *Paradise Lost* I.17–26. On Milton's conception of Christ's nature, knowledge, and action, see Barbara Lewalski, *Milton's Brief Epic: The Genre, Meaning and Art of Paradise Regained* (Providence, R.I., 1966), pp. 157–8.

34. For a discussion of what Milton may have meant when using the terms of relation common in seventeenth-century theology, see W. B. Hunter, "Further Definitions: Milton's Theological Vocabulary," in Hunter, Patrides, Adamson, *Bright Essence: Studies in Milton's Theology* (Salt Lake City, 1971), pp. 15–25. Whatever Milton took to be the nature of "Complete Glorification," it was specifically not narratable; see *Paradise Lost* III.60–2, where the sight of God is said to produce "beatitude past utterance" in the heavenly host; and *CP*.VI.626–30.

35. See *CP*.VI.478, and I.520 *(Of Reformation);* Calvin, *Institutes* (Bk. IV, Chap. 2, Par. 7); and Augustine, *City of God,* 2.2.

# INDEX

Abdiel, 96–8, 100–2, 128, 143, 219
n10, 220 n21, 234 n10, 236 n21
Adam, and "conformity divine," 7, 9,
11, 17, 141, 160, 181, 183, 190; and
rhetorical tropes, 26–7, 205 n1; soliloquy in Book X, 155–7; see also
Adam and Eve, creation
Adam and Eve, as "authors to themselves," 1–9, 13, 23, 35–7, 46, 57–8,
67, 75, 91, 93, 124, 127, 129–30,
141, 150, 160–1, 167, 192; conversation of, 81, 89, 113, 121, 132; fall
of, 14, 105, 109–10, 125, 127–50,
191–2; and propagation, 69, 75,
87–90, 113, 118, 121–2, 130–2, 140,
148, 155, 214 n10; separation of in
Book IX, 138–43, 226 n17; subjectivity of, 69, 78–81, 91, 116–27,
144, 163, 188
Adamson, J. H., 217 n21
Addison, Joseph, 151, 228 n1
Aeneas, 23
allegory, 43–6, 130–1, 219 n14, 235
n15
Ames, William, 108, 110, 179, 190,
214 n8, 222 nn31,35, 233 n5, 237
n24
Anderson, Judith, 199 n13
Appleby, Joyce Oldham, 202 n31
Aquinas, St. Thomas, 20, 54, 59, 179,
190, 212 n17, 237 n24
Aristotle, 5–6, 128, 134, 136, 144, 147,
198 nn9,10, 232 n2
arminianism, 13, 202 n29

Athanasius, St., 52, 211 n13
Auerbach, Erich, 24, 205 n45
Augustine, Saint, Christian Doctrine,
188–9, 219 n11, 236 n23; City of
God, 209 n24, 238 n35; Confessions,
200 n22, 207 n7, 217 n19;
Enchiridion, 167–8, 231 n19;
authorship, see metaphor

Bacon, Francis, 14, 33, 202, n30
Baker, Herschel, 198 n7
Barker, Arthur, 147, 228 n29
Barthes, Roland, 204 n43, 212 n20,
232 n28
Baxter, Richard, 218 n6
Beelzebub, 30–3, 34, 37–8, 42, 57, 96
Bell, Millicent, 134, 226 n12
Benveniste, Emile, 233 n4
Benjamin, Walter, 177, 233 n3
Bennett, Joan, 222 n34
Broadbent, J. B., 91, 210 n4, 214 n3,
217 n1
Brooks, Cleanth, 215 n15, 228 n31
Browne, Thomas, 229 n6
Burden, Dennis H., 215 nn13,15
Burke, Kenneth, 205 n1, 236 n19
Bush, Douglas, 210 n4

Cain and Abel, in Paradise Lost, 172–3
Calvin, on faith, 238 n35; on knowledge, 226 n8, 237 n32; on the sacraments, 106–9, 221 nn26,29, 214 n8,
222 nn30,32,35, 237 n27; on salvation, 167; and the war in heaven,
99–100, 220 nn17,18, 221 n22

239

# Index

chaos, 43, 111, 113–14, 153
Christ, as antitype, 18; and "being-
toward-death," 148, 171–2; and
Eve, 144, 158; and the Lord's Sup-
per, 106–11; and the rhetoric of me-
diation, 10, 17, 27–8, 41, 49, 56, 60–
3, 164–5, 171–2, 187–9, 193–6, 205
n1; and salvation theory, 50–1; *see
also* the Son, transfiguration of
Christ
Christopher, Georgia, 203 n33, 205
n1, 222 n30, 230 n11
Circe, 142
Cirillo, Albert, 210 n9
Collins, Christopher, 206 n2
Cope, Jackson, 225 n6
Courtès, J., 232 n1
creation, of Adam, 119; of Eve, 83–8,
120–2; of the world, 91, 111–16
Crosman, Robert, 215 n11
Culler, Jonathan, 197 n4, 232 n24
Curry, Walter Clyde, 217 n3, 221 n24,
237 n25

Damrosh, Leopold Jr., 208 n15, 17
Danielson, Dennis, 202 n29
daughters of Cain, in *Paradise Lost,*
9
Davies, Horton, 221 n27
Death (as character), 41, 43–6, 88,
130–1, 136, 153–4, 161, 167, 174
de Man, Paul, 233 n4
Derrida, Jacques, 211 n11, 230 n12,
231 n23, 237 n25
Descartes, René, 207 n10, 235 n14
Donne, John, 13, 202 n30

Earl, James, 217 n22
Empson, William, 43–4, 55, 60, 209
n25, 210 n4, 212 nn18,26,27
Eve, dream of, 68, 83, 91–2, 134–5,
142, 162, 228 n22; soliloquy, Book
IX, 145–6; syntax of, 145, 192; *see
also* Adam and Eve, creation

the Father, as presented in Book III,
49–66; subjectivity of, 55–62, 68,
152; *see also* God, rhetoric
Ferry, Anne, 199 n13, 207 n9
Fineman, Joel, 198 n6

Fish, Stanley, 50, 210 n6, 215 nn11,
12, 228 nn24,27
Foley, Jack, 206 n5
Fraunce, Abraham, 205 n1, 222 n33
Freeman, James A., 209 n23
Freud, Sigmund, 207 n12, 213 n31,
216 nn16,17, 225 n7, 229 n8, 231
nn22,23
Frye, Northrop, 226 n9, 231 nn21,24,
232 n2

Gallagher, Philip, 209 n27, 218 n7
Genette, Gérard, 224 n4, 228 n3, 229
n4
Giamatti, A. Bartlett, 214 n10, 215
n15
Gilman, Ernest B., 197 n3
God, activity of, in man, 12–16, 52,
53; dialogue within the Godhead in
Book III, 59–65; emanation of, 75,
88–9; foreknowledge of, 1–6, 11,
154–5; and light, 51–4, 58–9, 211
n10; *see also* the Father, the Son
Goldberg, Jonathan, 204 n39
Goldman, Jack, 221 n24
Greenblatt, Stephen, 199 n13, 218
n9
Greimas, A.-J., 232 n1

Harding, Davis P., 209 n23
Harrier, Richard, 197 n3
Hartman, Geoffrey, 221 n23
Hegel, G. W. F., 212 n28, 213 n1, 236
n21
Heidegger, Martin, 127, 148, 200
nn20,22, 223 n2
Helgerson, Richard, 199 n13
Hercules, 142
hermeneutics, 8–9, 15, 97, 104, 110,
139, 162, 191, 219 n14, 223 n2; *see
also* tropology, typology
Hesiod, 209 n27
Hill, Christopher, 202 n31
Hughes, Merritt Y., 210 n9
Huguelet, Theodore, 219 n11
Hunter, William, 210 nn8,9, 211 n10,
238 n34
Huntley, Frank L., 213 n33
hypocrisy, in *Paradise Lost,* 67, 97,
112, 114, 169–70

240

# Index

# Index

Patrides, C. A., 52, 198 n7, 200 n21, 210 nn3,4, 211 nn12,13, 217 n21, 229 n5, 236 n16

Paul, St., 3, 99, 178–9, 220 n16, 236 nn21,22

Peter, John, 210 n4, 214 n4

Philo Judaeus, 214 n8, 234 n10

Plato, 227 n18

prospect, as a concept in *Paradise Lost*, 77, 83, 87, 90, 109, 164–6

*protevangelium*, 142, 153, 157, 160, 161, 165, 176, 229 n5, 230 n11

Quilligan, Maureen, 45, 209 nn28,29,30, 228 n22

Radzinowicz, Mary Ann, 199 n11, 203 nn32,35, 233 n39, 226 n14

Rajan, Balachandra, 203 n36, 204 n44, 230 n15, 231 nn18,21

Rapaport, Herman, 208 n17, 209 n28, 237 n29

Raphael, 90–119, 123–5, 128–30, 140–3, 152, 179, 186–9, 219 n13, 228 n3, 236 n20

realism, 36–7

rhetoric, analepsis, 10; chiasmus, 5, 10; of the Father, 63, 170; of feeling, 48, 50, 61, 127; prolepsis, 9–10, 17, 19, 30, 38, 40–1, 48, 56, 153, 180–1; of Satan, 34, 35, 42, 73, 76, 132, 143, 144; and time, 68, 179; *see also* irony, metaphor, metonymy, synecdoche

Ricks, Christopher, 215 n12, 223 n1

Ricoeur, Paul, 8–9, 24, 185, 198 n10, 199 n14, 200 nn16,17,18,19,20,22, 201 n25, 207 n7, 212 n15, 223 n2, 232 n1, 235 n13, 237 n24

Riggs, William, 215 n14, 218 n13

Ryken, Leland, 209 n1, 212 n16

Samuel, Irene, 210 n4, 212 n21, 218 n8, 226 n10, 234 n8

Satan, and Abdiel, 96–7; animal forms of, 79–81, 137–8, 143; escape from hell, 55–6, 59, 71; fall of, 48, 73, 96; and fall of man, 66, 68, 71, 83, 91, 93–4, 110, 130–1, 143–4, 191–2; and historical consciousness, 6–7, 28, 31;

and Lucifer, 30–1, 44, 76, 95–6; and Sin, 121, 153, soliloquy in Book IV, 71–6; soliloquy in Book IX, 132–4, 137–8; subjectivity of, 7, 25, 26–47, 58, 63, 66–8, 72–3, 78, 82, 131–3, 163–4; syntax of, 29–30, 57, 132–3, 138, 145; and Uriel, 53, 66–7, 70, 113, 165, 169, 218 n9; *see also* rhetoric

Savage, J. B., 135, 226 nn13,14

Savoy Declaration, 107, 221 n28

Sessions, William, 23, 204 nn41,42

Shaw, William, 224 n3

Shoaf, R. A., 208 n20, 209 n28, 226 n17, 228 n2

Shumaker, Wayne, 226 n12

Sin (as character), 41–6, 88, 121, 130–1, 136, 151, 153–4, 161, 167, 175, 209 n28

the Son, and creation of the universe, 112–15; incarnation of, 187, 191, 193–4; as judge, 142, 144, 151–3, 160; as mediator, 58–65, 101, 147, 163; and the war in heaven, 98–101, 111; *see also*, Christ, God

Spenser, Edmund, 22–4, 142, 203 n37, 204 nn38,39,40, 228 n21

Steadman, John, 98, 208 n18, 220 n15

Stein, Arnold, 209 n26, 219 n12, 226 n14, 229 n9

Stone, Lawrence, 202 n31

Struever, Nancy, 218 n8

Summers, Joseph, 45, 209 nn31,32, 223 n39, 227 n19, 230 nn11,13

Svendsen, Kester, 157, 230 n11

Swaim, Kathleen, 144, 217 n20, 228 nn23,26

synecdoche, 26–8, 35, 41, 54, 63, 77, 108–9, 123, 131, 180, 186–8, 194, 205 n1

Tasso, Torquato, 142, 228 n21

Tayler, Edward, 198 n8

Thucydides, 96, 218 n8

Todorov, Tzvetan, 199 n12, 214 n7, 232 n2

tragedy, 6, 124, 126–8, 131, 134–8, 150, 165, 227 n20, 232 n2

transfiguration, of Christ, 100, 111

242

# Index

transusbstantiation, 104–12, 115, 123, 188–90
tropology, 12–13, 15, 19–20, 22
Tung, Mason, 219 n10
typology, 13, 15–26, 94, 131, 149, 162, 165, 178, 180, 234 n10

Uriel, 53, 84–9, 113, 169, 218 n9

Vaughan, Henry, 214 n9
Vergil, 22, 23
Volpone, 15

Waite, Tom, 207 n10
Waldock, A. J. A., 207 n11, 210 n4, 214 n4, 226 n12
Walker, Julia, 209 n22
war in heaven, 91–102, 111, 124, 130, 138, 140, 176, 187, 219 n14, 220 n20
West, Robert H., 217 n3
Whaler, James, 208 n21
Whitaker, William, 19, 203 n33, 234 n10
White, Hayden, 233 n4
Williamson, George, 218 n6